Memories of the Spanish Civil War

Memories of the Spanish Civil War

Conflict and Community in Rural Spain

Ruth Sanz Sabido

ROWMAN & LITTLEFIELD
Lanham • Boulder • New York • London

Published by Rowman & Littlefield
A wholly owned subsidiary of The Rowman & Littlefield Publishing Group, Inc.
4501 Forbes Boulevard, Suite 200, Lanham, Maryland 20706
www.rowman.com

Unit A, Whitacre Mews, 26-34 Stannary Street, London SE11 4AB

British Library Cataloguing in Publication Information Available

Library of Congress Cataloging-in-Publication Data

The hardback edition of this book was previously cataloged by the Library of Congress
as follows:

Names: Sanz Sabido, Ruth, 1983- author.
Title: Memories of the Spanish Civil War : conflict and community in rural Spain/ Ruth
    Sanz Sabido.
Description: New York : Rowman & Littlefield International, 2016. | Includes
    bibliographical references and index.
Identifiers: LCCN 2016020903 (print) | LCCN 2016021483 (ebook) | ISBN
    9781783483686 (cloth : alk. paper) | ISBN 9781783483693 (paperback) | ISBN
    9781783483709 (electronic)
Subjects: LCSH: Spain—History—Civil War, 1936-1939—Social aspects. | Spain—
    Rural conditions—20th century. | Collective memory—Spain.
Classification: LCC DP269.8.S65 S26 2016 (print) | LCC DP269.8.S65 (ebook) | DDC
    946.081—dc23
LC record available at https://lccn.loc.gov/2016020903

♾™ The paper used in this publication meets the minimum requirements of
American National Standard for Information Sciences—Permanence of Paper
for Printed Library Materials, ANSI/NISO Z39.48-1992.

Printed in the United States of America

*In loving memory of my grandparents, Francisco Sabido
(1919–1983) and María Rodríguez (1923–2006)*

Contents

List of Illustrations

List of Tables

Acknowledgements

First of all, I would like to thank the residents of Arroyomolinos de León (Huelva, Spain) who agreed to participate in this project. Not only did they give me their time, but the opportunity to scrutinise their memories, their opinions and their emotions. I am grateful to all of them for revisiting the horror, for sharing the sort of insights that come with age and experience and for all the tears (there were many) and all the smiles (there were some of those too). Their memories have provided the foundations for this book, and the process of engaging with them has been enriching in many ways. I would particularly like to thank Santiago and Blas Campos, who took a keen interest in the project from the beginning, and Lorenza Rodríguez López, who did not hesitate to open the doors of her home so that I could review the files compiled by her late husband, Rafael Cid. I am also grateful to the local council for granting me access to the local archive and for putting all their resources at my disposal.

In addition, I would like to thank the members and collaborators of the Asociación para la Recuperación de la Memoria Histórica (ARMH), Todos los Nombres, Asociación Salamanca Memoria y Justicia, Associació per a la Recuperació de la Memòria Històrica de Catalunya and Mesa de Catalunya d'Entitats Memorialistes. Although this book is not based on the parallel project (a documentary film) that I have conducted with them, their kindness and the opportunities they gave me to learn about their work from within has contributed to the overall shape of the work. This book is ultimately dedicated to all the people I encountered: the victims, their relatives and the volunteers who selflessly devote their time to mitigating the impact of an unjust system that has endured for too long. My thanks also to Ana Lumbreras, Carmen, Luis, Angelito, Manolo, Francisco, Lupe, Sol and her wonderful family, Jill, Terri, Rob and so many other friends and comrades (too many to mention) who have contributed to the development of this and other parallel projects in one way or another.

My mother, Pepa and my brother, Enrique, are my compass. Without their generosity and endless patience I would not have been able to complete the book. I am also grateful to my mother for introducing me to the little universe of Arroyomolinos, and for helping me decipher the complex map of local nicknames and family connections. Donald provided the encouragement that I needed to complete the work, while Penny's feline contributions made the editing process so much more fun.

I am also deeply indebted to Stuart Price, whose enthusiasm for this project has been evident from the first time I mentioned it, in 2012, to the final production of the book. His intelligent insights and unwavering support have been crucial throughout the entire process, and I am grateful for his time, feedback and moral support.

I would also like to thank my editor, Martina O'Sullivan, for her interest in the book, and the reviewers who read my proposal for their useful and encouraging feedback. I am also grateful to Professor Richard Barker, Dr Ángela Cenarro and Professor Helen Graham for their support and kind comments. Some early papers based on the research were presented at three events: a research seminar at Canterbury Christ Church University on 13 November 2013; at the conference 'Generations of Protest: Marxism Matters?' (20 November 2013, De Montfort University); and at the public talk 'Memory and Ideology in the Spanish Civil War', held during the Cultural Exchanges event at De Montfort University in 2014. During the final stages of the project, on 5 November 2015, I delivered another research seminar at Canterbury Christ Church University. I am grateful to all the colleagues who attended these events and kindly offered their useful comments and questions. Finally, I would like to thank the School of Media, Art and Design, the Faculty of Arts and Humanities, and the Research and Enterprise Development Centre at Canterbury Christ Church University for their encouragement and for continuing to support my research.

An earlier version of some of the material in this book has appeared in Sanz Sabido, R. (2016) "Local memories: Conflict and lived experience in the Spanish Civil War". *Catalan Journal of Communication & Cultural Studies*, 8(1): 11–30.

Ya no se aclama y se grita,
aunque el dolor sea muy fuerte,
pero ante la cruz maldita
al que pregunta se advierte
que ahí yace la doncella
que vilmente fue violada
una oscura madrugada
antes de darle la muerte.
Y allí yacen los mineros
que arrancaron el carbón,
los metales y el acero,
debajo de este higuerón.
Y allí, junto a aquel estanque,
mataron a un abogado
por sentirse enamorado
de una España más brillante.

…

Cielo azul de Andalucía
¿qué no dirá tu llanura?
¿qué no dirá tu montaña?
de esta sombra negra y fría
que la voz de cobardía,
alardeando bravura,
llama grandeza de España.

Santiago Campos, 2003
Arroyomolinos de León (Huelva)

Participants from Arroyomolinos de León

ANTONIA

Antonia comes from a very humble background. Although she does not explicitly identify with any political parties, she takes a critical stance towards Franco's repression. She is now in her early eighties.

AURELIO

Aurelio Domínguez Silva was Secretary of the Libertarian Youths in Arroyomolinos in 1936. He is Magdalena's brother, and Blas and Santiago's uncle. Aurelio passed away in 2010. This interview was conducted by Rafael Cid on 9 September 2002.

BLAS

Blas Campos is Santiago's brother. He defines himself as a communist. He is now in his early eighties.

CARLOS

A devout man, Carlos is in his seventies and comes from a right-wing family.

CUPIDA

Cupida defined herself as left-wing, but she clarified that she had respect for the 'saints'. She passed away in 2015.

ELENA

Elena is in her seventies and comes from a right-wing family. She is Carlos' cousin.

FRAN

Fran is now in his mid-nineties. He managed to participate in the interview without making any explicit remarks. His descriptions were very useful to understand the socio-economic context of the village during and after the war.

FRASQUITO

Frasquito defines himself as left-wing, but admits that he pretended to support the regime while his father and uncle were hiding in the family home. He is Lorenza's brother, and is now in his nineties.

JUAN

Juan was born in 1940 and explains that, even though he did not live through the Civil War, he was very much aware, as a child, of the legacy of desolation that the conflict had left in the village.

JUAN MANUEL

Juan Manuel was given his name after his two grandfathers, Juan Sánchez Carrasco and Manuel Fernández Rubio, who were executed in 1936.

LORENZA

Lorenza is Frasquito's sister. She defines herself as left-wing. Her father was hiding in the family home when her mother became pregnant with her. He eventually turned himself in to save his wife's reputation in the village.

LUIS

In his early sixties, Luis has always had a keen interest in learning about the local past by talking to older generations. He defines himself as left-wing.

MATEO

Mateo is in his late fifties and his knowledge of the events is based on what his family and other villagers have told him about the war.

MERCEDES

Mercedes was born in the 1950s and, having migrated with her parents when she was a child, she knows what her close relatives have told her about the conflict. She defines herself as left-wing, and has a critical view of her experience growing up during the dictatorship.

MIGUEL

Miguel has a libertarian mindset, although he does not necessarily describe himself as such. He refuses to own anything and, despite his lack of resources, he gives away most of the products that he grows in a borrowed plot of land. He is in his late fifties, but he knows everything that older generations have shared with him over the years.

PEDRO

Pedro does not put a label to his politics, although he is clearly on the left. He is in his early seventies and has learnt about the local events through his family.

RAFAEL

Rafael is in his late seventies and is known to have a very good memory. His knowledge was very useful to trace local family connections and backgrounds.

RAMONA

Clearly critical of the regime, Ramona is in her early eighties. Some of her relatives, including her mother, were direct victims of Francoist repression.

SANTIAGO

Santiago Campos is Magdalena's son and Aurelio's nephew. He is an outspoken communist who, years ago, ran as representative of Izquierda Unida in local elections. Santiago passed away in 2015.

SILVIA

Silvia describes her politics as 'whatever is best for the working people'. She attended school in the 1940s and remembers the class differences that existed between different children in the village.

VALENTINA

Valentina is in her early eighties and comes from a left-wing background.

VALERIA

A very devout woman, Valeria is in her late seventies and comes from a traditional right-wing family.

Chapter 1

Introduction

Memory, Conflict and the Rural Context

On 24 August 1944, General Leclerc's command, the Ninth Company of the Second Armoured Division (commonly known as *la Nueve*, or 'the Ninth'), was the first military formation to enter Paris after the Nazis had vacated the city. Newly liberated Parisians watched as armoured columns passed through their streets, led by a vehicle that carried the Spanish Republican flag. The tanks that followed were marked with the names of famous battles from the Spanish Civil War (1936–39), like Madrid, Brunete, Guadalajara and Teruel (Mesquida 2014; Pons Prades 1975; Pons Prades 1985).

This landmark event has not, however, passed unaltered into the History books. According to accounts that have prevailed until very recently, Paris was not liberated by the Ninth as such, but simply by the Second Armoured Division. Of course, the Ninth was just one component of a much larger army, but its near disappearance from the narrative can be explained by two inconvenient realities. The first is that the Ninth, led by Captain Raymond Dronne, was composed for the most part of Spanish rather than French combatants. These men – almost exclusively members of the CNT and FAI[1] – were just some of the thousands of Republicans (anarchists, communists and socialists) who had fled their homeland in 1939. The Second Armoured Division as a whole, however, contained a majority of French soldiers: therefore, any reference to the Division would inevitably reinforce the notion that the liberation was an exclusively French affair. The second reason for this neglect relates to a shameful episode in the history of France itself. Having suffered for three years at the hands of a right-wing military insurgency, thousands of displaced Spanish men, women and children made the arduous climb across the Pyrenees to escape persecution (Matthews 1939). Edouard Daladier, the French premier, closed his country's borders to avoid the avalanche of refugees, but had to reopen them when Franco, the victorious Nationalist dictator, refused to countenance the creation of neutral zones. Although masses of refugees continued to arrive in France, they were not received with compassion. Most of them ended up in concentration camps, where they were imprisoned and forced to live and work in horrific conditions (Caamaño 2015; Macciuci 2006; Mesquida 2014; Rafaneau-Boj 1995; Riera 2016; Vilanova 2003).[2] The testimonies of the survivors help to illustrate the situation. For example, Fermín Pujol, who would later become part of *la Nueve*, recalls his experience:

> When we arrived, they disarmed us. They took everything away from us, rings, jackets, wallets, everything, and they sent us to a beach, in the open air, with no protection, surrounded by a wire fence and guarded by armed soldiers. Scabies and lice soon became our companions. If anyone escaped, the Senegalese colonial troops would shoot to kill. (in Mesquida 2014, my translation)

More than 15,000 refugees died within the first few weeks, and many more would never be able to return home. Despite the treatment they received, many of the adult males volunteered to continue the struggle against fascism by joining the French army, taking part in numerous battles and fighting alongside other foreigners during World War II. The Ninth, with its contingent of 146 Spaniards from a total of 160 men, were for the most part barely out of their teens when they first took up arms in Spain in 1936 (Mesquida 2014). Such was the preponderance of Spaniards in the company that all commands were given in Spanish. Their character was depicted by Captain Dronne, who described this group of fighters as

> individualists, idealists, courageous, showing an almost foolish bravery. They did not have a military spirit, they were even anti-militarists, but they were magnificent soldiers, brave and experienced fighters. … If they embraced our cause voluntarily, it was because it was the cause of freedom. They really were fighters for freedom. (Dronne 1984, 262–63, my translation)

As Mesquida (2014) points out, had *la Nueve* been comprised of Americans, dozens of films would have been made about them, because they exhibited extraordinary dignity, courage and solidarity. Yet, the significance of their struggles and achievements was not only underplayed, but also progressively forgotten, starting from the very day after the liberation of Paris, when Charles de Gaulle, speaking at the Hôtel de Ville, announced that Paris was

> liberated by herself, liberated by her people with the help of the armies of France, with the help and support of the whole of France, that is to say of combatant France, the only France, the true France, eternal France. (de Gaulle 1944, my translation)

From this moment, the version that prevailed was that Leclerc's Division had freed the French capital. De Gaulle's statement sought to foster a patriotic sentiment among the French population, one that would serve to unite France, which was characterised at this critical time by division and instability.[3] The problem was that, in doing so, the contribution that non-French fighters made to History was obscured. As Beevor and Cooper note,

> There was not the slightest mention of American or British help in the Liberation. In the eyes of the Allies, this was a churlish and grotesque rewriting of history; nevertheless, it was an inspired message, creating an image of national unity where none existed and binding the sorely wounded pride of the country. (Beevor and Cooper 2004, x)

The attempts of the French to nationalise the victory, Mesquida points out, meant that the foreigners were marginalised and made to disappear from History and from Memory (with the capital 'H' and 'M' denoting that these are official, state-sanctioned versions of the past). In this respect, Beevor and Cooper's assessment, by focusing on American and British aid alone, also fails to acknowledge the active contribution of Spanish men to the liberation of Paris and, more broadly, to the fight against fascism. This process of forgetting was exacerbated further by the campaign of repression and 'memory management' within Spain itself, through which the dictator, Franco, attempted to erase all traces of his enemies' existence. Yet, the worst form of insult inflicted upon these Spanish soldiers was not the fact that their efforts had become invisible: it was the fact that France and the other Allies would not assist them in their fight against Franco's regime, even though the Spaniards had been instrumental in the Allies' struggle against the Nazis. After World War II, Spanish ex-combatants, unable to return to their country, had to remain in France, while fascism in Spain became more entrenched.

LOCAL, NATIONAL AND INTERNATIONAL CONTEXTS

This book, though it begins with a reference to World War II, focuses on the terrible event that preceded it: the Spanish Civil War. Of course, the fact that both wars involved some of the same people and, in some cases at least, a shared consciousness of the evil they opposed, is arguably a good indicator of the continued importance of the earlier conflict. Numerous scholars have discussed the historical and ideological meaning of the Civil War, its impact on European political and military developments in the 1930s and 1940s, and the military interventions made by several external governments (see, e.g., Beevor 2006; Graham 2012; Preston 2012). Between 1936 and

1939, Spain became a battlefield where fascists and anti-fascists fought what has been described as a 'rehearsal' for World War II, in which the former had the opportunity to test their new weapons (Bowers 1954). The pact of non-intervention that was agreed in August 1936 by twenty-four countries (including Britain, France, the Soviet Union, Germany and Italy) was effectively broken when Franco's forces gained the support of the German and Italian war machines. Meanwhile, the Second Republic, an elected and therefore legitimate government, did not obtain the same amount of support from those nations that were supposedly in sympathy with democratic principles. In addition to the assistance of the Soviet Union and Mexico, the Republican government counted upon the volunteers who filled the ranks of the International Brigades.

Notwithstanding the international character of the Civil War, it is not my intention to dwell upon this aspect of the struggle. Any discussion of the war requires some knowledge of the broader effects and consequences of foreign intervention. Nonetheless, a central purpose of this book is to reclaim the conflict as one that was eminently Spanish, for the majority of the lives lost and ruined – not just at the battlefronts but also in the repression that followed – were those of Spanish civilians. This book thus reflects on what the conflict meant to ordinary people whose lives were disrupted by the military coup of 1936 and the subsequent waves of violence that lasted for decades after the Republic's defeat. The purpose of my narrative is to redirect the broad international and theoretical perspectives towards a more localised and 'lived' approach, focusing on the 'civil' aspect of the war, while attempting to demonstrate that the local, regional, national and international dimensions are interrelated and should therefore be considered alongside one another.

HISTORY AND TRUTH

The experience of the men who composed *la Nueve* illustrates a number of issues in the conceptualisation of, and relationship between, History and Memory, as well as other notions such as truth, consciousness and justice (some of the key concepts with which this book engages). In the first instance, the 'historisation' of significant events includes not only the straightforward recounting of what happened, but also a certain degree of calculated organisation and even strategic 'management' of information that defines what is and is not presented. The way in which the Ninth was 'historicised' is one example of this process. It may be argued that covering up the achievements of a particular group of men was a necessary political manoeuvre in order to achieve a 'greater good', but historians' complicity with the perspective adopted by de Gaulle (supposedly on behalf of the French state) seems to indicate that the apparent factuality and reliability of (official) History is, in fact, littered with state-sponsored inaccuracies.

This is not, therefore, an attack on the work of historians, but a critique of the History that is promoted (and imposed) by powerful agents at particular historical moments. In Spain, after the end of the war in 1939, and even from the very moment when they began to seize Republican territory, the National-ist propaganda machine went to great lengths to manage the information that was released to the general public. Meanwhile, anyone who was suspected of sympathising with the Left was persecuted, with the ultimate purpose of purging any dissenting ideologies. For the defeated, Franco's mechanisms of information management, and the creation of his own approved History, marginalised their voices and diminished their chances of writing their own narratives.

More recently, the work of a number of historians has helped to challenge Franco's version of the past. For example, Spanish historian Francisco Espi-nosa Maestre, who has authored a number of in-depth historical analyses of the Spanish Civil War (in particular, work on the south-western provinces of Seville, Huelva and Badajoz), has analysed the figures that pro-Franco historians published when estimating the numbers of victims of fascist vio-lence (Espinosa Maestre 2005; Espinosa Maestre 2011; Espinosa Maestre 2012a). In order to illustrate his approach, Espinosa points out the inac-curacies in General Ramón Salas Larrazábal's book *Pérdidas de la Guerra* (1977), which was an attempt to deal with issues such as the use of repressive practices during and after the war. According to Salas' supposedly 'exact' enumeration of victims, 176 people lost their lives in the province of Bada-joz between 1936 and 1940, including those who lost their lives in 'irregular executions' (139 people) and 'judiciary executions' (37 people). Espinosa's view is that this type of historicising relies on numbers to make bigger fic-tions seem credible:

Salas' work reminds us of those tall tales that Goebbels liked so much: the scien-tific tall tale, in which lies appear so wrapped in numbers, charts, equations and details that they seem to be true. All in all, this reveals a fascination for numbers [Goebbels 1998, 35]. Salas' figures were, in addition, accompanied by an allu-sion to the 'harsh reprisals that, according to all testimonies, were carried out by the occupants of Badajoz in 1936' and by the remark that 'there is no doubt that the reach of these [reprisals] has been greatly exaggerated, but it seems that the 91 civil executions recorded in 1936 and the 26 executions of 1937 may be too few'. This is evidence of how reality can be distorted and history falsified. It is hardly surprising that before his 'final rectifications' Salas asserted that in the *whole province* of Badajoz the *gubernamentales* [the government representa-tives] killed 1,466 people and their opponents 989. Had he analysed the data in the civil registry properly, he would have known that more people were killed

in the *city* of Badajoz alone, than the number he ascribes to the entire province.
(Espinosa Maestre 2011, 357–58, my translation and emphasis)

When Espinosa discovered that the number of assassinations in the west of
the province was twice the figure given by Salas for the entire province, he
noted that this did not include the names of individuals that had not been officially recorded. He also pointed out that the research that had been conducted
in other provinces had consistently invalidated Salas' figures, although half
the country had yet to be fully investigated. Nevertheless, Salas' study is still
being used by various authors as though it is a valid source (Espinosa Maestre
2011, 358).

Reig Tapia (1986), for instance, presents an ambivalent assessment of
Salas' figures. Despite his argument that only some privileged individuals
(such as Salas) were allowed to consult the archives (on the basis of their
affinity to the 'right' type of ideology), Reig Tapia states, nonetheless, that
there is no reason why, in principle, Salas' evidence should be doubted. He
even agrees with Salas' claim that there were not as many death penalties as
commonly assumed, and that the number of executions was even lower than
that (Reig Tapia 1986, 23; see also Salas Larrazábal 1977, 128). The problem
with Salas' data is that it only takes into account the 'official' figures, based
on information gathered by analysing legal documents. This approach tends
to ignore both the realities behind each case and the vast amount of people
who became the victims of repression through 'unofficial' channels. Reig
Tapia argues, quite rightly, that the only way to achieve the required precision
in the quantification of victims would involve an exhaustive analysis, going
from village to village and studying every type of archive, including hospital, war, prison and cemetery registers. The addition of all the local analyses
would then provide a more reliable picture of the repression. Yet, at the same
time, Reig Tapia seems prepared to accept Salas' skewed figures as believ-
able and to present them as the only systematic study, one which represented
the 'greatest individual effort' that had been developed up to that moment
(Reig Tapia 1986, 29).

MEMORY AND HISTORY

The focus on quantitative precision sometimes leaves the 'histories' (in plural
and with a lower-case 'h', to indicate their multiplicity and heterogeneity)
that are gathered from other sources (such as oral reports) seem somehow
inferior to official documents. It is in this context that scholarly debates have
developed about the ability of the separate but interconnected disciplines of
History and Memory, to make the past accessible to contemporary audiences.

In this respect, Phillips notes that one of the conditions that have led to the development of Memory Studies is, precisely, the increasing mistrust of 'official History' (Phillips 2008, 2). From this perspective, memory is understood as a way of valuing those histories that have not entered the 'annals' of History. These memories can be described as alternative versions of the past that have not received the sanction of those in power. Similarly, Ramoneda (1997) argues that 'memory is one of the few resources with which we can defend ourselves from history, which is always written by the victors' (my translation). In the race to establish a coherent narrative, the law of the strongest often prevails: following any conflict, the winners often try to impose their views on the defeated.[4] Through official and unofficial mechanisms, all of which operate under the aegis of the state and other agents that work on its behalf, the voices of the losers are silenced. One important countermechanism that is available, the one that may serve to resist the imposition of the victors' History, is frequently found in the collection, analysis and publication of oral testimonies, which give expression to, and magnify, silenced and oppressed memories (Portelli 2006).

So, for example, Miguel, one of the participants in this study, mentioned the massacre of Badajoz that Espinosa has examined (see above):

> Here, in the village, they killed more than forty people, but they killed 3,000 in the *plaza* in Badajoz [in reference to *la plaza de toros*, that is, Badajoz's bullfighting ring]. In Segura, they killed 500, at least. They did not have the balls to take Badajoz. They killed women, children, old people. ... They killed everything that moved in front of them. They caught them and executed them, just like that. (Miguel 2014a, my translation)

The figures and the precise details of the executions may not be relayed accurately, but it is remarkable that, despite the efforts to erase the event from (official) History and from (official) Memory, knowledge of this massacre has been transmitted orally among people who have not had an opportunity to learn about it in school or by reading books. Here, we find the connection between histories, memories and orality. Orality provides us with a window into past events or, rather, with multiple windows that allow us to take account of the myriad histories of which the past is actually composed. This book does not argue that establishing the exact number of victims is unimportant (see the argument on Salas' figures, above): in fact, an attempt to reconstruct the list of victims in a village in Southern Spain appears in Chapter 4. My main emphasis is, however, on 'local' memories related by members of a community – the residents of Arroyomolinos de León in the province of Huelva – that suffered persecution after the coup of 18 July 1936. My goal is to rescue their memories from the oblivion promoted by the state.

MEMORY IN SPAIN

Seventy-one years after the liberation of Paris, a contemporary initiative to pay homage to the Ninth Company (see above) provided an opportunity to recall the momentous events of 1944. This commemorative act, held on 3 June 2015, was organised by the mayor of Paris, Anne Hidalgo (a descendant of Spanish migrants), and paid tribute to the Spanish Republicans who liberated the French capital. Besides its significance for scholars of Memory Studies, this occasion was particularly interesting because King Felipe VI and Queen Letizia of Spain were invited to the ceremony. The mayor said in her speech that 'this monarchy embodies the young, reconciled Spain. ... That a king pays homage to a group of Republicans is the best proof of this new Spain, which has turned the page on its darkest hours' (Hernández Velasco 2015, my translation). She also claimed that the King and the Queen represented the face of a free and united Spain, and, in addition, that they were governing the country 'under the symbol of tolerance, diversity and modernity', embodying 'unity in diversity' (Hernández Velasco 2015, my translation). The presence of the Spanish monarchy on this occasion was intended to symbolise political reconciliation in Spain, a theme taken up by Prieto (2015) in an opinion column published in *El País* under the title 'Un buen gesto real hacia los republicanos' (A positive royal gesture towards the Republicans). Prieto declared that the act served to recognise

> those Spanish people who were defeated by the Francoist army and whose memory has remained crushed for decades, first because of the weight of the dictatorship and later, during the democratic period, as a consequence of the tenacious resistance of many individuals who should have taken steps to heal the wounds caused by the already distant Civil War. (Prieto 2015, my translation)

Prieto correctly draws attention to the perpetual erasure of the memory of the defeated, not only under the dictatorship but also during the democratic period. Yet, while seemingly reasonable, Prieto's summary of the fate of 'those Spanish people who were defeated by the Francoist army' includes several remarks that have assimilated a number of Francoist myths, legends that are still often taken for granted, emerging explicitly or implicitly within various types of public discourse. In Prieto's case, for instance, it is unclear who 'those Spanish people' were, why they fought, why their memory had been crushed, and exactly who was responsible for mounting such a 'tenacious resistance' to the process of reconciliation. The allusion to a 'Francoist army' adds to the confusion, particularly if we consider the fact that the legitimate army – the one that served the Republic – is not acknowledged.

Although these deficiencies may not have been intended, such references point, implicitly at least, to some of the widespread (and generally internalised) myths of the Civil War, namely the *discursive erosion* of the Second Republic's legitimacy. This government was, despite its considerable shortcomings, the first formal democratic system in Spain – a fact that is almost always obliterated by claims that the democratic period in Spain began after Franco's death. Even terms that are now in common use, such as the reference to the Civil War, fail to alert us to the fact that a military coup had been directed against this infant democracy, ultimately annihilating it. When the political realities of 1936 are disguised, as a matter of course, as a less severe phenomenon, we may begin to question the entire system of representation. So, for example, one of the main explanatory frameworks that has pervaded popular attitudes is that the three-year conflict was an unavoidable fratricidal struggle in which both sides committed all types of aberrations, equally and on the same level, since the context of the fight required – and perhaps even justified – extreme measures. This myth, and some of its variations, constitutes the basis of the Civil War framework, and is an integral part of the general understanding that exists of the recent history of Spain. If it is true that 'we' were all to blame in equal measure, then it is easier to promote the suggestion that nobody in particular should be made responsible for the consequences.

Prieto's assessment of the monarchy's participation in the act of commemoration (described above) adds to the reinforcement of this inadequate framework. The royal couple's gesture, Prieto claimed, was twofold:

> Not only do they pay tribute to the Spanish republicans that were in the vanguard of the troops that liberated Paris in World War II, but they also rescue them from the oblivion to which the French Republic had consigned them. (Prieto 2015, my translation)

It is striking that, having blamed 'many [*unnamed*] individuals' for the perpetuation of the conditions that the Republicans have endured, Prieto does not hesitate, at this point, to place the responsibility for exacerbating the problem on the French Republic. Here, and throughout the article, which consistently fails to address the core issues in a critical manner, there is no reference to the original causes of the problem, or to the lack of official attempts to recognise the Republican case. Far from pointing out the incoherencies of the commemorative event, in which a king pays tribute to a group of Republicans, the author emphasises the positive symbolic significance of the monarchy's participation in the act:

Nothing could have stopped this event from becoming public, even without the presence and support of the authorities. But the attendance of Spain's Head of State is precisely what gives the act of commemoration greater symbolic value, similar to the meeting that took place between King Juan Carlos and Dolores Rivas de Cheriff, the widow of Manuel Azaña, the last constitutional Head of State before the advent of the dictatorship. That particular encounter took place in Mexico in 1979 and became, at that moment, a powerful symbol of reconciliation. Many years later, Felipe VI is taking another step in the same direction, uniting the exiled Spain with the civil and political society that constitutes today's Spain. The powers of the Head of State may be symbolic but, without spectacle or commotion, they contribute to the moral maturity of our society, bringing the effects of that distant civil conflict to a close. (Prieto 2015, my translation)

The symbolism that Prieto describes is called into question if we assess the participation of the Monarchy within the *international* context of the commemoration. We might consider, for example, a different type of event, one that took place on 21 May 2015, less than two weeks before the tribute to the Ninth was held in Paris. A group of archaeologists, forensic anthropologists and volunteers from the Asociación para la Recuperación de la Memoria Histórica (ARMH, Association for the Recuperation of Historical Memory) gathered in the cemetery of Teilán, a village in the north-western province of Lugo, in order to exhume the remains of Bernardo Álvarez Trabajo, 'el Gasta', who was gunned down by civil guards in 1949 (Sabugal 2015).[5] Exhumations often take several days to complete, and they sometimes have to be put on hold if resources are exhausted before the graves are discovered. On this occasion, however, the association knew exactly where the remains were, as they had already exhumed another body in the same place in 2012. On that day, they were able to complete the work and proceed with the scientific analyses that follow an exhumation.

When a body is exhumed, the association carries out an in-depth forensic and anthropological study of the remains, as well as a genetic test (conducted without charge in Argentina) that can be used to confirm the victim's identity. This process, which takes months to conduct, is followed by a ceremony to 'deliver the remains' (*entrega de restos*) to the nearest surviving relatives. The burial of the victims is normally a private matter, but the organisers of these ceremonies purposely invite people with 'official' status to represent the public administration, in an attempt to give the event a public dimension. This is meant, in effect, to emphasise the fact that the exhumation of Franco's victims is not a matter that merely concerns the private sphere of the relatives: their family member will, at last, be buried with dignity, but the whole occasion is also a public issue and, more specifically, a matter that the state should resolve. Organisers usually invite local representatives from all parties, regardless of their points of view. There are variations from locality to locality, but it is often Izquierda Unida (the United Left, composed of radical parties and groups), and sometimes PSOE (Partido Socialista Obrero Español, on the centre-left), that tend to accept the invitations, thereby providing a clear indication of the ideological charge that is attributed to these events.

To provide another example, on 30 May 2015, only three days before the event in Paris, another *entrega* ceremony was held in Valderas, a village in the north-western province of León. The remains of nine men were returned to families who had spent nearly eighty years hoping to find their missing relatives. On both occasions, and in the hundreds of other scientific exhumations and *entregas* that have taken place since 2000,[6] local residents, descendants of the victims and local politicians have been present as the remains were revealed. Yet, neither the current king, nor his father, has ever attended any of these ceremonies. The examples of exhumations and *entregas* mentioned here have been chosen for illustrative purposes only, but entire books could be dedicated to recounting each exhumation, *entrega*, demonstration and other forms of public commemoration that have taken place in Spain, and which have never been attended by representatives of the monarchy or the central government (with the exception of cases when the Ministry of the Presidency, during José Luis Rodríguez Zapatero's government, has funded commemorative monuments).

If we consider the process through which authorities are asked to attend these events, the first question that springs to mind is why, if the exhumations are really a matter for the state, it would be necessary to make a formal request for official public recognition. An obvious parallel to this question is why the head of state or the central government are not involved in these acts as a matter of course. The answer to these questions is the same as the one that explains why memory associations have received no official support since 2011 (assistance was limited between 2007 and 2011, and was non-existent before 2007), while international bodies such as the Abraham Lincoln Brigade Archive (Bierzo Diario 2015) and the Norwegian trade union Elogit (InfoBierzo 2015) recognise their work with awards and donations that enable the ARMH to survive. The answer also helps to explain why, eighty years after the beginning of the Civil War, there are still around 114,000 *desaparecidos* (disappeared victims) (Bierzo Diario 2015).

The answer to these questions lies in the *institutionalisation of oblivion*. The 'pact of silence' that was agreed during the transition to democracy meant that the problems caused by the military coup (that led, in turn, to the Civil War and the dictatorship) remained unresolved long after Franco's death. This refusal to examine the past helped maintain the deep-rooted divisions between the 'two Spains' (Juliá 2004) that can be traced back to the catastrophic experience of the 1930s. The consequences of the war and Franco's repression have not been addressed properly, and this means that the topic remains highly contentious. The struggle between the different sides has therefore become an integral part of Spain's collective identity, often re-emerging in contemporary political and socio-economic debates. The Law of Historical Memory, which was passed in 2007 by PSOE (technically a centre-left party), provides guidelines on issues related to memory, from the exhumation of mass graves to the elimination of street names that still refer to agents of the dictatorship. However, the limited scope of this law, and the fact that there is no obligation to enforce it (it provides, instead, the grounds for localised debates), has led to further political polarisation, particularly when the right-wing government of Partido Popular, or PP, have stopped applying it.

In the meantime, thousands of families are still searching for the graves of their relatives, while none of the culprits have ever been brought to justice. Before the 2007 Law of Historical Memory, the Amnesty Act of 1977 – which is still in force today – guaranteed the protection of the repressors. The Act was the legal expression of the pact of silence agreed during the transition: it committed all sides in the conflict to forgive and forget, but served, in effect, to exonerate Franco's high-ranking officials and civil servants from any crimes they had committed. Consequently, in Spain, the concepts of 'amnesty' and 'amnesia' have frequently been conflated as synonyms (Escudero et al. 2013, 9). This is how oblivion became institutionalised in Spain, and public Memory was defined accordingly.

What we are witnessing is, in short, a national strategy of forgetfulness and oppression that hides behind an international façade of harmony and respect. An additional example, one that is in keeping with the 'transnational' narrative that grew around the king's speech in Paris, is provided by the Minister of Foreign Affairs and Cooperation, José Manuel García-Margallo, who paid tribute to the Spanish Republicans who died in the concentration camp in Mauthausen[7] (Austria) during World War II (EFE 2015a; see also EFE 2015b). During his visit to the camp, García-Margallo emphasised the importance of 'honouring and renewing the universal duty of memory against acts of brutality' and claimed that 'we need memory to be a constant part of our learning' (EFE 2015a, my translation). The minister further claimed that the Spain that pays tribute to the victims today is 'an open country, democratic, supportive, inclusive, where respect for the other, for the different, is the norm. A country that rejects any form of intolerance, of intransigence, of brutality' (EFE 2015a, my translation). These words epitomise the stance of the Spanish government towards an international act of commemoration – involving Spanish prisoners in Nazi concentration camps – that hides, nevertheless, the policy of neglect that they pursue at home.

Indeed, it is striking that this minister was speaking on behalf of a government that has done its best to obstruct, through discursive and material means, the work of the memory movement. All government subventions for exhumations were stopped (they are now funded by public donations, international awards and by the relatives themselves), while those who dare to investigate the historical facts are condemned. Both the king's and the minister's speeches are characterised by the same defining quality: the fact that they were both made abroad. This meant, in effect, that they needed to include the necessary references in order to make their interventions acceptable for an international audience. This discourse is designed exclusively for external consumption and, as discussed above, is entirely unsupported by any 'pro-memory actions' within Spanish borders. In Spain, the official discourse – and, indeed, the actions that accompany it – is quite different (see, e.g., the articles published by Amnistía Internacional 2015; CEAQUA 2015; Chientaroli 2014; and Junquera 2015, regarding the United Nations' condemnation of Spain's failures on the subject of historical memory).

Against this backdrop, the call to remember the past is a particularly contentious issue, one that is strongly defined by the development of a number of myths perpetuated during the dictatorship (see above). The transition to democracy was conducted in a way that ensured the preservation of these myths within contemporary Spanish culture, and they are now accompanied by the stance, predominantly defended by PP and its followers, that the past is best left untouched: it is unnecessary or inadvisable to 'reopen the wounds of the war' (*'reabrir las heridas de la guerra'*). Partido Popular (known as Alianza Popular until 1991) embodies the democratised version of Franco's propaganda machine and is, unsurprisingly, opposed to anything that would 'stir things up' (*'remover las cosas'*). It is no coincidence (as illustrated by several examples that appear throughout the book) that this expression is often used by my own interviewees, who often voiced doubts about their participation in a study of this kind. Individuals may indeed have legitimate reservations due to a variety of personal factors or feelings, such as fear or shame, but the official discourse of PP on this matter – essentially, that it is unnecessary to pursue the issue – is defined by the desire to protect the post-Franco status quo. In this sense, the two main political parties, the right-wing PP and the centre-left PSOE, are not that different. Both parties have demonstrated, in their own ways, their unwillingness to revisit the issues that were not only left unanswered when the war finished in 1939, but also remained unresolved after 1975, when Franco died.

This neglect gives renewed strength to the argument that revisiting the past is a necessary first step in dealing with the terrible effects that the repression had on thousands of families and, to use the 'wounds' metaphor once more, to close *'las viejas heridas'* (the old wounds) that still persist today. The motto of the ARMH, '*verdad, justicia y reparación*' (truth, justice and reparation) encapsulates both the aim of healing these wounds and the method of doing so: to admit the truth of what happened, to achieve justice for the victims and to repair the damage in any way possible (see Chapter 3 for a discussion of these principles). Most memory associations insist that every aspect of this process must be conducted publicly, insofar as the damage was not only inflicted on particular individuals by specific executioners (which would confine the issue to the private sphere), but was conducted as a systematic act of state terror (so the state needs to redress its effects publicly).[8]

MEMORY, ORALITY AND THE LOCAL

Memory is, by its very nature, a site of struggle and, in the specific national context of Spain, is clearly one that continues to provoke a great deal of anger and contention. The unheard voices of the past mainly began to gain attention at the turn of the century, although they remain, on the whole, obscured by state-sponsored versions of history (Sanz Sabido et al. 2016). In this book, I examine some of those hidden narratives through the interdisciplinary frameworks of Memory and Critical Ethnography. The Critical Ethnography of Memory proposed here aims to gain access to 'local' memories – that is, individual memories of local events – through a process of immersion in the small communities where specific incidents occurred. The methodological underpinning of the approach is discussed in greater depth in Chapter 3, but the method depends on a critical analysis of the narration *and* performance of oral testimonies about past events. The purpose is to give voice to those who have been silenced by the imposition of repressive political, legal, economic and cultural mechanisms during the war, the dictatorship and after Franco's death in 1975, through ostensibly democratised channels of control. The Critical Ethnography of Memory therefore provides a tool that can be used to uncover what Foucault (2004) described as 'subjugated knowledges', which he defined in two different ways:

> On the one hand, I am referring to historical contents that have been buried or masked in functional coherences or formal systematizations. … Historical contents alone allow us to see the dividing lines in the confrontations and struggles that functional arrangements or systematic organizations are designed to mask. Subjugated knowledges are, then, blocks of historical knowledges that were present in the functional and systematic ensembles, but which were masked, and the critique was able to reveal their existence by using, obviously enough, the tools of scholarship. (Foucault 2004, 7)

From this perspective, a critical approach to knowledge requires a close examination not only of the content of History, but also of the official processes, principles and institutions that have determined which 'knowledges' are sanctioned and which are suppressed. On the other hand, Foucault also considered an additional form of 'subjugated' knowledge, which he defined as

> a whole series of knowledges that have been disqualified as nonconceptual knowledges, as insufficiently elaborated knowledges: naïve knowledges, hierarchically inferior knowledges, knowledges that are below the required level of erudition or scientificity. And it is thanks to the reappearance of these knowledges from below, of these unqualified or even disqualified knowledges ... that made the critique possible. (Foucault 2004, 7–8)

Certain types of knowledge are therefore hidden, while others are declared ineligible before they have even acquired the status of knowledge. For Foucault, these knowledges consist of what people know at a local level:

> this is by no means the same thing as common knowledge or common sense but, on the contrary, a particular knowledge, a knowledge that is local, regional, or differential, incapable of unanimity and which derives its power solely from the fact that it is different from all the knowledges that surround it. (Foucault 2004: 7)

Following a similar principle, the primary concern of a Critical Ethnography of Memory involves immersion in local milieus and the critical analysis of oral testimonies, an approach that is closer to the second definition given above, although it also takes into account the first perspective, since they are both useful in facilitating critique: they are both oriented, in other words, towards unearthing hidden stories on behalf of the people who experienced them, and validating them against the systemic, long-standing marginalisation of their voices. To put it differently, this method contrasts local events and experiences, as remembered by those who lived them, with those national memories nurtured by official state channels. In this respect, oral testimonies play a crucial role since, in Fraser's words, they help to 'articulate the experiences of people who, historically speaking, would otherwise remain inarticulate' (Fraser 1979, 31).

The histories that form the basis of this study emerge from an ethnographic study conducted in the small Andalusian village of Arroyomolinos de León (situated in the southern province of Huelva). Twenty-two villagers recalled the events that took place locally, in their rural community, in the 1930s and early 1940s, expressing their memories through particular narratives and performances in semi-structured interviews (see Chapter 3 for a more in-depth discussion of the methodological framework). The immediate objective of this analysis is to provide a description of the participants' accounts, while noting the ways in which inhabitants of the community remember the *same* events. The point of this approach is to examine the ways in which the meanings of particular events circulate within public consciousness, with particular reference to a category I refer to as the production of 'local' memories, which assume both individual and collective forms: first, because individuals remember events within the range of their own cognitive abilities; and, second, because individual memories add up to the social memory of the particular community that experienced, witnessed and 'shared' those events. By examining the testimonies of local protagonists, I also delve into the broader discursive frameworks at a national level, which have mythologised the entire period (see above). In Chapter 3, I provide a discussion of the interplay between local, regional, national and international levels of memory.

Admittedly, contemporary oral testimonies about the past will reflect how events are remembered and understood *in the present*: they will not necessarily reveal the variety of meanings that they may have had throughout the years and, above all, what they meant when the events first occurred. In fact, memories and meanings rarely remain fixed, as they are constantly exposed to new developments and are shaped by various forms of social influence (see Chapter 2). So, for example, drawing upon Assmann's reference to the history of Moses, Harth (2010) points out that 'the effective normative, symbolically coded "truth" of a great memory figure' is not to be found in the past of that figure, which

> can be reconstructed by comparatively rational means, but rather in the perspectives from whose vantage point later generations have interpreted and incorporated into their own self-image his history, passed down in writing, and the story of the exodus associated with his name. (Harth 2010, 91)

The 'truth' that becomes available to us after any historical process is therefore defined by the various subjective perspectives that can be obtained in the present. Harth further notes that the memory metaphor has a twofold function: 'On the one hand it designates the cognitively simplified visualization of the past, and on the other hand it provides a symbol for the formation of ideological convictions' (Harth 2010, 91). Theoretically, from the perspective of History as a formal discipline, both the 'simplified' and 'symbolic' qualities of this type of 'truth' render it ineligible as a meaningful contribution to a scientific and objective narrative. We have already seen, however, that official History does not necessarily consist of pure accounts of the past, as they are often underpinned by ideological standpoints. Morris (2007), for example, talks about a process of 'mnemonicide', or assassination of memory, that takes place in official History. I would add that a similar process – the assassination of 'memories' – takes place in the establishment of 'official' Memory, since both official History and official Memory are, in fact, very similar in their state-sponsored mechanisms and ideological intentions. The *critical* element of Critical Ethnography of Memory is directed at these 'official' ideological and rhetorical constructions.

There are a number of options available to counteract the self-ascribed validity and superiority of the dominant perspective over the myriad subjugated knowledges that remain buried in local milieus. For historians an initial step would be to separate the description of the past from any ideological interpretations (such as Salas' work cited above), particularly when these are produced in the service of oppressive systems, and to write a History that is inclusive of the multitude of histories that comprise the past. In the absence of these actions, and as long as the contingency of History (and of Memory) is not at least acknowledged, the subjective nature of local memories is precisely one of its key values, as it provides a counterweight to the totalising nature of official versions. However, the subjectivity and fragmentation that exists in this plurality of memories is, as mentioned above, what makes these raw recollections unsuitable for more forensic approaches to the study of the past. In this regard, Ortiz Heras sees the potential in creating a *social memory* that – based on the desire to understand, rather than to settle scores – describes, analyses and interprets oral testimonies in an effort to turn these fragmented and plural memories into a critical History, one that has justice and the formation of free and tolerant citizens as its primary goals (Ortiz Heras 2006, 191). Izquierdo Martín and Sánchez León (2008) also argue in favour of a more citizen-oriented History, which can only happen if positivist and definitive approaches are rethought. Moreover, Portelli (1991) points out that any discrepancies between (proven, objective) fact and (malleable, subjective) memories do not amount to a weakness, but a strength: memories *also* contain facts, and not only that, but a range of narrative details and forms of meaning. As one of the participants reiterated during his interview, 'This is what I have heard, it may not be true, but it is what I know.'

While oral testimonies do not consist of purely objective and reliable facts, this does not mean that they should be considered to be entirely subjective and fictional, and certainly, they should not be neglected for that reason. The narration and performance of memories constitute, at once, a narrative of a moment in history *and* the way in which that moment is remembered through a particular subjectivity (Madison 2012). Oral contributions therefore combine references to events that occurred – so there is, at least, some degree of factuality in them – with deeper meanings that would otherwise be lost. Events may be described inaccurately, some of its aspects may be forgotten or re-arranged, and descriptions may include references to other seemingly unrelated happenings, some of which belong to an entirely different time period. 'Errors, inventions, and myths', Portelli (1991, 2) notes, 'lead us through and beyond facts to their meanings.' These are some of the analytical categories that can be used, not only to identify how individuals remember specific events, but also to examine the socio-political underpinning of those memories, which can be accessed through a deeper engagement with the testimonies, their narrators and the temporal contexts within which they are expressed.

The localised view presented here is drawn from two main sources: first, a collection of oral testimonies, offered by inhabitants of Arroyomolinos de León, constitute the primary vehicle through which the social memories of the villagers are accessed; and, second, a number of documents, discovered in local and private archives, add further detail to the oral narratives. As I will argue in Chapter 3, the use of documents is not at odds with ethnographic endeavour, but serves to strengthen the case for a method that combines different sources in order to understand the past and the contemporary legacy of that past. Admittedly, a historian dedicated to purely archival work would make a much finer analysis of these documents, which would also have been compared with a greater variety of files in other archives. Here, however, my primary goal is to examine the local memories of a small rural community in order to understand the interplay between different levels of memory, particularly between local (or social) and national (or public) ones. It is worth clarifying at this point that the localised approach taken here is not meant to suggest that all villages had an identical experience: quite to the contrary, this perspective is designed to emphasise the variety of contexts that exist within the national context. My contention is that, despite the commonalities that can be found between localities across the country, the Civil War was far from a monolithic event that can be described with a few select or 'totalising' statements.

RURAL COMMUNITIES

> It is unbelievable, what a war does in a village. Such a tight-knit community, and you see… People in the village that you see every day, you see them in the street and you know they killed your father, and have done other things too. Those things remain inside you. That thorn is still there… People may not talk about it, but they know it, they still remember. (Carlos 2014, my translation)

The rural experience of the Civil War is important because it is character-ised by the imposition of repressive practices that divided relatives, friends and neighbours who inhabited relatively small, close-knit communities. The intimate focus on a small community in a rural area differs, to a certain extent, from larger urban contexts. Different forms of repression and violence developed in all localities throughout Spain, but the typical features of rural environments shaped the experiences, and the perception of those experiences, in particular ways. Cintas Guillén, for example, notes how, despite the continued strikes in large cities such as Seville, the revolutionary environment persisted more deeply in rural Spain, which remained a focal point of socio-economic and political struggles, particularly in deeply agrarian Andalusia, where conditions were especially harsh (Cintas Guillén 2006, 69).

Del Río (2014b) also provides an indication of the impact that the war had on the rural environment, in contrast to the urban one. When describing the fate of the Andalusians who ended up in German concentration camps, del Río points out that most of them originated from rural Andalusia: only 200 approximately of the 1,500 Andalusian prisoners came from one of the nine main urban centres in the region, including the eight capital cities and Jerez de la Frontera (del Río 2014b, 76). This is not surprising if we consider that most of those captured were landless farm workers and peasants, or others who occupied humble positions such as cobblers, barbers, bakers and miners, among other small trades. The figures present, in addition, an uneven distribution across rural Andalusia due to the way in which the occupation developed in different territories. The province of Huelva fell shortly after the coup, with the exception of the mining district where Minas de Riotinto sits. Here, workers managed to organise themselves quite well, thanks to their revolutionary background and combative abilities, but they found themselves trapped in a space surrounded by rebels. Only a few of them managed to escape and, of the ones who did, the majority had to walk across the mountains in the north of the province, towards Badajoz and then on, in most cases, to Madrid, Aragón and Cataluña (del Río 2014b, 77). Reaching these destinations was, however, a difficult objective to achieve. Two participants have recalled how one villager joined a column that was travelling to join the front on the Republican side. When these volunteers arrived at Llerena (in the province of Badajoz), they walked into an ambush:

> Prospe joined a column that was also joined by men from Riotinto, and from … many other villages around here, all left-wing people. The column was picking up men who wanted to fight against the fascists. They were tricked though. '*Compañeros*' [Comrades], they said. '*Compañeros*, there is food over here'… and they followed in. Suddenly they started shooting. They killed everyone who was at the front of the group. Prospe was at the back and survived. They had set a trap for them. In Llerena … I think they were killed in Llerena. (Miguel 2014a, my translation)

Fran (2015) also mentioned this incident without referring to the fact that Prospe was part of the column. Luis (2015), however, thought that several people from the village died in the ambush, including Manuel González García 'Comecuerdas', the father of 'Molía', and others.

Hazack defines the traditional rural society, with its basic social units (community and family) as

> a closed universe, relatively stable and homogeneous, in which the predominant norms are beyond individual motivation and form an oral culture that is sustained in a relative economic and cultural autarchy based on the practice of subsistence economy. The traditional society model manifests itself more as a series of axioms than as verifiable observations. (Hazack, in Sánchez Jiménez 1975, 11, my translation)

Without making the mistake of examining rural life from the perspective of urban existence, it is safe to say that rural environments have their own internal idiosyncrasies, sharing some commonalities across different rural communities while, at the same time, retaining characteristics that are specific to each village. In Spain alone, there are approximately 7,000 villages, and each of them has its own identity as a separate community.

In rural societies, time and family are organised around agrarian activities: these activities not only constitute modes of production or business, but a whole way of social life that is progressively built upon through the rehearsal of long-standing customs and traditions (Sánchez Jiménez 1975, 12). In this environment, it is possible to observe the emergence of some apparent contradictions. On the one hand, there exist among the villagers strong networks of solidarity. These relations function on a daily basis: whenever a person or family needs some assistance, whether in an ordinary situation or during times of adversity, villagers do their utmost to help their neighbours. On the other hand, however, tensions and divisions are also bound to appear in a context where every individual knows everyone else and one another's family roots and connections. The circulation of rumours and gossip is frequent, particularly when there are moral judgements to be made about the behaviours of others. In a small community, social conflict can accumulate until major scandals erupt, which in some cases transcend its borders. In contexts such as these, private events such as a divorce, losing a job or – in an environment that still remains very traditional – becoming pregnant out of wedlock, acquire a significant public dimension. Solidarity and social divisions are, in effect, two faces of the same coin. In these types of localities, it therefore becomes essential, in the interest of social cohesion, to elude anything that may cause major divisions. For this reason, certain conversations – such as those about the Civil War – are best avoided.

In practice, a community may be defined in relation to its *place*, which may be understood literally, as a term that denotes a geographical location, or as the *direct* social relations that exist *within* geographical spaces. So, for example, a town or a city can be considered to be a community insofar as it exists within certain territorial and administrative limits, and as long as there is a collective sense among citizens of belonging to that particular place. However, considering the number of inhabitants that live in these larger localities, people normally develop direct social relations with a far smaller number of fellow townsmen and women. In these cases, we may think about smaller places within the city that may constitute communities within the larger one, such as neighbourhoods, where people gather around specific streets, shops and schools to conduct their daily activities. Individuals may develop their direct social relations within the context of that particular community, while also maintaining social relations elsewhere, with colleagues in the workplace, with relatives and friends who live in the same or another locality, and with other acquaintances.

Let us consider an example that can be extrapolated to other smaller communities, such as villages, when they confront an event that takes place within their boundaries (geographical, administrative or imagined). An individual who lives in a given street may decide to commit suicide in a way that is witnessed by passers-by, for example, by jumping off a balcony. This is a traumatic event that will affect, above all, his or her own family and friends, but will also have an impact on anyone who has witnessed the actions, and any passers-by who may encounter the aftermath of his or her fall (including his or her family's first reactions, the arrival of the ambulance, his or her being declared dead, and so on). People – most of them, presumably, residents or frequent users of the area surrounding this street – will normally gather around sites, or sights, such as this, and will engage in spontaneous conversations about what has happened and what they know about the individual. Details about his or her life, background and supposed reasons for committing suicide are circulated among a group of people whose feelings may include shock, sadness and bewilderment. This traumatic event will be commented upon and remembered as part of the particular neighbourhood's fabric of social relations. Most people outside this community will not know about this event, although some accounts of what happened may leak out of the community through the relations that exist between its members and members of other neighbourhoods. Primarily, however, it will be remembered as a local event, becoming part of the collective consciousness of that community. The larger the community, the more 'dispersed' this consciousness will be.

As mentioned above, every local community has its own history and its own identity as a social group. In order to understand these neighbourhoods, it is necessary to know which events have come to define their particular sense of community, and the place of this 'self-awareness' in a broader context (the province, region, country and so on) in which it is embedded. Examining the details of the economic activities that are conducted within the community, for example, is essential, because they provide a good indication of the opportunities, challenges and struggles that its members tend to face on a daily basis. For example, a village that is primarily devoted to agricultural labour will be very different from the one whose main source of income is tourism, fishing or leather manufacturing. The typical problems that villages face, the natural environment that surrounds them, the types of social relations that develop within their boundaries and the ways in which they organise their life and work activities are all component parts of their particular histories, traditions, struggles for survival and identities as communities.

Local traditions also provide an important source of social cohesion. For instance, annual festivities, which are often linked to religious rituals and to stages of agrarian production (such as sowing and harvest times), offer opportunities for villagers to come together as a community and to build on existing social relations. So, for example, a number of such celebrations take place throughout the year in Arroyomolinos. One of the main festive occasions occurs on 15 August, the day of the village's patron saint (*la patrona del pueblo*), the Virgin of Remedies (*la Virgen de los Remedios*). On that day, numerous Spanish towns and villages celebrate local festivities across the country. In Arroyomolinos, neighbours join a ceremonial procession through the streets of the village, before going to the esplanade square to have some tapas, dance and chat with their friends and relatives. A combination of religious and secular activities take place over a period of four days, which end with the release of four or five wooden bulls, packed with fireworks, that are pushed at speed up and down the main road. This popular occasion, which is known as '*toro de fuego*' (fire bull), is well known in other nearby villages and is therefore attended by *forasteros* (foreigners or outsiders). Events like this exemplify the ways in which a village may develop its own traditions and identity, for which they become known, setting them apart from other localities while still fitting within the broader patterns that are usually observed in similar rural environments.

THE VILLAGE

The village of Arroyomolinos de León is situated in the northern part of the province of Huelva, in the West of Andalusia. It lies between the province of Seville and southern Portugal, while Badajoz is further to the north. The municipal area, which contains 8,695 hectares, is part of the Sierra Morena, a mountainous range consisting of valleys and peaks that attain a maximum altitude of 1,000 metres. The locality owes its name (literally, 'Stream Mills of León') to the water mills that were quite common in the northern part of the province in the nineteenth century: the area benefits from a dense network of rivulets that, however, tend to dry up during the summer months. In this village alone, there were between 18 and 31 mills that were used to grind cereals (Jurado Almonte 1995, 162; Madoz 1835, 57). Its urban structure corresponds to the typical '*pueblo-calle*' (village-street) that is frequent in the area, and the modern centre of the village lies alongside a national road (N-434) which provides an easy route to other neighbourhoods and regions. Although Arroyomolinos belongs to the judicial area of Aracena, neighbours maintain stronger commercial and personal links with other nearby localities, such as Segura de León and Fregenal de la Sierra (in the south of Badajoz) and Santa Olalla del Cala (in Huelva, some twenty-two kilometres to the south), where the nearest national health clinic can be found. In addition to these smaller municipalities, neighbours also travel to Seville, which is closer to the village than the provincial capital of Huelva, and which offers better services and ease of transport (Jurado Almonte 1995, 173).

In 1835, Madoz described the village as consisting of 190 houses concentrated in a number of streets

> without pavements and quite dirty, with one square where farmers gather to domesticate young bulls; it has an unfinished municipal house with one room serving as a prison; in this house, there was a primary school attended by 20 or 30 children, whose teacher was paid the small sum of 800 *reales* per annum. The upkeep of the Chapel is maintained thanks to the parishioners' donations. (Madoz 1835, my translation)

Figure 1.1   Remains of one of the mills in Arroyomolinos de León. Family Archive.

Today, the two main buildings in the locality are of religious nature: a church (Iglesia Parroquial de Santiago el Mayor), which is located in one of the main squares, and a chapel (Ermita de la Virgen de los Remedios), which is found near the exit of the village, at the southern end of the national road. Both buildings, which date from the seventeenth century, are centres of religious and popular festivities throughout the year, and they are also two of the key sites that are often mentioned in the oral testimonies gathered for this study. The village, which presents the typical Andalusian style of white, stone-built houses, has in addition a council building, a market that runs on Thursdays, and a surgery. These buildings are situated in a modern area near the centre.

Just like other mountainous, agricultural villages, Arroyomolinos has always had a relatively small number of inhabitants, a number that has continued to fall, especially in the second half of the twentieth century. The first modern census, in 1857, included 852 inhabitants, but the locality increased its population, thanks to a larger number of births and the arrival of immigrants seeking the opportunities offered by the exploitation of wood and coal. Arroyomolinos began the twentieth century with 2,366 inhabitants, increasing to 2,666 in 1920 (Jurado Almonte 1995, 168). From that point, the village started losing inhabitants due to a reversal in migration flows: the local population began to seek new pastures due to the lack of resources in the village, which was evident even before the industrialisation of Spain – a

Figure 1.2   Iglesia Parroquial de Santiago El Mayor, the Church in Arroyomolinos de León. Photograph by Ruth Sanz Sabido.

trend that intensified in the 1960s and 1970s, when a significant number of families left the village to look for better prospects in more prosperous parts of the country. The municipal register of 1940 included 2,357 people who were present in the village, 97 absent inhabitants and one non-resident or passer-by. Between 1960 and 1975, the population was reduced to nearly half the size recorded in 1920, while the 1994 census counted only 1,240 inhabitants. One of the consequences of this migration is that a considerable number of houses remain empty or are only used at specific points during the year, mainly when people return to meet their families and friends during the local festivities, or when migrants decide to move back to the village after retirement. The fact that most migrants are of working age and the number of deaths in the village is higher than the number of births means that the village is strongly characterised by an ageing population (Jurado Almonte 1995, 168). In total, about 490 people contribute actively to the productive economy, mainly through agricultural labour, while the unemployment rate is very high (approximately 41% of the active population).

Although the economic situation is certainly challenging, these figures do not tell the whole story: in addition to the (small) subsidies received from the government, perhaps more important is the 'submerged' economy that exists in rural areas such as this one (Jurado Almonte 1995, 171). Exploitation of small plots of land for family consumption does not provide the necessary means for self-subsistence, but it gives a boost to the domestic economy, and goods such as vegetables, eggs or chorizos are also often exchanged informally among neighbours. People who work in construction, commerce or other services can also attend to their small plots of land in the evenings, providing an additional means of subsistence. Overall, the village exemplifies the typical socio-professional division in rural and agricultural communities, which includes, on the one hand, a majority of self-employed, occasional workers and, on the other hand, a smaller number of people who are in a position to employ others, or who have permanent jobs (Jurado Almonte 1995, 171).

As a 'mountain' village, Arroyomolinos' economy has always been, in the main, based on agriculture and the rearing of livestock. These activities have traditionally been maintained under precarious conditions, due to the rocky composition of most of the land. An agricultural area with orchards, benefitting from small streams of water running nearby, was developed over the years in the plots of land closer to the village (Jurado Almonte 1995, 162). The largest proportion of land, however, consists of forests of oaks and holm oaks, as well as olive trees, which are divided into plots and also generate income and resources for those who own them. For example, some years ago a cooperative, Unión Agraria, was set up in the village in order to trade in olives and produce olive oil, although it did not survive for long and has now closed. One of the participants refers to this cooperative as an example of a

Figure 1.3 View of Arroyomolinos de León from the road that leads to the cemetery. Photograph by Ruth Sanz Sabido.

failed project of economic and social justice in the village, insofar as it was a missed opportunity to create a system from which neighbours could benefit equitably.

In 1835 Madoz did not know that, by the end of the nineteenth century, local people would find work in Minas de Cala. Indeed, Arroyomolinos is part of the Mancomunidad 'Sierra Minera' (Community 'Mining Mountains'), an inter-municipal association of villages that also includes Cala, Santa Olalla del Cala, Cañaveral de León and Hinojales, all of them villages in the north-eastern part of the province of Huelva (Mancomunidad Intermunicipal de R. S. U. 'Sierra Minera' n.d.). In some ways, working in the mines provided better financial returns than working on the land, and this had some positive effects. However, working conditions in the mines were very poor and workers were exposed to long working hours in a dangerous environment. This was not only the case in Cala, but also in other mines in the province, such as the ones in Minas de Riotinto, just forty miles to the south, and in other parts of the country, such as the mines in Asturias. This type of working environment tended to support the growth of syndicalist movements, sharpening class consciousness and encouraging resistance to economic and political injustice (see Chapters 4–6).

NOTES

1. Confederación Nacional del Trabajo and Federación Anarquista Ibérica. See Mesquida (2014). In addition to the French patriotic reaction, another reason why the Spanish soldiers were not recognised was, precisely, because many of them were anarchists.

2. For accounts of Spanish people in German concentration camps, see Hernández de Miguel (2015) and del Río (2014a).

3. This type of strategy is, by no means, exclusive to France. See, for example, Kammen's (1997) discussion of the ways in which, for the sake of national unity, U.S. memories of its past have also been depoliticised and distorted.

4. Although it is frequently claimed that History is 'written by the victors', the aftermath of the Spanish Civil War provides a contradictory lesson: in Spain, a strong residue of Francoist propaganda still remains, while abroad the overwhelming interest is, and has been, in narratives produced by the Republican camp.

5. According to Sabugal (2015), Bernardo Álvarez, 'el Gasta', was already politically active during the Second Republic, when he was imprisoned in Astorga (León) in 1934. When the coup started in 1936, he was undertaking the military service in Cádiz, where he was arrested and sentenced to death. He was later released and, on his return to the Bierzo area, became active in the guerrilla. In 1948, he was wounded in a shoot-out with the Civil Guard, but managed to escape to Orense, where he hid in the mountains with comrades Elías López Armesto, 'Pájaro', and Manuel Fernández Soto, 'Coronel Benito'. A mole infiltrated in the guerrilla denounced them and, on 22 June 1949, the Civil Guard killed and buried them in an unidentified grave in the cemetery of Teilán. Their bodies were inscribed in the registry as 'unknown' (Sabugal 2015).

6. It is not possible to quantify the exact number, but hundreds of exhumations took place privately in the late 1970s and early 1980s. It was in 2000 when the first 'scientific' exhumations took place, when Emilio Silva organised the exhumation of his grandfather and twelve other men in Priaranza del Bierzo (known as '*los 13 de Priaranza*', or 'Priaranza's 13'). The ARMH was created and has, since then, helped hundreds of families to recover the remains of their relatives.

7. About 100,000 people, of more than forty nationalities, were killed in Mauthausen during World War II. Most of them died as a consequence of the inhumane working conditions. In this context, fainting with exhaustion or hunger was a sure way to be finished off by a beating or a bullet. Among the prisoners, there were approximately 7,500 Spanish Republicans: about two-thirds of them died in this concentration camp (EFE 2015a).

8. While my perspective is that memory is indeed both a private and a public matter, I argue that, even though the state needs to take responsibility formally and financially, memory associations should continue to be in complete charge of the work so as to avoid the different ways in which the state may analyse the evidence or control the process to protect its own interests.

Chapter 2

Memory, Politics and Lived Experience

We live in a transitory present that, despite its constant 'advance' towards the future, never attains the condition of 'futurity'. The present remains, therefore, the time and space within which we operate, a field of experience that functions as a nexus between the past that we have already lived (and can recall) and the future times in which we hope to live and towards which we work (Soto Gamboa 2004). It is only in the present that we can ensure *some* form of control over events, insofar as we can decide which actions to take or not to take, dependent on our understanding of the situations we face in each moment. In the present, of course, we can no longer change any of our previous actions or events. One certainty about our past is that we cannot return to it: crucially, for the argument advanced in this book, this observation is not the same as arguing that the past as such has disappeared altogether. According to Aróstegui (1998), the *historic* as a category is an inevitable dimension of what exists now, and is not merely the sum total of what has existed previously (see also Sanz Sabido 2016). If the constantly changing nexus of the present (the world that we inhabit) connects the past with the future, it is in one sense a continuation of what has already been. The present is therefore never quite a clean slate, a *tabula rasa*, which can be inscribed with new information, without any consideration of the phases that preceded it and no understanding of how it came to assume its current form. We are, as Saramago argues, 'made of the memories we have and the responsibilities we assume; without memory we do not exist and without responsibility perhaps we do not deserve to exist' (Saramago 1998, 246, my translation).

Indeed, with memory comes responsibility, including the duty to remember where we come from and the actions for which we are responsible. Here, we begin to see that time is more complex than a chronological concatenation of moments, or a mere 'fact of life': time is, as Adam (1990, 2) points out, 'implicated in every aspect of our lives and imbued with a multitude of meanings', in both everyday and exceptional circumstances. Similarly, taking responsibility for our actions should not be seen as an additional burden, but as an intrinsic part of our existence. The problem emerges when there is an attempt to break the link that joins the past and the transitory present, which takes place when, at a discursive level, this continuity is doubted, challenged or ignored. Any efforts that attempt to break away from the past and to create a clean slate can only be artificial, and are usually motivated by a desire to abandon any responsibilities. They are intentional attempts to erase an inconvenient past – or aspects of it – in order to suit current interests.

Yet, past events did occur, regardless of the discursive frames and politico-legal measures that might be used to deny their reality. In addition to the denial of what has passed, a parallel danger has the potential to develop: if we are to accept that the past has no bearing on the present, and there is no need to take responsibility for our previous actions, we may in effect be setting a dangerous precedent for the future. As Spanish philosopher Emilio Lledó (2015) once noted, those who want to forget what happened in the past are seeking to justify any vile act in the present in the hope that it will never be remembered later. Intentionality – that is, political intentionality – lies at the very core of public memory.

Based on these insights, Chapter 3 will present a conceptual and methodological framework which, taking into account the social and political nature of memory, enables us to understand the formation, maintenance and reproduction of memories by individuals in a given location. The chapter will also address the role that these recollections occupy in relation to national, public memories. What we remember, how we remember it, and the social processes involved in how we re-activate and offer an account of our experiences are some of the aspects with which scholars in Memory Studies have contended for several decades (Assmann 1995; Assmann 2010; Erll 2010; Halbwachs 1992; Misztal 2003; Olick 2010; Ricoeur 2004). Here, I argue that place, power and the 'self' are central to both the theorisation and the narration of memories. I will return to these notions later in the chapter and throughout the book. However, before developing this further, some characteristics of memory at its most basic level – the individual cognitive ability to remember – need to be substantiated. Although the field of Memory Studies is concerned with memory as a collective act, useful insights can be gained by reflecting on this concept from a more literal, individual perspective. In order to understand the role that memory plays in a person's life and sense of self, I consider the effect that the loss of this faculty has on an individual's quality of life and identity. The experience of María, a sufferer of Alzheimer's disease, helps to illustrate this point.

COGNITIVE MEMORIES

María was a woman who defined herself primarily as a wife, a mother and a grandmother. She had lived through the Civil War and the dictatorship although, like most people of her generation, she rarely spoke about it. As a consequence of the social attitude of her times, she was taught to function in a domestic setting, sharing the responsibilities of housekeeping with her four sisters. Following a socially appropriate period of courtship, María married a loving husband and had one daughter. Beyond the love that she had for her family, she adored the village where she was born and lived. She and her husband brought up the child in the same village until they decided to migrate to another location, closer to a town, so that the girl could attend a better school and have access to greater opportunities. Their daughter did exactly that: she studied, graduated from university, secured a permanent job and started her own family. Having accomplished their objective, María and her husband were ready to return home to the village, but at this point he was diagnosed with cancer and he passed away within six months. María's plans and goals, and her very reasons for living were, as far as she was concerned, suddenly destroyed. The period of mourning gradually passed but, although she continued to function, she never truly recovered from her loss. The rock upon which she had depended was no longer there to support her, and this showed in every aspect of her life. She temporarily found refuge in the house that they had built for their retirement, but this place, which had been filled with the joyous anticipation of a much longed-for return, had lost much of its meaning. She soon became a grandmother, and this began a chain of events that would lead to her going back again to the town to join her daughter and her new family, where she would live for the following twenty-three years, until she passed away.

Approximately six years before her death, María had begun to show signs of dementia. At first, she would forget to switch off the lights, and would also repeat the same comment or ask the same question every few minutes. She then began to describe events from a time when she was younger, often repeating the same stories in a short period of time. One day, she described an occasion when several men and women were collecting and pressing grapes, a process that was carried out annually. In one particular year, someone had slipped and had made a mess, leading to a comic situation which she clearly still enjoyed remembering. The event, which still made her laugh, was narrated for her captive audience several times.

An otherwise kind, generous and affectionate woman, María also went through a period of extreme distrust and stinginess, openly accusing everyone of stealing from her and sometimes becoming aggressive. Towards the end, when she had become completely dependent on her daughter and other close relatives to meet her most basic needs, she became increasingly quiet and absent-minded, occasionally calling her son-in-law by her husband's name, and asking her own daughter who she was. 'I am your daughter, mum,' her daughter would say. 'I don't have a daughter,' María would respond. By that point, her remaining long-term memories were fixed on a time when the birth of her daughter had not yet taken place.

This description provides a brief snapshot of how María gradually lost her cognitive abilities, a development that not only made her become dependent on those around her, but which also made her forget who those people were and, indeed, who she was herself. Dementia, the progressive degeneration of basic brain functions such as memory, perception, judgement, understanding and other cognitive faculties (Morrissey 1999, 54), manifests itself through a number of symptoms, which include disorientation, confusion, hostility, hallucinations and personality alterations, among others, all combined with a deficit in memory functions (Sabat 2001, 274). Studies of dementia and Alzheimer's disease have considered the process of bereavement that relatives and carers go through, while the person they are grieving for is still alive (Jones and Martinson 1992). This helps us to understand the sense of loss that is associated with the degeneration of memory. While patients of other life-threatening illnesses are aware that a fatal end is possible, in the case of dementia sufferers, an irreversible process is at work, one that takes away the individual's ability to understand their own decline. Even though the individual may still be present physically, they cannot regain their sense of self. Morrissey notes how Alzheimer's disease affects almost everything related to being a person, robbing them of their dignity, independence and individuality. He points out that 'it is true to say that the person is disappearing and, frighteningly, in some cases is already gone' (Morrissey 1999, 45).

This book is not about Alzheimer's disease or people who suffer from this condition. However, the effects that this illness has on individuals enable us to understand memory as a cognitive function and to appreciate the essential roles that this faculty plays in a person's life. 'Just about everything we do or say', Schacter (1996, 3) points out, 'depends on the smooth and efficient operation of our memory systems.' The description of María's transformation shows us how a woman who could function independently, and who was fully aware of her life trajectory, had turned into a dependent person who could not recognise *who* she was, *where* she was and even *when* she was meant to be living. Her confidence when insisting, to her own daughter, that she did not have a child, indicated that her mind had travelled back to a stage before this child existed. However, the fact that her daughter was sitting in front of her (the fact of her very existence), was proof that this past had actually occurred, and that it had certainly been a central part of María's life. María did not remember where she came from (understood here not strictly in geographical terms but, more generally, in the sense of her life development), but this forgetfulness does not negate the fact that she had experienced that particular life.

Her inability to remember did not make any of the major events of her existence, and the consequences that flowed from these events, any less real. She had married, she had become a mother, she had migrated, she had hoped to return, she had mourned her husband and she had celebrated the birth of her grandchildren. These, and all the other events that comprised her life, including the incident with the grapes, which she once found so funny, had *really* happened and had been important to her. Some of these events are still remembered *now*, in the mutable present, by those people who also experienced them, or became aware of them, in their own individual capacities through their direct connections with María.

SOCIAL DEMENTIA

In the same way that memory acquires a symbolic meaning when applied to collective experience, so does the concept of amnesia, where this is understood as the effect of forgetting the past. In Memory Studies, the disconnection between past and present has often been described as 'social amnesia' (Jacoby 1975). This notion is adapted from another individual condition, of either permanent or temporary forgetfulness, which then acquires a wider symbolic and collective dimension. Yoder (1997), for example, uses the concept of 'amnesia' to describe contemporary American attitudes towards slavery, in a context where racial inequality coexists with a discursive (hence superficial) commitment to equality. In Spain, the term 'amnesia' has also been used (in the context of the 1977 amnesty) to designate the parallel imposition of continued silence and oblivion that accompanied the application of political and legal measures supposedly designed to reinforce the transition to democracy (Aguilar 2000). Although this, and other related notions are useful, this book suggests the term 'social dementia', a concept that highlights the negative and 'degenerative' consequences that the loss of *social* memory may inflict on a particular group or community. Whichever label is employed, the parallels between an individual's ability (or inability) to remember, and the ways in which memories exist (in symbolic terms) in wider society, are useful as theoretical and analytical tools. After all, no memory can ever be recalled outside the human brain: societies as such do not actually remember, because they do not have the necessary neurons, organs and systems to be able to do so.

The question is then how the collective outlook of a society is actually formed and maintained. Reference to the fate of individuals and groups is therefore relevant for two reasons: the social order is composed of smaller individual units and, as outlined above, the transposition of individual memory to a social level (in terms of both the powerful capacities and imperfections of the human mind) may help us to understand the uses of the past in contemporary Spain, and indeed in any other context. Take, for example, the situation that arises when a person is cognitively unable to remember his or her past. It is, as Morrissey points out, almost as though that individual is disappearing, despite the fact that he or she is still alive in a purely physical sense. Although this form of basic existence seems to represent the continuity of life itself – in the sense that the victim can be said to have a past, a present and a future – the disease forces the sufferers to break the link between their past and their present, making it impossible to imagine a future as well. The more the illness advances, the cleaner the slate becomes. The sufferer loses his or her bearings: the consequence is a loss of direction, sense of purpose and meaning, all of which are grounded in the past. The German title of Schacter's book, *Wir sind Erinnerung* (1999), notes that 'we are recollections', encapsulating the crucial part that memory plays in our lives. Without memory, all those around us would be strangers, any symbolic forms would become meaningless, we would not be able to perform any activities and our sense of personal identity and self-awareness would disappear (Schacter 1996, 3). Similarly, a society that forgets its past, and the very process of its own formation and development, is a society that goes through a degenerative process through which its direction, purpose and meaning are lost. The argument, advanced in certain political sectors, that the past has disappeared and does not need to be remembered tries to provoke this rupture, a *social dementia* of sorts, which is instrumental in avoiding responsibility for what has happened before.

The difference between forgetfulness in dementia sufferers, on the one hand, and socio-politico-legal oblivion, on the other, is choice (or the lack of it): a person does not choose to suffer dementia, and has no control over the effects and reach of the disease, which are imposed upon him or her. In the best of cases, treatment may help to slow down its progress. The matter becomes more convoluted when we consider political and legal oblivion, which is a choice for those who impose it, and is welcomed by those who agree with, or benefit from, the erasure of the past. For those who do not support this form of suppression, but are forced to forget their own history, there is no question of choice. For them it is an imposition, one that both reflects and reproduces an imbalance in power. The crucial difference, therefore, lies in the socio-political nature of memory and oblivion that can be observed at a collective level.

THE SOCIAL AND POLITICAL NATURE OF MEMORY

The distinction between individual and collective levels of memory reflects the demarcation between neuroscience, which is concerned with what happens in the brain, and Memory Studies, which attempts to describe how the basic characteristics of physical memory are manifested metaphorically when, for example, groups of people 'remember' events collectively. An understanding of neuroscience is useful because, although the act of remembering really only takes place in a neurological sense, this does not mean that memories are isolated in an individual's neurons, protected from external influence. In fact, the mechanisms involved in the cognitive retention and reactivation of memories include a number of external factors that shape the details that we remember and how we recall them at a later stage. At any time after a particular event has occurred, interactions with other agents (including friends, relatives, acquaintances, politicians and the media) play an important part in the ways in which memories are stored and narrated, shaped and reshaped, which in turn leads to an emphasis on some of their constituent elements while other details become dormant. This is why memory is always social, and why the cognitive and social aspects of memory must be considered in conjunction with each other.

In addition, as mentioned above, some of the traits and mechanisms belonging to this cognitive function are reproduced symbolically at a *collective* level. In normal circumstances, a person tends to remember the most crucial moments that have marked the course of his or her life, as well as other events that they have lived through, witnessed or heard about. Some of these events may be remembered more or less often, more or less vividly and in more or less detail, while other memories may seem to be forgotten until they are re-activated and brought to the fore. Similarly, in our societies, we frequently commemorate key dates and events that have determined, in one way or another, the course of history. The more significant the occurrence, the more likely it is to become a point of reference for politicians, the media, activists and other social agents, re-activating the relevant memories for years to come. The dominant social and political actors are the ones who define the relative significance of the event, and therefore how it will be remembered. In practice, there are unwritten categories that establish whether an event is worth commemorating or not. The degree of public attention given to it (e.g., the amount of media coverage it receives) also varies depending on these tacit categorisations, which ultimately depend on the extent to which they are politically convenient, timely and beneficial to specific groups of social actors.

So, for example, if the event matches the established criteria that deem it worthy of public commemoration, then it is not unusual to see allusions to it in the news media, and in programmes specially produced to mark the occasion. Public agents, such as politicians and other known personalities, normally pay tribute by attending acts of remembrance, which may then be mediated extensively. In many cases, the political usefulness or timeliness of remembering these events goes hand in hand with the need of the media to attract higher circulation or audience ratings, so events are also more likely to be covered if they meet the (also unspoken) criteria of newsworthiness (Galtung and Ruge 1965; Harcup and O'Neill 2001). In contrast, events that are not considered to be sufficiently important in terms of public remembrance become invisible or near invisible in the public sphere, so their sponsors or advocates have to work harder to attract attention. In these cases, commemorative events may be organised by smaller groups, but they often receive comparably less publicity and, as a consequence, attract fewer opportunities for public awareness and discussion.

The differential treatment of events by the media and other agents exemplifies the contentious uses of public memory. By analysing the nature of this unequal coverage, it is possible to observe how the dominant assumptions held by media institutions are not only defined by socio-political struggles, but also contribute to their reproduction and perpetuation. Competing perspectives on the meaning of public memory also become part of the mediated debate, where some individuals may question the need to hold commemorations or the meanings attached to specific events. For instance, Spain celebrates one of its bank holidays on 12 October, to mark the anniversary of Christopher Columbus' 'discovery' of America in 1492. This is, in fact, one of Spain's two national days, both of which are similar to the bank holidays on England's St George's Day, France's Bastille Day, or the United States' Independence Day. This particular bank holiday in Spain was officially known as *Día de la Hispanidad* (Day of the Hispanic community) until 1987, when the name was changed to *Fiesta Nacional* (National Holiday) in an attempt to remove the reference to Spain's colonial connection to Latin America. In other words, the official name change was an effort to manage the public memory of the historical event (although the day is still commonly referred to as *Día de la Hispanidad*).

The second national day in Spain is celebrated on 6 December, *Día de la Constitución* (Constitution Day), in commemoration of the referendum, held in 1978, during which the Spanish people voted 'yes' to the new Constitution (this was written during the period known as the 'Transition to Democracy'). This is therefore a day that symbolises *el consenso* (the consensus) that was reached between different ideological perspectives during that period (91.8% voted in favour of the text, with a participation rate of 67.1%). The debates and disagreements that arise in the context of these commemorations are driven by fundamental differences of opinion about the meaning of what is remembered and the political repercussions that are attached to them. So, in the case of Constitution Day in Spain, the official meanings ascribed to this day are related to efforts to support the development of the new democratic state. In practice, it serves as the 'democratic' alternative to earlier national days that are no longer recognised, which some sectors of society may none-theless wish to reinstate. One such example is 14 April, the 'Day of the Second Republic' (an option that would have been welcomed by those Republicans who did not agree with the restoration of the monarchy after Franco's death). Another might even be 18 July, the 'Day of the National Uprising' when, in 1936, elements of the armed forces rose against the elected government (a date that still creates a frisson among Franco's modern sympathisers).

Against this backdrop, the celebration of 6 December as a national day offers a symbolic 'middle ground', which is part of a broader programme of compromises intended to reach a 'final' consensus. The agreements that were reached during that period, including the choice of a neutral national day and the resolution of other more momentous issues, became part of a norm that is now meant to be unassailable, preventing dissenting voices from challenging any substantial aspects of the new system. The discourse of the consensus argues that the rules of the new game were laid out during the transition, and that we must now abide by those rules in perpetuity. This perspective – the one adopted by the state and, therefore, the official position – predominates over the perspectives of those who question the agreement and the basis upon which it was reached. Decisions over *what* the Spanish are meant to remember as a nation are in effect determined in large part by the exclusion of memories that are not sanctioned by the state. The choice of national days is, therefore, not a trivial matter, as it is intrinsically political and concerned with deeper struggles over meaning and power. Meaning, in these cases, is provided by the historical background and significance of the events that are commemorated, which are not regarded in one simple or homogenous way, and can therefore lead to confrontations and differences of opinion. The question of power is inherent in these tensions, insofar as competing viewpoints and interests lie at their heart. As in every power struggle, some of these perspectives become favoured over others, eventually establishing themselves as the norm.

What we learn from this discussion is that, even when commemorative acts and dates may seem innocent and devoid of any intentionality, formal, 'institutional' memory has a tendency to choose what should be retained and to discard inconvenient perspectives. Memory, as a cognitive process, is of course inherently discriminatory, in the sense that we never remember every-thing and tend to rehearse and reinforce certain incidents. Our brains protect us from the chaos that would ensue should we try to remember every single experience and detail: we forget, therefore, much of the stream of information to which we are constantly exposed, as our memory systems may consider them to be irrelevant or useless, even if this means that we sometimes also forget aspects that we need to retrieve at a given time (Schacter 1996, 4).

In addition, however, individuals can also choose to indulge in what is sometimes informally described as 'selective' memories, an expression that, beyond its ostensibly tautological meaning (because, by nature, memory is always selective), is intended to encapsulate the deliberate intention to remember or to forget specific events (the word deliberate is appropriate here because this happens, not through a process of 'natural' selection, but as the result of careful design and premeditation). In the same way that an individual can allege that he or she does not remember something in a certain situation, in an attempt to erase an inconvenient fact, broader top-down discourses can also try to achieve a similar aim when the past is of collective importance (Sanz Sabido 2015). There, at the collective level, some memories are also selected as suitable, becoming animated in public discourse, while others are 'forgotten' and buried under the manifestations of the official stance, revealing the socio-political nature of memory.

TYPES OF MEMORIES

So far, I have made a broad distinction between memory at a cognitive level, in its literal meaning, and memory at a collective level, in a metaphorical sense. On the one hand, from the perspective of neuroscience, there exist several types of memories that work in different ways, and which use various cognitive systems and neural structures to help us achieve different actions. Experts in this field have made considerable progress in trying to understand how these complex processes work neurologically, although they agree that many of these still require further investigation. On the other hand, the conceptualisation of memory at a collective level has also led to the emergence of numerous definitions and theoretical approaches that have attempted to explain the socio-cultural underpinning of memory, a debate that forms the very basis of Memory Studies as a discipline (see, e.g., Assmann 1995; Assmann 2010; Connerton 1989; Halbwachs 1992; Misztal 2003; Olick 2010; Phillips 2008). Even though there is an overall consensus that memory is generated, shaped and transmitted collectively, there is some divergence in the concepts that are used to present the various nuances and perspectives.

Notably, the term 'collective memory' is one of the key concepts that have been defined in different ways by various authors. Halbwachs' seminal work on the social construction of memory, which has been central to the development of Memory Studies, understands memory to be 'collective' because human memory, at the cognitive level, can never be isolated from the collective contexts in which it develops. Halbwachs (1992, 52) argues that individuals hold memories together because 'they are part of a totality of thoughts common to a group' so, to recall them, we need to 'place ourselves in the perspective of this group ... adopt its interests and follow the slant of its reflections'. He argues that memories are not stored and retrieved because they resemble one another, or because they are chronologically contiguous to other memories, but because memories play a role in a particular collective, reinforcing common attitudes and the ways in which the group thinks (Halbwachs 1992, 52). According to this view, a group's internal logic is based on their memories: first, their ways of thinking are centred around, and shaped by, their previous memories, which work as a framework that determines their thoughts and behaviours; secondly, once the group is used to functioning within that framework, the retrieval and reconstruction of all its other memories will follow a similar principle (Halbwachs 1992, 52). As noted by Halbwachs, the first group within which we shape our first memories is the family, but individuals then begin to associate with different groups simultaneously throughout their lives, which means that each memory is located 'within the thought of the corresponding group', in the first instance, and then, in relation to the combination of groups of which the individual is a member (Halbwachs 1992, 53). For Halbwachs, the term 'collective memory' was not intended to describe one specific type of memory: his contention was, to put it in simple terms, that memory *is* collective, thereby setting the social parameters of living memory – that is, a form of memory that can be communicated orally among members of the 'corresponding' group.

Nevertheless, throughout the recent development of Memory Studies, there has been an increase in the number of concepts that make distinctions between different types or forms of remembering, all of which are social or collective in the way proposed by Halbwachs, but nonetheless distinct according to various criteria, such as the ways in which memories are conveyed in the public realm, the characteristics of the social milieu within which memories exist, or the generational transmission of memory. For example, in his overview of the field, Casey (2008) distinguishes between four types of memory – individual, social, collective and public – based on the relative size of the group and how memories are communicated between the participants. For him, 'social' memories take place in the public realm (outside the privacy of our homes) but in contexts where people can maintain and share their common memories, as is the case with village life. According to Casey, 'collective' memories, however, involve a larger concentration of people, such as the number found in a town or city, in which social relations are less conducive to the development and conservation of memories that are equally relevant to all. Finally, the term 'public' memories describes the ways in which larger groups, such as nation-states, remember aspects of their past. The difference between Casey's concepts lies in the extent to which members of each group are able to share the same experiences, and can maintain a more or less direct connection to these points of reference after the experiences themselves are over.

As regards 'public' memory, Phillips (2008) proposes two frames that explain different ways in which the terms 'public' and 'memory' are linked: on the one hand, he presents a 'memory of publics' frame, which refers to 'public' as a sort of public sphere that remembers *together*, not as the sum of many individuals remembering the same thing, but as a sense of togetherness produced through the act of remembrance, and therefore as an essential part of their very constitution and existence. On the other hand, Phillips considers the 'publicness of memory', which describes the processes through which certain memories become public while others remain hidden from public view. Nevertheless, he does not intend to argue that both frames are strictly separate. In fact, Phillips (2008, 10) recognises that the act and sense of remembering together ('memory of publics') and the extent to which memories are public ('publicness of memory') are interrelated and can therefore occur simultaneously in what is usually known as 'public memory'. This is what I have previously referred to as 'official' Memory, and which I describe in Chapter 3 as a form of 'national memory'.

From a different perspective, Assmann (1995) introduced the concepts of 'communicative' and 'cultural' memory. He agrees that memory is collective in nature, but addresses the limitation of Halbwachs' approach, which only theorises memory up to the point at which it can be communicated orally. The average life expectancy of memory, if we follow Halbwach's analysis, would be no more than three generations, after which memory would become History. Assmann's contention is that, in fact, memory continues in the form of 'objectivized culture – whether in texts, images, rites, buildings, monuments, cities, or even landscapes', because 'a close connection to groups and their identity exists which is similar to that found in the case of everyday memory' (Assmann 1995, 128). The memory that Halbwachs understands as 'collective' is described by Assmann as 'communicative'. Communicative memory is social in nature, and describes the idea that memories can be transmitted directly among generations that share the same time and space (generally, grandparents, parents and their children). This type of memory is closer to what I define as 'local' memories, although my framework acknowledges the interrelations between direct or intergenerational transmissions of remembered events and other larger social processes involved in the formation and shaping of memories in general (see Chapter 3).

It is precisely in this way that we need to understand Assmann's concept of 'cultural' memory. This notion refers to the memories that are transmitted beyond the direct availability of oral testimonies, and are therefore concerned with the perpetuation of memory in the longer term and on a larger scale. Assmann (1995, 129) notes that cultural memory has certain fixed points, which consist of fateful past events that are maintained through cultural formation and institutional communication. This form of 'approved' memory is passed on through various channels, from architecture to the media, and plays a major role in the creation of unitary national memories (Erll 2010). Grainge (2003, 10–12), for example, has highlighted the interconnections between media and memory not only on the basis of representations (what he calls 'memory in film'), but also in terms of the diversification of memory markets, the growth of the heritage industry and the proliferation of time-shifting technologies like VCR and DVD (or 'film as memory').

Some authors have argued that the study of localised and individual approaches to memory may no longer be so relevant in such a heavily mediated world, since broader cultural references become more predominant both in terms of *what* is remembered and *how* it is remembered in a local context. The argument here is that the predominance of cultural or manufactured memories, which are produced entirely for the purposes of their mediation, may erode or even erase individual and social memories. Scholars such as Jacoby (1975) and Berman (1982) have argued that commodification contributes to the process of disconnection between the present and the past, insofar as the latter is substituted by saleable versions that make it more difficult to know the actual past. However, I would argue that the predominance of dominant forms of 'cultural memory' explains why we need to return to the physical base of memory (i.e. specific territories, communities and individuals). Bearing in mind that the various 'types' of memories (however defined) do not exist in a vacuum, we need to examine the interplay between each one of them, without overlooking the fact that they are all in perpetual interaction. While the focus on cultural objects has meant that Memory Studies has dealt with representations of the past, drawing on disciplines such as literature, film studies and cultural studies, the ways in which the past is represented *through* cultural objects can be considerably more abstract and detached than those offered by the familiarity and concreteness of lived experience.

Therefore, rather than examining cultural memories on their own, as if they were isolated from individuals and social relations, it is more useful to consider how they contribute to the construction of a culturally reconfigured past, from the perspective of audiences or citizens. This also suggests that some of the interdisciplinary potential of Memory Studies is not being fully explored (Hodgkin and Radstone 2014). Beginning from the firm assertion that different types or sources of memories are not entirely separated from one another, the analysis of oral testimonies about the past provides an entry point for understanding the ways in which people's memories may have developed, and may thus shed light on the extent to which different types of memory might have influenced them.

MEMORY AND EXPERIENCE

While conducting some interviews with victims of repression and their relatives across Spain, I spoke to two sisters about their grandfather's experiences during Franco's dictatorship. Although the information that I had been given *a priori* only referred to their maternal grandfather, it emerged that their father had also been a direct victim of the regime's repressive practices. This revelation came as a surprise as this aspect of their family's life had not been mentioned before or during the interview, and it was only after the formal setting of the meeting had come to an end that this became apparent. It was evident that they did not want to discuss it, perhaps because of the pain it elicited, which had made them choose to focus on the case of their grandfather instead. Looking at some family photographs that were on display on the sideboard, one of the women showed me who the people in the images were. She suddenly became tearful when she pointed at her father. That is when she muttered that her father had been arrested and forced to do construction work during the regime. She then explained that, many years later, when he was terminally ill, she had visited him in hospital. At that point, the illness and the medication were making him delirious. The man had some bruises from being in bed for a prolonged period of time and, when he saw his daughter, he said to her: 'They captured me and look at what they have done to me.' Startled, his daughter soon realised that he was confusing his current bruises with the ones he had sustained when he was imprisoned and tortured years earlier. When her sister heard this story, as it was being explained to me, she said that she did not remember this incident. The first sister, still in tears, answered back, slightly annoyed: 'You don't remember it because it happened to *me*. You weren't there, so how would you be able to remember?' (Beatriz 2015).

The connection between memory and experience is evident: one remembers what one has experienced or, at least, the most salient aspects of those experiences. In this context, salience works subjectively: within any given situation, different individuals may retain, consciously or unconsciously, a variety of aspects of the past depending on their previous knowledge and experiences, their skills and interests, and their relative position within the event. These factors would determine, physically or figuratively, their perceptions of what happened, and also what may later be remembered and how it will be remembered. The presupposition is, in any case, that the event was experienced first-hand by one or more individuals whose functioning cognitive systems enable them to store the information and remember it later. This view of memory is therefore closer to the cognitive notion of memory. Consequently, direct participants or witnesses of an event, each with their individual cognitive systems, may provide dissimilar accounts of what happened. This is, in fact, often the case, as different people may remember details that were unnoticed by others, or may be affected by a variety of other factors that may impact on their description of the event. It follows, then, that the larger the number of people who are able to remember and narrate an event they experienced, the greater the number of different versions and details that will be gathered. According to Luis, one of the participants in this study, the only way to know about what really happened during the Civil War is to look at the diaries that some combatants kept:

> They wrote in a … in a diary … they wrote the things that happened, what they saw. If they died, someone else would pick it up and continue writing. Everyone else can say what they like. Many people have told lots of untruths, but this is the only way to know the truth of what happened at the front. (Luis 2014a, my translation)

Not only do these diaries benefit from first-hand experience, but also from the immediacy of the events. Both factors translate into what Luis considers to be the 'truth' of what occurred during that period, which contrasts with the 'untruths' that 'many people' have told over the years.

By this point, however, we have discussed how memory, either social or collective, enables the possibility of the events being 'remembered' even if they have not been experienced directly, but have become known to the individual through oral testimonies or various cultural objects. Halbwachs, with his view of collective memory, and Assmann, with his notion of communicative memory, understand that lived experiences may form the basis of oral testimonies that have a life cycle of approximately three generations. Beyond that point, Assmann and other theorists of cultural memory have argued that memories can still be transmitted for generations, and across locations, through monuments, commemorative acts and other cultural channels including the media (Boyer 2011; Erll 2010; Garde-Hansen 2011; Koselleck 2011; Neiger et al. 2011; Samuel 2012; van Dijck 2007; Young 2011). Moreover, we cannot ignore the fact, discussed above, that these 'types' of memory, or different ways in which they are communicated, can also happen simultaneously when the living memory of an event and cultural forms of remembrance may be coetaneous to one another.

Indeed, while scholars have spent a great deal of time and effort in defining these concepts and setting boundaries between them, it would be a mistake to assume that they are separate processes. The fact that memories are not fixed is an inherent trait of the ability to remember, both at cognitive and collective levels. Cognitively, an individual's range of post-event experiences and social exposure can change the ways in which the person remembers and narrates that event. Similarly, from a collective perspective, more recent events and developments can re-define the terms of socio-political debates in the public sphere and the ways in which past events are read and interpreted. The co-existence of both 'types' of memory – when individuals remember their own experiences at the same time that the society remembers the events collectively – enables an additional layer of mutual reshaping and reactivation: the latter provides a broader source of opinions, information and new perspectives that may affect the way people re-read the reminisced past; the former can contribute material, in the form of oral testimonies, to the development of collective memory. We can observe this process of mutual shaping in a variety of cases, depending, primarily, on how long it has been since the event took place. When the memories are about an event that occurred eighty years ago, such as the Spanish Civil War, the number of individuals who experienced it directly dwindles with the passing of time, in comparison with a growing majority who, still within the three-generation cycle, did not live through the event but have become aware of it through direct grandparent–parent–child communication, through exposure to cultural objects and through a (generally deficient) formal education about the period that spans from the Second Republic to the present.

How does this process of mutual shaping work when the individuals who remember the event constitute the majority? This question involves two basic premises: first, the event is recent enough for it to have been experienced by individuals who are still alive; and, secondly, that this 'experience' should not be understood exclusively as direct or first-hand experience, but also as collective experience, that is, when the event is experienced, at a distance, by individuals who are not direct participants. So, for example, one date that the majority of the living Spanish population can remember is 11 March 2004. On that day, ten bombs exploded on four commuter trains in Madrid, killing 193 people and injuring 1,858. The attacks took place three days before Spain's general elections, hence altering the course of the electoral campaign in its very final stages. The political debate during those three days centred on the public identification of those who were responsible for the attacks. Even though there had been signs, from very early on, that indicated that it was an outrage inspired by al-Qaeda, the government at the time, led by Partido Popular, claimed that bombings were perpetrated by the Basque separatist group ETA (Euskadi Ta Askatasuna, or Basque Country and Freedom). José María Aznar's government adopted this strategy in order to circumvent any voices that linked the attacks with Spain's support for, and participation in, the Iraq war. In addition to the human toll and the shock that often accompanies the aftermath of this type of event, the Spanish people also had to deal with their government's attempts to cover up any political responsibilities that derived from their decision to take part in this conflict, against which Spanish citizens had protested in massive demonstrations. Despite Partido Popular's attempts to mislead the electorate, the news media played an important role in informing the audience about the truth of the matter. In the end, Partido Popular lost the elections and Partido Socialista formed a new government.

Twelve years later, the way the attacks are remembered at different levels and among different sectors of society has evolved, if only to accentuate some aspects of the event over others. From the individual perspective of each of the victims and their close relations, the memories of these events are primarily defined by their direct experiences of what happened to them and how the attacks affected their lives. While the majority of the population understands the events both in their human and political dimensions, for the victims, and perhaps for the next generations of their families, memories of the bombings are mainly based on their first-hand involvement in the events. This is not to argue that those memories are exclusively shaped by those events, but the weight of the direct experience is more significant for them than the political aftermath, to which they have also been exposed at a collective level. Meanwhile, the victims' testimonies sometimes contribute to the collective memories of that day, as they are included in anniversary special reports and documentaries, and victims are seen attending commemorative acts. Cultural interventions are therefore intertwined with personal ones, and all of them contribute, in turn, to the shaping of memory.

Chapter 3

Critical Ethnography of Memory

Scholars in Memory Studies have developed several approaches in order to explain the collective nature of memory, the relationship between cognitive processes and experience, and the ways in which memory is mediated through mass media and other channels. Much of this work is theoretical and, in many cases, authors have set out to develop theories of remembering that are not limited by specific case studies and from which general conclusions can be drawn (Bergson 2007; Ricoeur 2004). In producing work that is not concerned with the concrete analysis of specific communities, they have offered useful, though necessarily abstract overviews of the subject. Bearing in mind the ideological imbalances that underpin public memory, there is an argument to be made in favour of developing these general theories. As previously discussed, the impulse to remember or to forget events (or selective aspects of them) at a collective level is intrinsically political. Foucault (2011, 253) noted that 'if one controls people's memory, one controls their dynamism. And one also controls their experience, their knowledge of previous struggles'. The extent to which specific historical events are known to the population (as well as the kind of public interpretations that accompany those that do receive attention) demonstrates the need to consider the wider political environment within which oral testimonies about the past are shaped, and the ways in which memory is subsequently managed, negotiated and expressed.

As an approach, the Critical Ethnography of Memory intends to provide a conceptual and methodological framework that foregrounds local or indigenous accounts of major public events. This form of analysis combines theoretical and methodological insights from Memory Studies, Orality and Critical Ethnography, in order to gather the local memories of people who have lived through momentous historical periods, and to compare the narratives they produce with the state-sponsored reproduction of 'public memory'.

Local memories, as discussed later in the chapter, are defined as social memories that are strongly attached to a given place and the community that inhabits it. The framework proposed here examines how mechanisms of social control manifest themselves in the act of narrating local memories.

Writing from the perspective of oral history, Hamilton and Shopes have noted that Memory Studies has mainly focused on the creation, circulation, mediation and reception of broader cultural memories, but would benefit from the engagement with the 'more reflective work done by oral historians', which is based much more closely on lived experience (Hamilton and Shopes 2008, x). Oral history is concerned with the ways in which individuals produce meaning from their accounts of the past, and is therefore useful to take into account the dynamic nature of remembering, the gaps or silences in the transmission of memory, the collapsing of past and present in individual recall, and people's sense of historical and contemporary consciousness (Hamilton and Shopes 2008, xi). Far from merely collecting oral testimonies and using them descriptively as sources of data, oral history has a long analytical tradition from which Memory Studies can draw methodological and conceptual insights, namely in relation to the concrete events and experiences with which it is concerned: the ones that take place locally, at a given time and space, with a specific group of participants and witnesses, in a certain community based upon particular or local social relations.

One aspect that is intrinsic to memory is the fact that the recalled event occurred in the past. As long as the incident *really* happened, the question should not be whether it has taken place, but in what ways it is being recalled in the present. This enquiry should elicit a discussion that (i) begins from the fact that an event that occurred in the past should be acknowledged and remembered; (ii) recognises that there are multiple memories and a variety of perspectives that need to be considered; and (iii) understands that memories are not fixed and static but dynamic and in a permanent process of redefinition.

THE TENETS OF A CRITICAL ETHNOGRAPHY OF MEMORY

In attempting to construct a Critical Ethnography of Memory, the first challenge is to acknowledge the sheer complexity and volume of the narratives that are generated by respondents. The second is to recognise that the testimonies produced about a particular occasion can vary, not only because verbal accounts will differ from person to person, but because a single individual will often emphasise different aspects of the same event at different points in time. Once these variations in the quality and scope of testimony as a *practice* have been acknowledged, the basic principles that should govern the field can be described. A Critical Ethnography of Memory, therefore, should (1) outline what a 'critical' approach entails; (2) (re)assert the values of truth and oppose the drift to oblivion; (3) investigate 'local' territories while (4) making reference to other levels of memory; and (5) be grounded in both contemporary and historical modes of enquiry.

1. The 'Critical' in the Critical Ethnography of Memory

In the first instance, the Critical Ethnography of Memory is 'critical' precisely because of its essential concern with the 'forgotten' truth – or the truth of the forgotten – that is, with the subjugated memories of those who lost the war and were subsequently repressed. The aim is to draw attention to memories that have been ignored and silenced, in order to analyse existing social relations from the perspective of the powerless and, ultimately, to effect socio-political change in their favour. This approach pursues what Simon (1993, 76) calls 'insurgent commemoration', which he describes as 'attempts to construct and engage representations that rub taken-for-granted history against the grain so as to revitalize and rearticulate what one sees as desirable and necessary for an open, just and life-sustaining future'.

The examination of oral testimonies plays a crucial role in the accomplishment of this purpose. According to Hamilton and Shopes (2008, viii), oral history is a valuable tool to uncover 'unknown truths' or 'giving voice to the unheard, the secret', particularly where no other evidence is available. A critical analysis of narratives about the past enables us to identify how memories are ordered, which fragments are narrated, which ones appear as central, and how they are linked to other memories or pieces of knowledge. By examining the subjective act of remembering, we are also able to identify how broader discourses shape, and are activated within, those narrations. By exposing these discursive mechanisms, which are often taken for granted, we can make a critique of the political underpinning of memory as a first step towards addressing any injustices from the past that are perpetuated in the present.

In ethnographic terms, Chacko (2004, 61) notes that the acknowledgement of the ethnographer's positionality can make the researcher more vigilant about power relations at every stage of the ethnographic process, including the formulation of the research question, data gathering and reporting of findings. Hence, this critical approach must take into account the researchers' personal and professional background, their political stance, and any other factors that may have a bearing on their handling of the critique they produce (see below).

2. Against Oblivion: (Re)Asserting the Truth

I argued above that the present can never be disconnected from the past, and noted that the act of remembering the actions that have been taken should involve an acknowledgement of responsibility. Conversely, forgetting – or denying aspects of an inconvenient past – not only avoids these responsibilities, but can also protect current interests. In Spain, arguments that the Civil War and the dictatorship should not be revisited, are advanced in the main by right-wing parties, which justify their position by arguing that this process would simply reopen old wounds. However, parties that define themselves as 'centre-left' have also sanctioned these attitudes, directly or indirectly, through their reluctance to take determined action to address the issues (see, e.g., Alfaya 2003; Gavilán 2004; Ortiz Heras 2006; Richards 2006).

Despite any discursive and politico-legal attempts to erase the past, these events continue to have a bearing on the present. It is not possible to deny the uprising of 18 July 1936 and the subsequent chain of events that developed from that moment, including the thousands of victims who died or whose lives were irremediably affected. The controversy stems from the fact that Franco's dead were given proper burial in 1939, as soon as the Civil War finished, while most of the dead on the anti-fascist side are still waiting to receive a similar form of recognition while their descendants are forced into an endless cycle of neglect and subjugation. The Critical Ethnography of Memory (re)asserts this 'truth' against any systemic or institutional attempts to forget it. The ethos of the framework can be encapsulated in Ortiz Heras' (2006, 181) statement that 'oblivion is not the opposite of memory but the antonym of truth'. In this sense, memory and truth are near synonyms.

This form of truth includes those stories about the past that are pieced together in certain ways, and encompasses the form in which they appear, such as the moment when they are narrated or performed. The focus on truth should therefore be understood in terms of the certitude that the events happened, and that the essential facts of the matter should not be forgotten or erased.

3. Immersion and the Local

A Critical Ethnography of Memory is based on the premise that memories are attached to particular territories and, as such, that their collection and analysis must also be grounded in those same places. The act of considering local memories in *their own right* means that we must establish what they mean to residents, taking into account their sense of collective identity and community. This is the closest point of entry into the real materiality of past events, the advantage of which is noted by Ashford (1960, 119, in Finberg 1973, 29) who, in his local history of High Wycombe, points out that 'we are in danger of falsifying history if we fail to realize that for people of places [*sic*] like Wycombe their own borough was still the foreground of their view of the world, even in times of great national crisis'. According to Finberg, the local historian has the opportunity to investigate details that are not abstract or expressed in general terms, but relate to specific events, in specific landscapes, involving specific groups of people. The focus on the local enables the production of a knowledge that would otherwise be overlooked, or lost in the impulse to create an all-purpose, general narrative, such as the national, Historical narratives that aim to fulfil an important purpose in the construction of a country's identity and sense of unity. The example that opens this book, which described de Gaulle's discursive reconstruction of the liberation of Paris, is only one of numerous instances in which History has been written to meet a national purpose.

The findings unearthed by Ethnographers of Memory would, in many cases, contribute details that would be of use to local historians. However, ethnographers not only benefit from accessing local contexts, as would historians, but in fact *depend* on that access to be able to conduct their work. As Drake (2003) notes, the past is only accessible through private and publicly articulated memories, narrated, in every case, through the perspective of the present. Therefore, immersion – the process through which the ethnographer embeds him or herself in the group that he or she wishes to observe and understand – is only possible in the relevant place or places that are currently accessible. The closest route into the past of any given community is to absorb as much of that past as possible by acquiring an in-depth understanding of that community in the present time, so as to recover and map this past with the details that are still available.

Meanwhile, the focus on local contexts does not mean that insights are discontinuous with work in other localities, or irrelevant to the development of findings that can be applied to a broader social environment. It should be clear, however, that the intention of the framework is not to formulate a totalising theory that is infallible in all cases – the approach that Foucault (2004) describes as resembling 'totalitarian theories, or at least all-encompassing and global theories'. Rather, the purpose is to suggest some ideas that can be tested, amended and reformulated as necessary according to each local milieu, its particular characteristics and the circumstances surrounding the past events that are narrated. As Foucault argued, the local character of the analysis does not mean

> soft eclecticism, opportunism, or openness to any old theoretical undertaking, nor does it mean a sort of deliberate ascetism that boils down to losing as much theoretical weight as possible. I think that the essentially local character of the critique in fact indicates something resembling a sort of autonomous and non-centralized theoretical production, or in other words a theoretical production that does not need a visa from some common regime to establish its validity. (Foucault 2004, 6)

In Spain, local circumstances during the Civil War differed from village to village, even though all localities were embedded within a similar climate of systemic repression. In Arroyomolinos, for example, one participant stated that

Mayors were in charge of making those decisions [to execute people] in the villages. Here, Trenado, the son of a bitch, signed the [death] sentences. In Hinojales, however, they didn't kill anyone, and in Hinojos, or Niebla, I am not sure which one, they didn't kill anyone either. It depended on the mayor, because they were the ones who authorised the executions. (Miguel 2014a, my translation)

Miguel's testimony highlights the fact that, even though people were targeted and killed 'here' (and in many other places), it was done differently elsewhere. Likewise, it has emerged that decisions regarding the execution of women were also made locally in ways that diverged from how they were treated in other places (see Chapter 6). Each locality, therefore, experienced specific incidents that marked the course of events in particular ways, thereby providing a unique basis for local memories to develop.

4. Local Memories and Other 'Levels' of Memory

I have discussed some of the levels at which memory operates, from the individual or cognitive level to wider social environments, including the family, the immediate social surroundings, and the public or national context. We have seen that individual memory is not only a psychological phenomenon but also a socially shared experience that has been classified differently by various authors. Consequently, Memory Studies has seen a growth in the number of terms that are used to describe different manifestations of remembrance, depending on the factors that determine their development and circulation across the social spectrum. However, the boundaries between different 'types' of memory, which scholars spend so much time demarcating, sometimes become blurred (see Sanz Sabido 2015).

In a Critical Ethnography of Memory, memories are attached to particular territories and, accordingly, the framework interprets each type or level of memory in relation to the place to which it refers. The five levels of memory through which this framework operates are: individual memories, local memories, regional memories, national memories and international memories. As noted earlier, the main focus is placed on local communities, which are defined as 'social' memories by Casey (2008). This level of memory is based on the individual recollections of people who have a cognitive record of events that took place in a given locality or geographical area. It is within communities that inhabit specific territories and lived particular experiences that memories are created, evolve or disappear.

By contrast, regional, national and international levels of memory (which might otherwise, in Casey's view, be known as collective or public memories) enable us to examine the interplay between these various spheres and to identify the extent to which each of them affects the rest. The ultimate objective of the framework is to examine how the mechanisms of social control, which are activated at these higher levels, manifest themselves in the narration of local memories. For example, the prevalence of region-specific politico-cultural references (the regional level), the emergence and perpetuation of state-sponsored myths (the national level), or the production of discourses about memory from an international perspective (the international level) may be manifested in individual and local narrations of memory, reproducing them or challenging them, in explicit or implicit ways. In sum, the critical analysis of these memories seeks to interpret the re-emergence and continued propagation of those official and approved perspectives that continue to subjugate the disadvantaged, or to identify any cases when this process has been reversed in favour of the oppressed.

5. Contemporary *and* Historically Grounded Investigation

Conducting a Critical Ethnography of Memory involves working on at least two 'moments' in time: the time in the past when the events that are recalled originally took place, and the time when the memories are narrated. The framework therefore takes account not only of the core substance of the memories (which is found in the references to events in the past), but also of the subsequent factors that may have altered the narration of those memories (including, among other factors, the conditions in which the narration is delivered in the present).

Since our experience of the 'present' is of a condition that is subject to renewal (rationalised as either constant change or the movement of time past a certain point), and memories and their interpretation are also created within a shifting context, it is necessary to consider the moment when a certain narration was formed, and the time at which it was analysed, so as to make an appropriate evaluation of their meaning. So, for example, when Fraser published his landmark study, *Blood of Spain*, Franco had only just died and, in Fraser's (1979, 32) words, 'the dictatorial regime created by the victor of the Civil War began to be dismantled. A new era was opening to Spain'. From an historical point of view, Spain certainly began a new era with the implementation of the transition to democracy, the approval of the 1978 Constitution and the instauration of a Parliamentarian Monarchy. The fact that Franco's death had marked the end of the dictatorship and had given way to a new system is unquestionable. Nonetheless, the anticipation and optimism in Fraser's statement, which was written in the early days of this transitory phase, have to be understood within the context of that period. Today, Fraser's positive outlook has been replaced by much more critical stances.

The original events that constitute the basis of memories are grounded in history, but it is the contemporary context of the narration that determines the relevance of the material. This point is particularly important when the source of current social injustices is found in the past and has been perpetuated over the years. For this reason, we may argue that this approach is both contemporary *and* historically grounded. Furthermore, the 'transmission' of memories from the 1930s to the current context is an intrinsically generational process. As Cuesta Bustillo (2007a) notes, three generations – those of the Second Republic, the dictatorship and the transition – bring their different experiences and perspectives together, thereby contributing to the overall shaping of memories over the years.

METHODOLOGICAL OPPORTUNITIES AND CHALLENGES

The combination of perspectives from Critical Ethnography, Oral History and Memory Studies provides the present framework with a number of advantages. These include theoretical and methodological factors that affect the ways in which memories are formed, transformed and performed, the collection and interpretation of testimonies, the verification of data, the role of the researcher and his or her relationship with the participants.

The task at hand – in this case, to review the local memories of a traumatic period in a Spanish village – consists of much more than merely conducting interviews and identifying common themes. Barker (2007) reflected on this point in his work on Castilleja del Campo, a small village in the province of Seville. His intention, he explains, was to produce a book based on oral testimonies in order to show the 'human face' of the Civil War. However, when Barker completed the first draft of his book, nobody was convinced by its approach, with some critics insisting that it was written in 'the wrong style', while more politically infused attacks argued that it had the potential to 'stir things up' in the village. Barker himself felt that many pieces were missing (including a full list of victims of the repression) and, for him, this had a negative effect on the overall coherence of the narrative. When attempting to fill in those gaps, he knew that interviewing more people would lead to the repetition of the same stories, so he also consulted a variety of archives to supply the material that the participants' narratives had not been able to provide (see also Barker 2012).

Barker's example illustrates the complexity involved in a project based on oral testimonies as the primary source of data, which nonetheless strives to meet the criteria of facticity while also taking into account the variety of contextual factors that have moulded oral testimonies. The rest of this chapter is an attempt to analyse the methodological opportunities and challenges that have shaped the application of the current framework, which include (1) the ethnographer's positionality; (2) the overlaps between his or her personal and academic roles; (3) the ethnographer's (semi-)local connection to the locality;

(4) the narrator's background; (5) the context of the interview; (6) the role of 'informal gatekeepers'; (7) the importance of reflexivity; (8) the emergence and treatment of emotions; (9) the ethnographer's responsibility and ethical perspective; and (10) the use of archives to recover, among other useful data, existing testimonies about the past recorded at an earlier period. These are all elements that have had a bearing on the research, from inception to delivery, and therefore play a crucial part in the development of a Critical Ethnography of Memory.

1. The Ethnographer's Positionality

The non-positivist nature of ethnography means that there is not a single authoritative reading of a body of qualitative data. The ethnographer is – and acts as – a subjective being, thereby defining the entire project, from the original motivation that prompted the research, to the choice of location, to the conscious decision to take a 'critical' approach on behalf of the powerless and subjugated (Savin-Baden and Howell-Major 2013). In addition, one of the key notions in ethnography is that of positionality, which 'forces us to acknowledge our own power, privilege, and biases just as we are denouncing the power structures that surround our subjects' (Madison 2012, 8).

In order to assume a critical perspective, the ethnographer needs to acknowledge their positionality and the extent to which it affects their decisions and the overall management of the research. According to Fine (1994), ethnographers may take a number of different stances towards their research, thereby defining, at once, aspects of their positionality *and* the extent to which the ethnographic activity is critical. Critical Ethnography involves stepping away from what Fine describes as 'ventriloquist' stances, according to which subjects are treated as objects and all politics are denied 'in the very political work of social research' (Fine 1994, 19). A subtler form of the ventriloquist stance, which she defines as 'voices', also fails to be critical because, in appearing to allow the marginal but 'liberated' subjects speak, the ethnographer fails to acknowledge the power relations around those subjects, their spaces and what they have to say (Fine 1994, 19–20). In her view, therefore, critical ethnographers should

> critique what seems 'natural', recast 'experience', connect the vocal to the structural and collective [and] spin images of what's possible. In such work, the researcher is clearly positioned (passionate) within the domain of a political question or stance, representing a space within which inquiry is pried open, inviting intellectual surprises to flourish (detachment). The text itself is conceived and authored with a critical eye toward 'what is', attending seriously to local

meanings, changes over time, dominant frames, and contextual contradictions. Within these texts, researchers carry a deep responsibility to assess critically and continually our own, as well as informants' changing positions. (Fine 1994, 23)

This position within ethnography, which Fine describes as 'activist', must also concern itself with the question 'what could be', denaturalising 'what is', and imagining other possibilities in order to help members of society recognise their responsibility. When memories are examined from the perspective of Critical Ethnography, we are giving those memories a useful purpose – what Todorov (2000) calls an 'exemplary' use of memory – insofar as memories are not invoked for their own sake but are used to secure more equitable social relations based on the principle of justice. Furthermore, in a Critical Ethnography of Memory, the question 'what is' should not only include 'what could be', as Fine suggests, but also 'what has been', 'what is being' and 'what could have been'. With these questions, we are not only taking account of the relentless passage of time, in which memories are constantly made and remade, but also recognising that past actions have long-term consequences.

Having acknowledged the ethnographer's subjectivity, it is worth remembering that there is a difference between a subjectivity that is materialised in *statements* of fact (based on the ethnographer's own perceptions), and subjectivity that is grounded in sound theoretical and empirical data. Thomas (1993) makes this point, in favour of the latter, when he notes that

We let the data speak to us, we do not prejudge or impose our own preferred meanings, and we make sure that we do not say is when we mean ought. ... As scientists, we are simply forbidden to submit value judgments in place of facts or to leap to 'ought' conclusions without a demonstrably cogent theoretical and empirical linkage. (Thomas 1993, 22)

In light of one of the framework's key tenets – that it seeks to (re)assert the 'truth' against systemic and institutional mechanisms of oblivion (see above) – it is important that the ethnographer's work is not tainted with his or her own subjective fabrications. It is the data, and the critical assessment of the data, that should form the basis of the contribution.

2. The Ethnographer's Personal and Academic Roles

Two inherent aspects of the ethnographer's positionality are given by his or her personal and academic roles and trajectories. From an academic perspective, the researcher needs to consider his or her disciplinary background and, as part of the ethnographic process of reflexivity, review the ways in which it informs not only his or her interpretations (Lewis and Russell 2011, 399), but also the overall theoretical and methodological approach to the enquiry.

The perspective that underpins this project is based on an analysis of the ways in which structures of power are both manifested and perpetuated in narratives within particular political, economic and social contexts. The development of this process was also strongly marked by my personal connections with the community within which I worked. Ethnography is often thought of as an activity that is performed somewhere else, a place to which one needs to travel before undergoing a process of immersion. The current project, however, involved talking to people I already knew, in a setting that was familiar to me. My existing personal relations with these villagers – now turned into participants – were determining the way in which I perceived my research. This is not to suggest that I had forgotten about my commitment to rigour as a researcher, but the boundaries between the academic and the human, who had complex social relations with, and emotional investments in, the community became unclear. The research aspect was always present and, yet, at the same time, it was qualified by the fact that the personal dimension could not be erased. From a researcher's perspective, it was important, nevertheless, to yield reliable and valid findings, based on a thorough understanding of the relationship between the personal and the professional.

In fact, I would argue that, rather than blurring the boundaries between the academic and the human, a more accurate approach would recognise the fact that these dimensions actually overlap. So, for example, even though my family did not live there on a permanent basis, the Church at Arroyomolinos de León is the place where my siblings and I were baptised. In fact, the story of my baptism provides an illustration of the predominant ways of thinking in the village in the 1980s (which, in many ways, still linger today). When my parents began the process to baptise me, a group of *beatas* (excessively devout or overpious women) reacted negatively to the idea on the grounds that my parents had married in a civil – not religious – ceremony. As far as they were concerned, my parents were not legitimately married. In their mind, therefore, their daughter was illegitimate and to baptise her in the house of God would constitute nothing less than sacrilege. This group of women communicated their concerns to the priest and subsequently asked him not to conduct the ceremony.

These and other cultural influences shaped my view of the village and the local community. Yet, I never knew, neither as a child nor as a young adult, that the Church had been a site of violent confrontation between villagers in the 1930s, and that this and other events had marked the lives of many residents. I only discovered this when, as a researcher, I listened to my friends, neighbours and fellow villagers describe a succession of incidents to which I had never been exposed, even though they were known to people who were so close to me. I was also unaware of the fact that some local residents would never go to the Chapel because eighteen men were arrested in this building before their execution in 1936. As I listened to my participants' testimonies, my views of the village began to undergo a transformation from the notions I had acquired during my childhood. The point that I would like to emphasise here is the fluidity that exists between the human and the ethnographic role as the research proceeds.

3. On Being (Semi-)Local

The overlap between the ethnographer's academic and personal existence becomes even more noteworthy when the 'object' of study is directly related to his or her own personal life. While ethnographers often become involved in various types of communities with the sole purpose of researching them, my argument here is concerned with those cases when the researcher's involvement with the community pre-exists the research. My incursion into ethnography fits this scenario: Arroyomolinos de León is the place where the maternal side of my family comes from and, consequently, where I spent all my school holidays as a child. This means that, even though I was not born or brought up in this locality, I gradually became acquainted with the villagers, the local customs, the landscape and, in sum, everything that comprised this micro-world, unaware that I would one day conduct this project.

Heley (2011) emphasises the advantages of carrying out 'backyard ethnographies' in which researchers already have a significant amount of knowledge about the culture or environment that they are studying before the research begins. In fact, the extent to which the researcher is 'local' is a central aspect of his or her positionality, as it can potentially affect the ways in which that culture is interpreted. Once this existing relationship is reflected upon, being local offers a number of opportunities and advantages that can benefit the overall project throughout each of its phases.

The nature of my connection with the village could not, however, be described as that of a 'local' as I was born in the capital of the province, Huelva, and did not grow up in Arroyomolinos. This makes me an outsider in the eyes of the local community. A brief example should illustrate this point. On one occasion, while interviewing a woman called Lorenza and her brother, one of their neighbours, Ramona, arrived and asked Lorenza about some medical tests that her husband had taken earlier that day in Seville. This type of encounter is typical, where villagers walk in and out of their neighbours' houses unannounced, nurturing their relationships daily through exchanges of tokens of care, gratitude and attention. When Lorenza had finished sharing the details of her husband's visit to the doctor, Ramona looked at me and asked: 'And who is this girl? *A foreigner?*' ('*¿Y esta muchacha quién es? ¿Forastera?*'). For Ramona, and for the majority of the local residents, I was, in the first instance, a '*forastera*' or 'foreigner' (an outsider) to the village. Yet, the fact that I have ties with Arroyomolinos means that I was

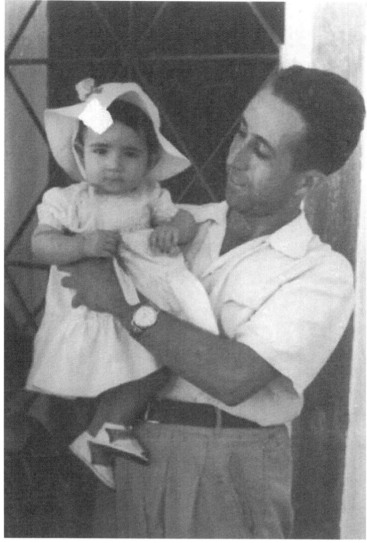

Figure 3.1 My grandfather, Francisco Sabido Suárez, holding my mother, in 1957. Family Archive.

not a complete stranger, since to those who know the history of my family, I was *la nieta de Suárez,* or Suárez's granddaughter. This meant, in turn, that my interaction with my respondents could have developed without needing to refer to the formal elements of the research project, while my semi-local position in the village also generated a number of opportunities that might otherwise have been unavailable.

In practice, the notions of 'insider' and 'outsider' are relative and unstable. It is not possible to delimit, in precise terms, the boundaries that separate them, nor is it realistic to try to calculate how much of a connection a person needs to have with a given community before he or she can be accepted (see Katz 1994, and Surra and Ridley 1991). Although I had not followed the standard practice associated with the ethnographic tradition of scholars such as Malinowski (1922), which posits travel to an unknown environment, I was nonetheless immersed in a fairly remote locality. I had not only to understand the depth of the social relations that existed within the village, but to appreciate the connections between Arroyomolinos and other regional and national centres.

When the topic of conversation is something as traumatic as the Civil War, which still produces a certain level of uneasiness and hesitation, the relative familiarity between the researcher and the participants helps them to engage in conversation, speak more freely and share more details about their memories. What is more, when word about the project spread, some neighbours came to me – rather than waiting for me to approach them – and began to describe what they knew, sometimes before specific questions could be framed. This willingness to participate, however, does not always correspond with a desire to remember and discuss these sensitive issues, which are normally avoided. Rather, the reaction of some villagers is better explained by their collaborative attitude and eagerness to help, particularly when they knew that they were assisting the cobbler's granddaughter. For this reason, some of the conversations did not take place in traditional interview settings, such as domestic (and private) environments, but in more informal and improvised contexts, from conversations in the street to spontaneous chats with labourers on their way to the countryside.

4. The Narrator's Background

It was noted above that memories are inherently socio-political, so a Critical Ethnography of Memory must consider the participants' background in order to gain a deeper understanding of the narrators and their points of view. This includes gathering information about any processes (private or social) that may have defined their stances and shaped their memories. The narrator or respondent is the vehicle between the ethnographer and the past, and the testimony provided helps the interviewer to comprehend both the event that is remembered, and the participant's stance towards it. Consequently, a critical analysis of the narration and its performance is central to the operation of the Critical Ethnography framework. Researchers need to examine the narrator's interpretation of the past, which should include an understanding of the role that he or she is supposed to have taken in specific events. So, for example, a participant might talk about an event as though it happened to others (describing his or her part in the drama as essentially passive), or might offer a narrative that highlights his or her individual activity. Here, the critical questions would be: according to the narrator, who experienced the event, who were the actors and the subjects, and where is the narrator situated in relation to this incident?

The narrator's background becomes even more important when the research is concerned with a controversial and contested political history (Sanghera and Thapar-Björkert 2008, 544). As Thomas notes, critical ethnographers 'begin from the premise that all cultural life is in constant tension between control and resistance'. This is reflected in 'behaviour, interaction rituals, normative systems, and social structure, all of which are visible in the rules, communication systems, and artefacts that constitute a given culture, imposing one set of preferred meanings over others (Thomas 1993, 9). The more tumultuous the socio-political background to the issues being studied, the more likely it is that discrepancies, suspicions and conflicts may appear throughout the ethnographic process.

5. The Context of the Interview

The context of the interview refers to the immediate circumstances within which the narrator provides his or her testimony. All these aspects form part of the 'narrative event', which takes place in the present time and cannot be separated from the rhetorical dimension of the participant's testimony (Freeman 2001, 289). The conditions of the narrative event, according to Bauman's (1986) definition, determine the ways in which the 'telling' of the testimony takes place. This is what Langellier and Peterson (2004) call 'situated constraints' which, in their view, include the relationship between the researcher and the participant, as well as their respective backgrounds and positionalities (see above).

In practice, these considerations include the time and space of the interview, which in turn also involve the narrator's own relationship to that time and space. So, for example, an interview may take place at the participant's house in the evening, but it is also worth noting whether the narrator has just arrived from working in the countryside all day, or whether, at that time of the day, they still have to return to the fields to feed the cattle. In addition, there may be children or elderly parents that need attention, causing disruptions that may affect the course of the conversation. In these cases, it may also be worth considering the distribution of work within the particular household, as in certain contexts (such as the one on which this study is based) there tends to be a traditional division of labour, by which women mainly attend to housework, occasionally assisting on the land, while men take most of the responsibility in the fields. Moreover, the domestic setting is, in this rural context, a semi-open space that neighbours tend to visit as a matter of course. The arrival of a new person in the context of the interview may lead to a significant alteration in its development, with regard to content, performance or both. For example, when I was interviewing Valeria (2014) in her patio, one of her neighbours, Valentina, called Valeria from her main door and entered the house. When Valeria (from a traditional right-wing family) realised that Valentina was approaching us, she pointed out, in a whisper, that Valentina had probably seen me coming into her house and 'she may just want to find out what is going on'. The interview continued and Valentina (a left-wing voter) also participated, but Valeria's contribution acquired a less conservative tone in her presence.

6. Informal Gatekeepers

During an interview, participants are likely to mention other villagers in their narrations, referring to the actions they took or the injuries they suffered. On some occasions, they may also point out that a certain individual may be able to contribute an additional testimony to the project. Furthermore, in a village where information circulates fairly quickly, some residents may make an informal suggestion about individuals or stories that may be of interest. So, for example, the names of a couple of individuals were often mentioned as local 'authorities' on the subject, while other potential narrators were identified due to their direct personal connections to the events. Their names and nicknames were offered alongside an indication of their address, in case I wanted to pay them a visit. At the beginning of the project, I started by interviewing four people and, through this process of snowballing and word of mouth, I ended up speaking to twenty-two individuals.

While local residents, in their willingness to collaborate, helped to recruit a larger number of participants, no formal permission was needed since, in principle, everyone in the village is relatively accessible and welcoming, without the need for official introductions. In this respect, there were no gatekeepers in this project, at least in its literal definition of 'sponsors or individuals who smooth access to the group. They are the key people who let us in, give us permission, or grant access' (O'Reilly 2009, 132). Nevertheless, the role of these loosely defined 'informal gatekeepers' provides a crucial contribution to the project, and must therefore be acknowledged as an integral part of the research process.

Informal gatekeepers can also influence an ethnographer's decision *not* to contact certain villagers. In these cases, the gatekeeping role does not facilitate further contacts, but attempts to prevent the development of contact with those they think unsuitable. For instance, Miguel, one of the villagers with whom I often spoke during the course of the project, uttered the following warning:

> Don't talk to those people. They are fascists. Those people will only tell you that they killed because the saints were burnt. Forget it. They won't tell you anything else. Don't mix with those people. I don't want to have anything to do with them. They killed because we burnt the saints? No way! (Miguel 2014a, my translation)

During another interview, Miguel referred to the group of local *beatas* and, in a similar vein, stated that

> These women, whatever they tell you, I don't know … I don't believe any of it. 'My father, my father' … What about your father? Your father stayed here and the others were the ones who died. Here there are very bad people … here, in this village. (Miguel 2014b, my translation)

Miguel was referring to a number of villagers whose testimonies would not fit in with the libertarian stance that he promotes, or even with a broader left-wing perspective. On a different occasion, another participant mentioned a villager who might be willing to participate and provide an additional testimony. When I asked Luis, another interviewee, whether this villager would be happy to speak to me, he hesitated, unsure of what to say, only to respond:

> That guy is very weird. You can try to talk to him and he may speak to you, but he is weird. Be careful, because some people seem one thing and they are another. He was young when everything happened and he knows stuff, but he is weird. (Luis 2015, my translation)

Luis did not clarify exactly what he meant when he insisted that this person was 'weird'. He simply reiterated that I should be careful. When I asked him whether he would accompany me to conduct the interview, he replied with a resounding 'no'. He was not going to this individual's house, he said, because he did not want to hear what he might say. Luis could have put me off speaking to this person, but I decided that I needed to investigate further. It emerged that Luis' reservations against this prospective participant were caused by the fact that the latter had publicly pretended to be in favour of the fascist cause in order to divert the attention of the authorities away from his family, since they had already suffered a number of repressive measures. What this individual considered as a necessary mechanism of survival for him and his relatives, Luis interpreted as a betrayal. Consequently, as far as he was concerned, I should not trust what he might say to me. His informal 'reverse' gatekeeping role was thus motivated by his ideological and moral perspectives.

Miguel's advice not to speak to the now grown-up children of those who were known to be fascists was also clearly defined by his political views. As with Luis, his 'reverse' gatekeeping efforts also went unheeded. Although the essential goal of the research is to position itself on the side of the social groups that have been disadvantaged, repressed and forgotten, this does not necessarily translate into the automatic exclusion of participants who might be able to provide other perspectives. There is a moral dilemma in this approach, since one plausible argument against it is that, by allowing the oppressors to speak and express their views, we are simply enabling them to extend their reign over a space that is supposed to be reserved for their victims. The intention behind the engagement with such views is not, however, to support their cause or to facilitate its perpetuation – for that, they already have all the necessary political and legal structures at their disposal. Quite to the contrary, the purpose of these interviews is to contribute further to the analysis of meaning-making in specific local communities and in relation to wider social structures and power relations, so as to 'get beneath the surface of oppressive structural relationships' (Harvey 1990).

7. Ethnography and Reflexivity

Earlier in the discussion, I have mentioned that the participants in this project are people with whom I was already familiar to varying degrees. This became one of the core aspects of my own reflexivity as an ethnographer. Reflexivity refers to the honesty and openness that is required when explaining how the parameters of the project are defined, the extent to which the research process is governed by the subjectivity of the researcher and how and where the data was collected (Ryan and Golden 2006). As part of this process, the ethnographer identifies how his or her background and experiences are brought into the processes of design and analysis, and acknowledges the extent to which the entire approach to the project is unavoidably shaped by them (Kingdon 2005). Within this project, I needed to acknowledge the fact that the locality with which I was engaging was known to me and thus was part of my consciousness. My knowledge of the village, and the village's knowledge of me, became parts of a reciprocal relationship that impacted positively on the research, particularly in relation to the exchanges that it facilitated (see above). Yet, at the same time, some of the challenges that I faced during the completion of this project were also related to my proximity to the locality. One of the key matters that arose was that, due to my emotional investment in this village, I needed to negotiate my role as both a human being and a researcher so as not to jeopardise my 'personal' position in this community. Here, reflexivity plays a crucial role in ensuring that, despite my family and emotional ties to the place, the research remained transparent and was performed in a methodologically rigorous way (Guillemin and Gillam 2004).

In addition, as a consequence of the research, I had to *relearn* the culture of the village, reshaping my views with new layers of socio-historical fabric. The Church, the Chapel, the School for Adult Education (formerly the local prison), the village council, the old people's home (formerly the Civil Guard headquarters) and the cemetery were some of the key local sites that I had come to know in certain ways, but which were now being transformed in my mind – a process that was determined by the new insights that my participants had produced. Likewise, my perceptions of the daily activities that are performed in the village, and those related to the festivities and special occasions, also began to evolve from the more superficial views that I had formed from my childhood, to a new-found awareness of the various layers and depths that actually make up the community.

Reflexivity also includes accounting for any 'emotional baggage' (Knowles 2006) that the researcher may be carrying, and which will inevitably affect the way they design the research, conduct the fieldwork and interpret the data. For example, in a project involving war, the ethnographer needs to make explicit the extent to which his or her private sphere has been affected by the conflict. Here, we need to consider both the direct and the indirect effects of the potential trauma, which may indeed pertain to the private sphere (such as the experience of repression within one's family) or to the public sphere (when the effects are the consequence of social trauma and systemic conditions understood more broadly).

In the case of my private sphere, there were no *direct* losses or victims of violence in my family, neither did any of my relatives take part in the acts of repression that were conducted in the village. My grandfather, however, was called to fight in the war, and had to do so on the Nationalist side because, according to my mother (and like many others), 'that's how fate determined it' (*'donde le tocó'*). He, unlike some of his contemporaries, returned home and was able to resume his life within the terrible socio-economic circumstances of the times. Although he survived, the hardships endured by his family also made him a victim. His father, who had been a miner, passed away when he was a child, leaving his mother to raise him and three other brothers, one of whom was disabled. Life was already difficult before the war, but became even more gruelling when the fascists took over the village after the coup. In these circumstances, losing a pair of hands within the household, on account of the war, put additional stress on an already unbearable situation. On his return, there was even more scarcity to deal with than before he left, now under new social, political and economic conditions that were progressively becoming the norm.

In this description, we see how personal circumstances are indivisible from the broader political and socio-economic context. Yet, it is also worth considering a traumatic event in its own right. My grandfather was, of course, not the only one in these circumstances. The entire village – and, also, the entire country – was inhabited by men and women who were struggling with comparable hardships, with the exception of the oppressors and of those who took advantage of the newly imposed conditions. Marcos Ana, who holds the tragic record of being the political prisoner who spent the longest time incarcerated (twenty-three years),[1] captured this notion of collective suffering under Franco's regime in his remark that 'all of Spain is a prison'. From this perspective, everyone can be considered to be a victim of the conflict, even if they did not suffer any losses within their family. At this point, we can distinguish between a private and a collective sphere of grief. When studying a matter that pertains to the realm of 'collective' grief and, by extension, of 'collective' memory – understood in the broad sense of symbolic remembering on a large scale – the extent to which the ethnographer can realistically detach themselves from the collective act of 'remembering' is rather limited, particularly if they are part of the community or society that is under scrutiny. All the members of that community share a common fate, in one way or another, regardless of their relatives' actions and of their own perspectives towards its politics, conflicts and identities. Even if an individual is a firm believer in the simplistic and non-committal argument that 'the past is best left in the past' – a point of view often promoted by the Spanish Right – they are still a constituent part of the community as a whole.

When the members of a community can still feel the (material or symbolic) effects of a conflict, and the ethnographer is part of this collective, he or she must be fully aware of, and be explicit about, the ways in which their perspectives towards the research are informed by their views on any contemporary 'memory struggles' (Sanz Sabido 2015). Any pre-existing assumptions in this regard must also be taken into account as part of this 'reflexive' exercise (Hubbard et al. 2001; Rolls and Relf 2006).

8. Ethnography, Memories and Emotions

From the beginning of the research, my main concern was that prospective participants would not necessarily want to talk about what happened in village during the war, mainly due to lingering fears caused by the memory of the repression. My assumption was, however, that once they decided to open up, the interviews would develop without any complications and the material would simply start emerging, ready for analysis. The way I had imagined this process was determined, to a great extent, by my familiarity with the participants, and I envisioned the interviews as developments of 'normal' conversations. It did not take long to realise, however, that the variety of responses would be more complex than that. For example, questions about Franco and the war were met, overall, with a higher degree of approval than initially expected. In fact, some participants seemed to welcome the opportunity to talk openly about these issues, and even thanked me for listening to them.

While this reaction initially took me by surprise, it was not difficult to comprehend: the interviews were already helping to release forms of subjugated knowledge, even before the content of the conversations had been shared beyond the walls of the participants' homes or the immediate confines of the exchanges. In this sense, the Critical Ethnography of Memory was already underway from the very moment when it facilitated opportunities for silenced memories to emerge.

There were, nevertheless, hesitations on the part of some participants, although these were better explained within the local context of the village, rather than from a national perspective. In particular, some villagers did not want to appear overly political, while others were worried that their testimonies might create new, or renewed, breaches within the community. Participants managed and negotiated this aspect in different ways (see Chapter 4). In addition, I had foreseen that people's responses would centre on rational descriptions of what happened during those years, together with implicit or explicit indications of the participants' political stances, or their stance towards the war and the way its legacy has been managed. However, my concerns that participants would be weary of participating, or choosing their words carefully, made me overlook another potential type of response: the emotionally charged testimony.

Indeed, the research elicited a number of emotional responses from some villagers as they recalled the experiences of their own parents and relatives. In those cases, the emotions were linked to their respective private spheres. Yet, in other cases, participants expressed their thoughts and emotions with regard to the experiences that the village, as a whole community, or specific villagers within it, had to endure as a consequence of repression. Whether these feelings arise in relation to private or public circumstances, it is unrealistic to expect that a scholar researching violence, death and murder can maintain a complete sense of detachment from the people or places associated with it (Woodthorpe 2011). The emotions that emerge from memories of extreme hardship are also difficult to ignore, particularly when participants become visibly distressed. At this point, the researcher, who has an ethical responsibility towards the participant, needs to take steps to relieve some of the built-up tensions and emotions, and to give the participant the opportunity to terminate the interview or change the topic of conversation. What the researcher does to alleviate the situation, and how the participant responds, depends on the needs of the latter and on the specific conditions of the interview. The question resurfaces later, during the analytical stage, about how to use this material for the purposes of the research, while remaining ethical and showing the participant respect. For this reason, it is important to ensure that the interviewee is aware of the objectives of the conversation, and to guarantee that the source is anonymised and protected. Nevertheless, when an interview becomes particularly distressful or challenging, it is always advisable to check with the participant whether they still consent to the use of their testimony.

A question still remains as to the appropriateness of revealing certain aspects of ethnographic activity, such as the deeply emotional moments that sometimes develop during the interviews. In line with Mauthner and Doucet's (2003, 417) view that the 'reflexive turn' enables sociologists to examine aspects of the relationship between the ethnographer and the participant, Blackman (2007, 712) argues that it is necessary to pay further attention to the emotional relations and reactions that develop during the encounters, in order to 'advance more "open" reflexive approaches that explain how research is conducted and written', and to fully recognise the challenges and opportunities of qualitative research.

In a similar vein, Bloor and Wood (2006, 147) argue that it is important, in the name of 'intellectual honesty', to abandon the pretence that the author is absent from the text (see also Geertz 1988). Notwithstanding the fact that reflexive accounts should not be overdone (Atkinson 1992), the advantages of acknowledging them generally outweigh the risk of being challenged on the grounds of lack of critical distance. It is necessary, therefore, to strike the right balance between reflecting on these aspects of the research process, on the one hand, and upholding its credibility, on the other (Woodthorpe 2011). Engagement with emotional aspects of the research is not, in any case, at odds with credibility. Quite to the contrary, this form of acknowledgement enables a deeper level of critical analysis (Hallowell et al. 2005; Kleinmann and Copp 1993; Woodthorpe 2009; Woodthorpe 2011).

As discussed earlier, fundamental overlaps exist between the human person and the role of the researcher. Thus, when the human-researcher observes other people's grief, it is not unusual that they might connect with them on an emotional level. At this point, it is useful to distinguish between the different ways in which the ethnographer's perspective is shaped. In this regard, Landsberg's definitions of 'sympathy' and 'empathy' are handy. 'Sympathy', on the one hand, refers to the act of projecting

> one's own feelings onto the other. This act can be imperialising and colonising, taking over, rather than making space for, the other's feelings. In the act of sympathising, not only is the victimhood of the other reinforced, but hierarchies are established; sympathy implies condescension, for the sympathiser looks down on his/her object, and in the process reaffirms his/her superiority. (Landsberg 2003, 147)

'Empathy', on the other hand, is not emotional but cognitive, and involves

> an intellectual coming-to-terms with the other's circumstances. ... Any ethical relationship to the other requires empathy: a recognition of the profound

difference and unknowability of the other, and a simultaneous sense of commitment and responsibility toward him/her even in the face of such differences. (Landsberg 2003, 147)

The Critical Ethnography of Memory needs to engage with the other's emotions, but should do so from an empathetic perspective that is congruent with the underlying principles of fairness and egalitarianism that underpin the tenets of the framework.

9. The Ethnographer's Responsibility and Ethics

After eighty years, thousands of Spanish people still feel apprehensive about talking openly about the Civil War and Franco's dictatorship. Although this pathological silence has been broken in many ways in recent years, there still remain various degrees of resistance to these discussions, particularly when individuals are concerned that the old problems may resurface. The lingering traces of fear that Franco's repression left behind, and the fact that participants in this project are residents of a small village, where the sense of community is strong among its neighbours, are some of the aspects that the ethnographer must consider when approaching the research critically *and* ethically.

Critical ethnographers also need to decide how to handle the data that they collect, particularly when its public release may cause some harm or discomfort to the participants or to other people who may be mentioned in the testimonies. It is for the ethnographer to assess the ways in which the data may be consumed, and the extent to which it may do more damage than good if, once in the public realm, it is used in ways other than originally intended by the researcher (Fine and Weis 1998, 272; see also Madison 2012). The responsibility lies with the ethnographer, whose decisions about what data to release and how to present it involve, among other issues, ensuring the participants' anonymity and confidentiality. This not only applies to cases when anonymity is explicitly agreed prior to, and as a condition for, the participant's cooperation, but also extends to belated requests that may emerge during the interview. So, for example, while collecting testimonies in Arroyo-molinos, some interviewees gave utterance to their fear of being perceived as though they were 'stirring things up' in the village. By making requests such as 'please don't write his name' or 'don't tell anyone that I told you', just before describing an event that involved specific villagers, participants would express their concerns about the potential consequences of their narrations.

In other cases, the interviewees' apprehensions were communicated more vaguely through statements such as 'there is no point in saying who they are. We all know who they are anyway'. Here, there is no explicit request not to mention the culprits, but the participant successfully avoids having to provide their names in the first place. This avoidance mechanism is underpinned by a similar fear of being accused of causing problems among villagers, particularly when the descendants of the fascists may not even be aware of their relatives' actions. Barker (2007), for instance, describes an incident in which a young woman was taken aback by a villager who exclaimed that her grandfather was a murderer (see also Barker 2012).

In cases such as this, the ethnographer is faced with an ethical dilemma: one between protecting the relatives, on the one hand, and challenging the immunity that the culprits have enjoyed for decades, on the other. The question is whether releasing some of the information could have any impact on contemporary social relations in the locality, on the living (and innocent) descendants of the culprits, and on the narrators themselves. At the same time, choosing not to disclose those names in order to protect the individuals involved would continue perpetuating the silence that has worked against the victims, thereby failing to meet the essential principle of the framework, which is to challenge the long-standing causes of social injustice. The ethnographer needs to deal with this conundrum on a project-by-project basis and on an interview-by-interview basis, bearing in mind the particular conditions and potential consequences of each narration.

10. Archives: Recovering *Past* Testimonies About the Past

Ethnography is associated, most frequently, with the study of groups of people, communities and places, relying primarily on tools such as interviews, observations and field diaries. Even though the crucial cognitive mode is observation, other important roles include listening to the conversations of the actors, asking questions and so on. There is, however, another important tool that can help ethnographers to provide a more comprehensive view of the past: the use of archives containing historical documents (Gobo 2008, 5).

At this point, it is worth remembering that, in the analysis of memories, a fundamental tenet of the Critical Ethnography of Memory consists of its concern with the facts that underpin the participants' recollections. Fine et al. (2000, 62) state that critical ethnographers should 'dare to speak the hard truths with theoretical rigor and political savvy' so as to explain accurately why and how the difficult elements of life are intimately tied to historical, structural and economic relations. However, when the ethnographer works with memories, he or she needs to consider that these memories are potentially adulterated accounts of what happened, and may therefore provide inaccurate descriptions of the circumstances around the event and how it developed.

These adulterations present both potential challenges and opportunities in the course of the ethnographer's work. On the one hand, adulteration of memories is negative in the sense that it blurs the truth of what really happened. This is why, when presenting the findings, the ethnographer must be sure not to pass uncorroborated details as fact. The ethnographer's contribution to the study of the past should not add any further confusion, particularly to areas that may already be deeply contested. The researcher should therefore be aware of, and be clear about, the tentative nature of his or her findings. As Thomas (1993, 35) notes, empirically derived conclusions 'become working guidelines rather than truths to be proven, and critical thinkers must always be ready to modify or change their beliefs and theories if the data require it'.

During the course of the research, it soon became evident that oral testimonies could not provide a comprehensive account of the events, as they not only included contradictions, but also missed some details. Even though the primary aim of this study was to understand the ways in which individuals remember those events, the existence of a local archive provided an opportunity to substantiate and extend some of the aspects that the testimonies had exposed. Despite the fact that the most incriminating documents from this period have disappeared, the files that remain in this archive (everything from the local census to planning permissions) contain data that helps to contrast some details and to substantiate the role of the local administration, often at the request of other political and judicial bodies, in the management of official forms of repression. The archive does not include, however, lists of those who were executed extrajudicially. It is unlikely that such files ever existed.

The examination of these documents does not detract from the centrality of oral testimonies in this study, but it helps to complement the findings derived from the interviews. Rather than seeing both elements as separate, it is worth considering the advantages of marrying both approaches. On the one hand, the concepts and tools provided by Memory Studies help researchers to understand the process of social remembering. On the other hand, archives contain documents (such as judicial cases) that include names, dates, figures and information about agents involved in the events that unfolded, according to the versions that were facilitated at the time. So, for example, when a document indicates that a villager had been caught transporting goods with the intention of selling them illegally, we acquire some knowledge about the institutional procedure that was set in motion from the moment this person was detained: their name, their personal information, specific details of the products they were smuggling, the location where they were caught and the fine that they had to pay. The name of the person who oversaw this process and his or her signature, alongside the necessary official stamps and the date when the statement was processed, seals the official character of the documents and, with it, their historical value.

What these stamped sheets do not tell us, however, is the impact that this institutional process had on the person's life, and the reasons that led the individual to engage in the activities that resulted in his or her detention. At a time when hunger and food rationing were rife, such a procedure would have deprived at least one family of a source of income, with the additional problem that a fine would also have to be paid. These details are not held in any documents and, beyond the immediate effects that we may be able to imagine, they only exist in the memory of those who lived the experience directly or as a witness. For this reason, it seems appropriate to combine both types of sources, whenever possible, because they both contribute to the understanding of life in the village during this period.

FROM ORAL TESTIMONIES TO NATIONAL MYTHS

Having discussed the basic tenets of the Critical Ethnography of Memory, and the key methodological issues that define its application, it is worth returning to the objective of the overall process: to foreground the local memories of individuals who have lived through major public events, in order to compare the narratives they produce with the state-sponsored reproduction of 'public memory'. According to Brockmeier and Carbaugh (2001, 12), 'stories are collective or collaborative productions that not only take place under particular social conditions, but *are* social actions'. A critical analysis of the ethnographic interview, taken as a whole, seeks to uncover manifestations of broader discourses that promote a series of official national myths, which are not necessarily made explicit in oral testimonies concerning specific events (since they are hidden or taken for granted).

The analysis therefore consists of two levels: the micro-level of the narrative, on the one hand, and the macro-level of the socio-political discourse, on the other. The micro-level of the narrative is concerned with two main aspects. First of all, it conducts a discursive analysis of the narrative, that is, the actual content that describes the event and takes us closer to the past that we are investigating. It includes details about what happened, as well as depictions of the social, economic and political issues that defined the community at that point. This is what Bauman (1986) calls the 'narrated event', that is, the particular historical moment that is remembered. In this analysis, we pay attention to the facts of history, which are still of central importance, and to the 'discreet elements of signification' that enable us to capture 'the depth of their inferences, their over-reaching consequences, and their political nuances' so that we may gain 'a deeper realization, an added insight, or a reality "thwarted" or "undone"' (Madison 2012, 36). We analyse, therefore, not only what is said, but also how it is said and how meanings are formed: we look for any discursive and performative elements that indicate where the power struggles lie, such as terminological choices, repetitions, framing and contextualisation strategies, as well as omissions, expressions of doubt or certainty, and the narrator's self-presentation as an agent in the story, as an active participant, as a witness or as someone who heard about the events from someone else. We pay attention to the assumptions that underpin the participant's intervention, together with his or her values, and what he or she believes to be true in historical, political and cultural terms.

Secondly, the micro-level also needs to consider the ways in which any subjective and contextual elements emerge during the interview. Narratives cannot be taken out of the context of their telling, so the micro-level takes into account all the ethnographic work that occurs before and during the interview, including any information about the context of the exchange, any knowledge about the participant's background, and any other aspects that help the investigator to assess the subjective and contextual elements that shape the narrative and performative articulation of memories. In contrast to the context of the interview (the narrative event), which belongs to the present time, the content of the narration (the narrated event) belongs to the past. Nevertheless, this content about the past is always articulated from the narrator's current perspective. Consequently, not only do we need to consider the subjectivity of the participant and any immediate contextual elements, but also the fact that the descriptions are made in retrospect and may therefore differ from the narration we may acquire at other moments in time.

The purpose of analysing the participant's narration and performance of memory is, ultimately, to shed light on the ways in which socio-political discourses shape memories and perpetuate the promotion of certain perspectives over others. This is the macro-level of the analysis, which consists of the extrapolation of the participant's assumptions to the broader context within which those assumptions are circulated. The micro- and macro-levels need to be examined in conjunction with one another, as they both maintain a symbiotic relationship. A discursive analysis at the micro-level would be incomplete without an in-depth awareness of the issues that stem from the macro-level, which consists of the official discourses that are, and have been, promoted by the state. The micro-level enables us, in turn, to make a critique of the injustices and inequalities that have been sponsored within the broader context. This link between specific narratives and official discourses works on the basis that the official state-sponsored versions, which have been circulated through various media and educational channels, have permeated the collective consciousness and provided individuals with a given framework to understand the past. The participant's narration includes indicators of that framework, which may be challenged or reproduced, on purpose or uncritically, depending on the narrator's personal stance on socio-political issues.

NOTE

1. Marcos Ana is the pseudonym used by Fernando Macarro Castillo (1920–), a Spanish poet who was condemned by Franco's legal system for his involvement in political activities in the 1930s. Marcos Ana was one of the thousands of Republicans who fled to Alicante to board a ship that would take them to safety, but those ships never arrived (see, e.g., de Guzmán 2014). Instead, they were surrounded by Franco's land and naval forces with the support of the Italian and German armies. Although he managed to escape, he was captured in Madrid and accused of committing murders for which many other individuals had already been brought to trial and sentenced to death. Marcos wrote a number of poems while he was imprisoned. When these were circulated abroad, a movement for his liberation began. When, subsequently, the government passed a decree stating that all political prisoners who had been in prison for over twenty years would be released, Marcos Ana was the only person to whom this new measure was applicable (Moro 2006).

Chapter 4

'There Was No War Here'

Repression and the Civil War

This chapter offers an approximation of the events that took place in Arroyomolinos de León (Huelva) in the summer of 1936, combining the narration of local memories and the use of legal documents. The information provided here also helps to contextualise those events by describing the state of socio-economic affairs in rural localities during the Second Republic, and the way in which the 'war' began in the village. One of the key points that stand out from the testimonies is that, despite the arrest of a group of right-wing villagers and the organisation of local guards designed to pre-empt an armed coup, there was no 'war' as such in Arroyomolinos but, instead, a sequence of acts of repression that were conducted by the fascist insurgents. This fact, which is not exclusive to this locality but offers an accurate description of how events developed in many villages across the country, is important because it situates the military coup and its immediate effects on millions of Spaniards in their proper place. It therefore helps to deconstruct the discourse of a Civil War that was fought between two equally matched opponents.

Although there are a number of scholars who have examined the Civil War in several villages in the south-west of Spain, both from the perspectives of History and Memory, there is very little information available on Arroyomolinos de León. Most of what has been documented so far forms part of an in-depth study of the Civil War in the province of Huelva, by historian Espinosa Maestre (2005), whose work provides a useful point of reference. Here, I will discuss the findings of my investigation, which complement, in various ways, what this historian had already published (see below).

'THERE WAS NO WAR HERE'

During the course of my ethnographic fieldwork in several localities in Spain, I have met participants whose initial statement was that there was no war in their villages (*'aquí no hubo guerra'*). Some villagers in Arroyomolinos also uttered this remark. Despite the resistance organised by the Left during the days that followed the news of the military coup on 18 July 1936, it seems that there was no significant struggle once the troops entered the village on 20 August 1936. That there was no 'war', however, does not mean that there was no violence, for the horror of Franco's repression began in the village from that very day. By stating that there was no 'war', participants generally mean that there was barely any real fighting when the villagers came face to face with the troops. The rejection of the term 'war' as an accurate description of the local development of the conflict, is also sometimes explained by the participant's knowledge of the unequal levels of military force that existed at the national level, particularly with regard to training and access to weapons. Miguel described the problem as follows:

> The army was divided, and the Civil Guard was divided. If Franco hadn't had the weapons that were sent from Germany, they wouldn't have won the war, I am telling you. The people weren't prepared for war, they didn't know what they were doing. They weren't prepared, but on top of that, they also had to face the Germans. (Miguel 2014a, my translation)

When I asked Miguel to clarify what he meant by his statement that people 'were not prepared', he said:

> The *fachas* won because the Germans helped them, but these guys [the people] were taken by surprise. They made a sergeant out of a shoemaker, a blacksmith, a musician. ... It can't be. It can't work like that. I think that this was a plot. A plot by everyone. That war ... it was about manipulation ... by everyone. (Miguel 2014a, my translation)

In Miguel's opinion, this was not a balanced struggle. According to García Márquez (2013, 49), the problem was not only that the people were not given weapons, but also that a campaign to disarm them had already been pursued. Consequently, even though there were plenty of people who were willing to fight, they found themselves unprotected, in a vulnerable position and unable to defend themselves.

THE TROOPS ENTER THE VILLAGE

According to Espinosa Maestre (2005, 564), the troops led by Captain Manuel Comín Allende-Salazar entered the village on 20 August 1936.

None of my participants could recall the name of the captain or where the troops came from, although Santiago (who had not had access to Espinosa Maestre's book) remembers that the troops arrived on 20 August. The arrival of the column was witnessed by one of my participants' father, who was working in El Coscojal (some lands between La Vicaría and Puente de la Gitana). He saw a number of individuals from the village, whose names he refused to mention, although there were 'some principals' and others who 'were not principals, but were in agreement with them and volunteered to shoot people'. Miguel provides the following testimony about that summer day in 1936, indicating that there had actually been some clashes on the Puente de la Gitana, a Roman bridge situated outside the village that can be seen from the road that now leads from Cala to the southern entrance of Arroyomolinos:

> The bridge down there, the Puente de la Gitana ... someone got his eye busted when the forces entered the village. When the forces came in, some of the trade unionists went with the fascists. The trade unions! Listen to what I am saying. ... And the scum killed people from the village, people who had not done anything, and they accused them of whatever they wanted. In Cala, they killed 18 from here. One or two men are buried in La Parrilla, and one of them was killed because he had been a socialist mayor. His children were orphaned. And another one was killed because his brother was a fascist and he told the authorities about him. (Miguel 2014b, my translation)

Figure 4.1   Puente de la Gitana, a Roman bridge outside Arroyomolinos de León.
Family Archive.

The moment when 'the troops entered the village' is mentioned, in most cases, as a temporal marker, but details about the event are very scarce. The focus shifts quickly onto how the fascists began their programme of repression. Everyone agrees (regardless of their political stance) that the Left did not kill anyone in Arroyomolinos, neither before nor after the occupation of the village. However, when news arrived that the coup had taken place, twenty or thirty right-wing people were imprisoned and both the Church and the Chapel were vandalised (Espinosa Maestre 2005, 564). Some testimonies also described a series of events that took place in the village earlier, in 1932, although participants tended to conflate these occurrences with the developments of 1936.

THE VILLAGE'S INCIDENTS

The expression '*los sucesos del pueblo*' (the village's incidents) refers to a series of disturbances that occurred in Arroyomolinos de León on 5 October 1932. Participants were, in fact, unable to pinpoint exactly when they happened, but they were sure that they had taken place at some point before the war. Miguel, for example, refers to the incidents as a demonstration ('*una manifestación*'):

> There was a demonstration. The people demonstrated, down there at the road to Cañaveral. But there were also some blacklegs and the whole thing kicked off. One of the civil guards was shot. I don't know what happened there. It could have been worse, but there was a sergeant who was very good, and things settled down a bit. These were the village's incidents. (Miguel 2014b, my translation)

When I asked Miguel what the demonstration was about, he replied that

> The people rose up because they were very hungry. There was a lot of hunger in the village. The bad guys in the village were the middle classes. They deceived the people, they used them as they pleased, but people were hungry and they couldn't take it anymore. (Miguel 2014b, my translation)

During a conversation with Luis, a day labourer who heard the story from older members of his family, he alluded to an uprising, although he did not provide any further details about the causes that led to it:

> People rose up. There was a strike on the road to Cañaveral, but the blacklegs wanted to work. They were building the road, you see. They shot someone, and they broke a guy's arm at El Castaño. Yes, he was a goatherd and they broke his arm. It was mayhem. (Luis 2014a, my translation)

Blas, a communist who is now in his late seventies and knows what happened because his parents had described the events when he was a child, provides some additional details about the environment in the village during those days. He smiled as he recalled what happened to one of the civil guards:

> Someone threw a stone at a civil guard. ... It hit him here, in the head, and knocked off his tricorn [smiles]. I heard it from the old people, who used to tell me... the workers were very unhappy and they had to bring lots of civil guards from all the villages. The village was full of them, because the people were protesting, throwing stones. ... That guard got hit by a stone, here [points at his forehead, more smiles]. The whole village looked black because there were so many guards wearing their black capes. (Blas 2015, my translation)

When I asked Blas what happened to the man who threw the stone at the guard, he added:

> Nothing, because there were many people involved, many workers and many guards, it was a big mess, so the one who hit the guard got away with it. Later on, there was a man doing the harvest, because people were very hungry and there wasn't anything to eat, so they went to do the harvest. So, one day, he was doing the harvest in a small plot of land outside the village, and the same civil guard, who was from another village, came to him and said 'I think I have seen you in Arroyo.' He said, yes, I am from there, but I am working here. The guard told him that there are many brave people in Arroyo, because of what happened during the *sucesos*. (Blas 2015, my translation)

Another villager, Carlos, provides a different perspective. Besides the fact that one of Carlos' relatives took an active part in the story, the crucial difference between his narration and the rest lies in their diverging political stances:

> My grandfather was right-wing. He had a plot of land, near the road to Cañaveral. That's where the workers were making the road from Arroyo to Cañaveral. It was made of stone and, well, that's when the revolution started, the revolution of the peasants, the workers. So, there were pickets. Some of the workers wanted to work, and other people didn't let them work, the usual thing in picket lines. Then, they caught a couple of civil guards, they beat them up ... and they were half dead. My grandfather took them to his land, where he had a small house, in the countryside. My grandmother had a sheet, a used sheet, an old one, and used it to wrap their heads. The workers knew they couldn't have gone far, because they were hurt, and they came to my grandfather's place to finish them off. My grandfather was very nice. He said to them, defiantly: 'The one who has the balls to do it, come inside.' (Carlos 2014, my translation)

Carmen, who is also related to Carlos and his grandfather, narrated a similar story and proudly pointed out that his relative had been mentioned in a newspaper that featured the *sucesos*. The piece included two photographs: one of them was an image of the civil guards' rifles which, according to the caption, had been destroyed when the guards were 'attacked by a crowd of villagers in Arroyomolinos' (El Correo de Andalucía 1932, 3); the second image was a photograph of Carmen's grandparents and their children. The caption acknowledges that they protected Casildo Ortega, a civil guard who had been wounded, by hiding him in a barn (El Correo de Andalucía 1932, 3).

In addition, the pro-Republican newspaper *Ahora* dedicated one page to 'Los graves sucesos de Arroyomolinos de León' (The serious incidents of Arroyomolinos de León). The coverage includes several photographs with captions, describing the

> small farmhouse where the civil guard Ortega, seriously wounded by the rebellious, sought refuge. The villagers took him into a barn, and the door … was blocked with stones to make it look as though it was closed up, as the disruptive elements vigorously searched for the injured guard. (Ahora 1932, my translation)

According to this publication, four guards were injured in total. The rebels caught one of them, Juan Martín González, and 'barbarously hit him'. *Ahora* also includes a photograph of another wounded guard, Rafael Gálvez; pictures of two of the instigators (named Eugenio García Torrado 'Verdura' and José Silva Almendro); and a group photograph of the thirty-two men who were arrested as a consequence of the *sucesos*. This picture was taken in the countryside, where the events took place, while the men awaited their imprisonment: there were so many arrests that some premises had to be fitted out for this purpose (Ahora 1932).

While the press provides some useful details that help to supplement the information gathered from the testimonies, news articles can also become a source of conflicting reports when contrasted with official documents and individual testimonies. So, for example, a man nicknamed 'Verdura' was indeed involved in the *sucesos* but, according to the judicial case, his real name was not the one stated in the article, but Vicente García Martín (C-2468/39). After his arrest, Vicente was released again and he continued his involvement in political activities. His case was reopened after the war, when he turned himself in on 16 April 1939. On 8 May, Supriano, the local mayor, declared that Vicente had indeed taken part in the *sucesos* of 1932:

> During the domination of this village by the red hordes, he was one of the individuals who stood out the most, and one of the most dangerous. He took part in all the acts of vandalism committed by the red hordes, distinguishing himself by subjecting the right-wing prisoners to abuse, insults and crude talk. He was in favour of murdering them or burning them alive. Affiliated to the CNT [Confederación Nacional del Trabajo], he is a real propagator of extremist ideas,

which he has felt as his own for several years. He fled the village together with
the leaders in order to join the red army in Badajoz, being hostile to the National
Movement. (C-2468/39, my translation)

Corporal Millán Rubias also confirmed these details in his statement, describing him as 'one of the main scoundrels of the Marxist sort' and therefore
'dangerous for the National Cause'. He also pointed out that the accused had
been in the prison of Huelva for 15 months due to his participation in the
events of 1932.

A review of the judicial cases and oral testimonies confirms that José
Silva Almendro ('el Letrero') was also involved in the *sucesos*, as suggested
by *Ahora*. Like Vicente, he was released after a period in prison. However,
according to the Civil Registry in Arroyomolinos, José's death certificate
(which was registered '*fuera de plazo*' or 'out of term') indicates that he
died on 17 February 1937 as a consequence of the application of the '*bando
de guerra*' (a term used to indicate that he was executed). According to this
certificate, José was a forty-four-year-old labourer who was married and had
two children (his execution was mentioned by some participants – see below
for more details).

However, I have been unable to locate any references to Eugenio García
Torrado, the other 'instigator' of the *sucesos* that was mentioned by the newspaper. Other villagers who were mentioned in the judicial cases as having taken
part in the incidents include Francisco Agudo Pizarro, José Agudo Pizarro,
Aurelio Cordero Lobo, Cipriano Expósito Garrido, Manuel García Infante,
Antonio García Valero, Eduardo González Núñez, Francisco Marín Gil, Francisco Moya Ramírez, Salvador Núñez Romero 'Pollita', Francisco Romero
Tirado 'Panduro' and Emilio Sánchez García (Cid n.d.). In addition, a case was
opened against another villager, Adolfo Lozano Infante, accusing him of being

an individual who stood out in the CNT and had been brought to trial and condemned for the events that took place in this village in 1932. When our Glorious
Movement began, he participated, with others, in the burning and destruction of
sacred images in the local Church. He went to Cañaveral de León where he also
burnt, with others, the Church images and ornaments. He took two gentlemen
out of the prison (Cipriano Corona and José Rodríguez), who had been arrested
by the reds and, one at a time, told them in the outskirts of the village that he
would not kill them if they informed him where the fascists had hidden their
weapons. When he brought them back to prison, he warned them that they had
seventy-two hours to provide him with the details, and if they did not comply
he would shoot them dead. The village was *liberated* before the deadline was
up, so he fled to the red zone where he joined the militia despite his age [57].
(C-2382/39, my translation and emphasis)

The two 'gentlemen' who were taken out of the prison, according to this
case, were Cipriano Corona García and José Rodríguez Humanes, the local

judge and the local teacher, respectively. Both of them were strong adherents to the National Movement and the values that it imposed. Adolfo, who had threatened these men, was eventually sentenced to thirty years in prison. According to the auto-summary, Adolfo's threats against both prisoners are 'proven not only by the reports that were received from the authorities but also by the statements offered by witnesses'. The partiality of the sentence is demonstrated by the fact that these statements were provided by none other than the alleged victims themselves, and by Nicolás Martín Rocha (the local doctor), Manuel Supriano Vázquez (mayor and local head of Falange) and Manuel Millán Rubias (the leading military officer), all of whom were figures of authority within the village and thus able to provide the official seal of approval that the regime required.

THE 'MARXIST REVOLUTION'

According to Ordóñez (1968), the priest of the nearby village of Cala, Juan Chaves Molina, stated in 1932 that only 30% of the women and four men attended Mass (the religious service) in the village. This was an indication, according to Ordóñez, of the secularisation of the civil population. The priest had also pointed out that almost nobody received the last sacrament before dying, that the socialists were having civil burials, and that ten civil weddings were held in 1932. He added that the newspapers that people read were 'godless' and there were two centres, a socialist and an anarchist, where villagers gathered to discuss politics. This description could be applied, in broad terms, to other localities that went through similar processes of rebellion against the established political and religious order. In Arroyomolinos, we cannot ignore the existence of the *beatas* (group of overpious or excessively devout women) and a number of families that remained loyal to the Church. From a political perspective, there were socialists and anarchists, although the latter were more numerous. According to Santiago, there were about 500 men and women affiliated to the CNT, while the UGT (Unión General de Trabajadores) only had a handful of members (Santiago 2014a).

Against this backdrop, the news of the military coup of 18 July 1936 led to the organisation of several pre-emptive measures, such as the imprisonment of twenty or thirty right-wing villagers in the council building. Luis remembers the event as follows:

> The fascists were put in the Council. One guy who was doing the military service in Seville, I don't remember his name, went to the Council and poured water under the door. 'There you have water!', he said, only that it wasn't water. … It was petrol. And then those guys were released, and when the whole thing exploded, they went for him and shot him in Seville. I think that's where he is buried. (Luis 2014, my translation)

Similar actions were taken in other villages. For example, García Márquez notes that, in El Castillo de las Guardas, about twenty men – 'the most significant right-wingers in the village' – were arrested for about fourteen days following the news of the coup, with the purpose of preventing them from joining the uprising. As in other places, there were no reports of executions, beatings or degrading treatment (García Márquez 2013, 49–50).

Holding the local representatives of fascism in prison, and vandalising the Church and the Chapel were the main 'evil actions' that the *rojos* had committed in Arroyomolinos before the Civil War began (for discussions on other actions taken against the Church elsewhere, see Ledesma 2012; Lincoln 1999; Thomas 2014; Vincent 2007). In addition, according to some testimonies, the 'reds' were involved in other acts that, though seemingly inconsequential, served to scare some of the villagers at the time. For example, Valeria recalls the fear that her mother used to express when she knew that one of the most notorious 'reds' (in her view) walked down her street:

> There was a man, 'el Cojo de la Pata Palo' ['the lame man with the wooden leg'] … he had a wooden leg. He went into the houses to take the saints and burn them. I don't know if they came in here, but my mum told me many times … El Cojo is coming! And they hid because they were scared of him. He was *rojo*, *rojo*, *rojo* … bad, bad, bad. And they would turn around the pictures of the saints, or take them away to burn them. (Valeria 2014, my translation)

Valeria's emphatic description of the *rojos* as 'bad' is indicative of her conservative stance. Coming from a right-wing family, Valeria and her parents were at the receiving end of the actions that some individuals carried out during this period:

> El Cojo, he was one of the bad ones. He walked in the streets shouting 'come out, whores … whores, come out, do not hide'. He was red to the bone, one of those who didn't want the Virgin. My mum said that every time they saw him or heard him they got very scared because they thought he was going to kill them. My mum would say: 'ay, ay el Cojo, he was here in the street.' He was a revolutionary, very much so. (Valeria 2014, my translation)

Valeria's description contrasts with Ramona's testimony, which offers a completely different depiction of the individual and what he represented:

> That man … poor guy. They used to give him laxatives in prison so he would walk around the village … he couldn't control his bowels. By the time he got home, he was … The poor thing. He was just a poor devil. Some people laughed at him. (Ramona 2015, my translation)

Speaking from radically opposed positions, Valeria's emphasis is on the dubious morality of the 'reds', which she understands in religious terms. For example, she notes that some of the 'reds', who 'didn't baptise their children or anything', looted the houses, took paintings of the Virgin to burn them or turned them so they would face the wall:

> [They] went into the houses and looted them, they opened the drawers, and stuff like that. And I guess they did more than that, but I don't know, I mainly remember the stuff about the saints. They didn't want them. (Valeria 2014, my translation)

According to her account, however, the religious images and the churches were not damaged in Hinojales and Almonte:

> When they went into the Church, they threw everything around and they shouted the names of those who helped with the upkeep of the Church. When they went into the Church, they threw everything out, and they shouted the names of the people that looked after the Church. They also went into the Chapel. Then, later on, everything was repaired. In Hinojales and Almonte they didn't damage their saints, but they were not brave here. (Valeria 2014, my translation)

The fact is that the Republican mayor in Hinojales, Pedro Uceda, managed to circumvent the development of local clashes by encouraging villagers not to resolve their personal or political quarrels by accusing others. Consequently, not only did they avoid the destruction of the saints' images, but there was also no bloodshed.

However, Valeria's words regarding Almonte require a deeper review of the facts. Espinosa Maestre (2012b), in a thorough study of the *sucesos* (incidents) of Almonte in 1932, describes how a number of clashes developed after the local Republican government decided to remove some tiling that depicted religious images (Virgen del Rocío and Sagrado Corazón de Jesús). This decision was in keeping with the Second Republic's definition of Spain as a secular country. Yet, this was not accepted by the Right, which used it as an opportunity to challenge the Republic on the matter of the Agrarian Reform (see Chapter 5 for more details). The national plan to reform the ways in which lands are distributed took on a particular meaning in Almonte, a village that sits in the National Park of Doñana. These lands had been available to all until the nineteenth century, when most of the Park was privatised. The local council, sharing the same principles espoused by the national government, aimed to return those lands to the people, so all villagers could benefit from them for basic subsistence. Espinosa Maestre (2012b) argues that the *sucesos* of 1932 in Almonte were only the prelude to what was to come. After the 1936 coup, more than 100 people were extrajudicially executed.

Not only are Valeria's remarks mistaken with regard to the ways in which events developed in other villages, but her perspective focuses almost entirely on the protection of the saints, rather than people's safety. Her view therefore contrasts with Miguel's viewpoint – while Valeria values the fact that the images had been protected in other localities, Miguel emphasises that executions had taken place in those villages *regardless* of the reds' behaviour:

> The people they executed, they killed them because they just wanted to do it. I don't think the stuff with the saints was really a reason for doing it. Burning the saints was not a catastrophe. Maybe it was wrong, but it was not a reason. It was just an excuse. They wanted to kill people and that was it. (Miguel 2014b, my translation)

García Bañales (2015) has also argued, based on his study of Valderas (in the province of León), that the connection between these acts of vandalism and the subsequent acts of repression is doubtful, since fascist violence was unleashed in localities where the religious buildings and imagery remained intact. In Valderas, for instance, 90 people were killed even though no attacks had been directed at the Church. On a related note, García Bañales has also suggested that the workers' opposition to religion at the time was not as extreme as has often been described, and that this aspect has been exaggerated so as to justify the fascist 'reaction'.

Nevertheless, the events in Arroyomolinos resemble similar acts that developed in other villages. Based on the legal files examined by García Márquez, several indictments were issued after the war with reference to the participation of men, women and children in the Church fire that took place in El Castillo de las Guardas. According to the author, this was the people's way of protesting against the military coup. For many villagers, the Church was a representative of the Right and was therefore on the side of the military rebels and in favour of the coup (García Márquez 2013, 53–54).

Luis, however, also questions the link between the acts of vandalism and the subsequent repression, alluding to the lack of proportionality in the use of violence:

> They burnt the saints, but this was not a reason to kill people. But the *fachas* could see that they were getting on the wrong side of many people, so they sewed panic among the population. They had the power, so they did what they wanted. They entered villages and it is unbelievable, what they did. (Luis 2014b, my translation)

Despite the different stances that emerge in the testimonies, it is worth mentioning that even participants speaking from a right-wing perspective, such as Valeria, seem to condemn the acts of violence that followed when the fascists arrived later that summer:

Apart from burning saints, the *rojos* didn't kill anyone. Most of them were not guilty of anything, only those two or three *rojos* who were bad. The ones who killed were right-wing people. ... The saints could be replaced, after all. And my mum said that some of those men hadn't done anything. (Valeria 2014, my translation)

For Valeria, there is a difference between the 'reds' who had taken part in the events, and the individuals who did not agitate against the Church or, at least, did not take an active role in the acts. Behind her ostensibly 'humane' perspective, Valeria's words hint that her yardstick for measuring 'good' and 'bad' behaviour seems to be defined by the degree of an individual's attachment to religion. The remark that some men 'hadn't done anything' and 'were not guilty of anything' (and hence did not deserve to die) suggests that some other men had done 'something' and were guilty, thereby implying that perhaps those individuals deserved to be punished.

THE OFFICIAL VESTIGES OF SPAIN'S 'LIBERATION'

Although there are no documents about the extrajudicial forms of repression that were conducted after the coup, a review of official files, such as judicial cases, provides us with information about how certain events developed within the fascist struggle to 'liberate' Spain from the 'Marxist hordes'. Some of these are particularly useful because they include details that participants cannot remember accurately, while others draw our attention to facts that have not survived in local memories of the period. For example, a file contains details about the 'requisition', ordered by the socialist mayor, of the car that belonged to the villager Manuel García Sánchez. A closer look at the description of the events enables us to understand that this was not so much a 'requisition' as a request, on the part of the mayor, that Manuel drive him and others to nearby villages in order to conduct activities to support the anti-fascist struggle, following the uprising of 18 July.

Through the official documents, we learn the names of a number of men who took an active part in those journeys, according to various witness accounts. Yet, these descriptions, which are *past* testimonies about the past, do not necessarily provide accurate details. Some witnesses provided contradictory versions of what happened, either because they were trying to protect themselves or their comrades, or because they changed their declarations to criminalise certain individuals. Other accounts diverge drastically from one another, because of the frequent practice of asking 'reliable' witnesses to describe the political involvement, before and after the uprising, of the various people accused of left-wing sympathies. The degree of reliability of these witnesses was purely based on their political, social and moral standing as adherents of the Right, and did not necessarily consider whether these 'trustworthy' individuals had in fact witnessed the events they described. Consequently, their accounts were often based on hearsay, taking the form of statements such as 'the accused is said to have taken part in the events', or 'villagers say that he supports the Marxist cause'. Hearsay was deemed factual within Franco's justice system, as long as it came from 'reliable' sources, even though the information remained unverified. This systemic stratagem was reproduced across the country, from village to village, through the collusion of 'trusted' individuals who had earned, in the dictator's eyes, the honour of being relied upon, ensuring that their position of privilege was perpetuated. This form of connivance, which effectively helped to develop a deeply skewed justice system, is clearly observed in numerous judicial cases against anyone who was accused of supporting the so-called 'rebellion' against Franco. In order to gather evidence that could be used against individuals, official institutions issued requests for reports on the social and political conduct of named villagers before and after the coup. These bureaucratic procedures were part of the broader control mechanisms that contributed – alongside other repressive methods – to the creation of fear among the population (Gómez Bravo and Marco 2011). The archive in the Council of Arroyomolinos de León includes several folders containing dozens of these documents.

In the case of the requisitioned car, the owner, Manuel García Sánchez, declared that he had been given a copy of the Falange's manifesto about three weeks before 18 July, and had subsequently joined the party. However, he added that he had to burn the manifesto because he feared that the Marxists would find it among his possessions. On 18 July, the mayor, Manuel López Romero, delivered an order, authorised by the Civil Governor in the province of Huelva, explaining to García Sánchez that his car was to be put at the mayor's disposal, for it to be used as and when required (C-869/37). On 30 August 1936, García Sánchez declared that the car had been used to travel to Cala and Santa Olalla, carrying the mayor, Manuel López Romero, and other individuals from Arroyomolinos. Although Sánchez claimed to have been ignorant of the purpose of the journeys, he denied that the car was used to transport explosives, but declared that he did see his passengers in conversation with residents of neighbouring villages, including the mayor of Cala, Teodosio Riscos Ortín, and the doctor, Manuel Gutiérrez. According to Sánchez's testimony, he also drove them to Fregenal (in the province of Badajoz), where they sought updates on the threat posed by the National Movement.

Manuel Gutiérrez, the doctor, was eventually executed in Santa Olalla on 28 August 1936, alongside Juan Antonio Sánchez Carrasco (baker and the deputy mayor of Arroyomolinos). As regards the mayor of Cala, Teodosio Riscos, he was reported to have travelled to Arroyomolinos one night in order to participate in an attack against the Civil Guard headquarters. Teodosio, who was a member of the Provincial Executive Committee of Unión Republicana,

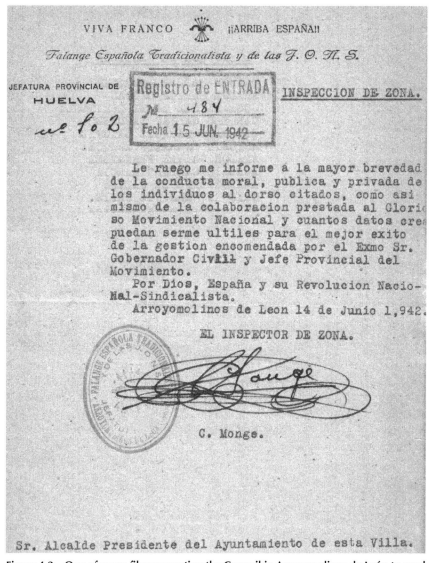

Figure 4.2 One of many files requesting the Council in Arroyomolinos de León to send reports on the moral, social and political conduct of named villagers. Ayuntamiento de Arroyomolinos de León.

became mayor of Cala in February 1936. His case is a prime example of the inaccuracies that can be found in the official registers, not only in terms of the tentative and highly charged content that was passed off as factual, but also as a consequence of the tumultuous circumstances through which individuals had to live. Teodosio disappeared on 3 August 1936 and, assumed dead, his death was officially inscribed one year later, on 5 August 1937. However, he had managed to escape to Seville, where he lived for years. For obvious reasons, his relatives never rectified the error.

Despite their myriad inaccuracies and gaps, official documents can be useful to gather details about the local society at the time. For example, by reviewing Adolfo Lozano's case, we learn that Domingo Darnaude Campos was the right-wing mayor in 1932, when the *sucesos* took place (C-2382/39). This detail helps to conjure up the political state of the village during the Republic. Domingo Darnaude Campos, a military man himself, came from the cacique family[1] in Arroyomolinos and was faithful to Franco's cause. The fact that this individual was mayor in 1932 not only highlights the sometimes forgotten fact – as far as Spain is concerned – that the Republic and the Left are not synonyms, but also provides a clear indication of the intimate connections that existed between official politics and the sources of military and socio-economic power and oppression. Domingo's nephew, Ignacio Darnaude, recalls how one night, visibly furious at something the 'reds' had done while he was mayor, Domingo had 'burst into the Casa del Pueblo [the House of the People], which was full of labourers, communists and libertarians, and screamed at them before taking out his penis and urinating with contempt in front of the livid crowd' (Darnaude 2006, my translation).

More typically, judicial cases contain details about the events that took place, how they developed, the people that were allegedly involved in them and the witness accounts that were used to incriminate the accused. These include the names of those who were accused of engaging in 'criminal' activities, as well as those who testified against them, hence providing a useful sketch of the local socio-political configuration. Not only do these files offer specific information that has been forgotten by participants when narrating their memories, but they also enable the identification of individuals who would otherwise remain unidentified due to my participants' frequent refusal to incriminate other villagers. So, for example, oral testimonies about the events surrounding the fate of the eighteen men that were taken to Cala (see further details below) often focus on what has emerged regarding the victims' experiences. The executioners, on the other hand, are always referred to as 'they', as a form of amorphous menace that soared over the village. What we are able to learn by listening to some of the villagers' narratives is that, when the fascists returned to Arroyomolinos after the execution, they were singing 'Cara al Sol', Franco's national anthem.

Only four participants made direct allusions to the local residents who executed the victims, but they all refused to identify them by name. When discussing the matter with Miguel, he referred to them as 'the volunteers' and, when I asked him who they were, he replied:

I don't know who they were, and if I knew, I wouldn't tell you anyway. But there were people who volunteered to shoot, their children are still around, some people still know who they were. They went to kill people, and then they came back singing, celebrating, as if they had done something good, or funny. (Miguel 2014b, my translation)

Later in the conversation, Miguel confirmed that he knew who some of the volunteers were, but he did not want to reveal their names: 'It's better to leave things the way they are. What's the point of going back to that?'. He had also refused to tell me who shot the civil guard during the *sucesos* (see above), so his unwillingness to provide names is not motivated by an intention to protect the Right or the Left but, simply, to protect people and avoid what he considers to be a potential problem: 'What can you do about it now, most of these people are now dead anyway, it's better to leave things the way they are, don't get into it.' Valentina also made an allusion to the executioners:

We know who they were, we all know. But, girl, what's the point of saying their names? They are all dead now, they are not here to respond, only their children and grandchildren. It wasn't their fault, the youngest may not even know about it. What's the point of stirring it up? (Valentina 2014, my translation)

Luis also referred to the volunteers who carried out the executions, so I asked him whether he could identify them. He ventured a couple of names, but he said that he was not sure (and I believe he was being honest about his doubts). For this reason, I have not transcribed the names that he suggested, as I am unable to testify to their veracity and mentioning them could lead to mistaken accusations. However, Darnaude (2006) notes that some of the civil guards who were involved in acts of repression were called Poveda, Casildo Ortega, Masero and Benito Cebrián Ruiz. The latter is the one whose name is still widely remembered in the village because of his vicious conduct during those years. Cabo Benito (Corporal Benito) is, indeed, often mentioned, contemptuously, in the testimonies I have gathered, and he is one of the very few individuals who are named by villagers without any reservations.

REPRESSION IN THE VILLAGE: THE ORAL VERSION

The lack of official documents detailing the names of all the victims of extra-judicial repression means that one has to rely on local memories of the period in order to trace and reconstruct the toll of the repression. Even when official death certificates exist, the details are not always reliable, due to the (often deliberate) omission or oversight. Espinosa Maestre (2005) provides a list of the victims of executions in the province of Huelva, including the ones in Arroyomolinos. His impressive historical work, always meticulous, is based on oral sources combined with the painstaking examination of archives and the thorough verification of various sources. However, Espinosa is aware that his list is incomplete and notes that there may well be some inaccuracies. This is not surprising if we consider that, besides the lack of, or unreliability of, official documents, local memories can also include a variety of errors.

While many villagers were quite certain that at least forty people from Arroyomolinos were executed during this period, some participants suggested that the total number of casualties may be between fifty and sixty. To begin with, the disagreement about the number of victims complicates the task, as we cannot be sure whether the list is complete. Espinosa Maestre's contribution was a useful reference during the interviews with participants, as the names offered by the historian helped to steer some of the questions that looked, more specifically, for names of victims and their stories. Some of the information offered by my participants differ from some of the details that were previously published by Espinosa Maestre but, just as this historian pointed out, the lists that follow are neither complete nor necessarily correct, as they are primarily based on what villagers could remember.

The following section is structured in three parts: executions conducted in Cala, executions conducted in Arroyomolinos and executions conducted in Santa Olalla del Cala. The killings that villagers have recalled took place in these three locations, although it is worth pointing out that Espinosa Maestre also mentioned that Amador García Suárez was executed in Aracena on 25 September 1937, while Vicente Ramos Tirado passed away due to an illness caused by the dreadful living conditions that he endured in the prison of Huelva, where citizens from all over the country were held (Espinosa Maestre 2005, 564).

Executions in Cala

One of the memories that has persisted most clearly in the local consciousness of Arroyomolinos is the fact that a group of men were kept in the Chapel before being executed in Cala. All participants have narrated, in greater or lesser detail, the experience of '*los 18 de Cala*' (Cala's 18). At the end of September 1936, eighteen men were driven to the nearby village of Santa Olalla del Cala, supposedly to make formal statements (Espinosa Maestre 2005, 564). However, the lorry did not arrive at its assumed destination. Instead, it stopped in Cala, a village located between Arroyomolinos and Santa Olalla, and all eighteen men were executed. Table 4.1 includes the names that I have been able to compile based on the participants' testimonies. However, as mentioned above, the list is incomplete and may still have some inaccuracies,

Table 4.1   Residents of Arroyomolinos de León who were executed extrajudicially during the early days of Francoist repression in Cala. Elaborated by Ruth Sanz Sabido.

Name	Comments
Claudio Díaz Corona's father	
Aurelio Domínguez	Councillor. Rosario's son
Francisco Domínguez	Ramona's uncle
Aurelio García Muñoz 'El Esquilaor'	Pitarro's older brother, from the 'Esquilaores' family
Manuel García Muñoz 'Pitarro'	'Esquilaores' family
José María García Rodríguez 'Tolón'	Terrible's father
Saturnino García Sánchez	
Faustino Picón Dorado	Milagro's son
Miguel Ramos Rodríguez	Antonio el Tropezón's brother. Antonio's tomb has the following sentence engraved: 'a tu hermano lo seguimos buscando' (We are still searching for your brother).
Antonio Rodríguez Santos 'Tomate'	
Manuel Sánchez 'el del Tío Mateo'	Mateo's father. Villagers were unsure whether his name was Manuel or Eleuterio
Nicasio Sánchez	Jerónima's husband (Nicasio Sánchez's father)
Antonio Silva	
Manuel 'el de la Concha'	The seamstress' husband
Sabidino's grandfather, 'Sieteculos'	His surname may be González
Francisco	Antonia Peralta's uncle

due to the difficulty in gaining reliable information. The table also includes some additional comments, provided by villagers, to assist in any future studies that may be conducted in the village. This list coincides in several ways with the one published by Espinosa Maestre (2005), although there are some divergences as regards the place of execution of some of the victims. The historian also includes some names that I have not been able to confirm, or who were not killed in Cala.

In addition to the value of recording the victims' names, the narration of local memories also facilitates information about the victims and the events surrounding their executions. About Manuel 'Pitarro', for example, we know that he was

> an eighteen-year-old [who] was killed because he used to sing. Pitarro, he was the stammerer in the village, and he was one of the 18. He sang things like 'Today we don't need shotguns because, in order to kill a bourgeois, you only have to mention communism, then he goes to bed for a month and dies of malaria.' Lyrics like that, and more. That man lived in my street, a bit further up from my house, he was not older than eighteen. His family was nicknamed 'los esquilaores' (the sheepshearers). He sang very well. The night he spent at

the Chapel ... he spent it singing. He didn't stop singing. (Miguel 2014b, my translation)

Pitarro's brother, Aurelio 'el Esquilaor', was also executed that day. Their brother José was not executed but was involved in local anti-fascist resistance activities and, according to Ramona, used to take shifts standing guard in case the fascists arrived. A fourth brother, Máximo, joined the column to fight in the war and never returned to the village (Ramona 2015).

It is remarkable how the war has remained a point of reference in informal sayings and expressions. So, for example, someone who wants to describe an object as being very old may claim that it dates from 'before the war' (*'esto es de antes de la guerra'*). Even more striking is the way in which allusions to the war may appear, unexpectedly, in any conversation with survivors of that period. During an improvised conversation with Antonia, which had focused on her health and her inability to look after her hens, I asked her how old she was. Unsure of her response, she determined to answer with the following words: 'My mother said to me that I was two years old when the war happened.' The reference to the war was unexpected, not only because of the unusual way in which she makes sense of her own age, but because this conversation was not planned or scheduled with research in mind.

I took the opportunity to ask Antonia what she could remember about that period. She explained that her mother had told her that her uncle, Francisco, was one of Cala's 18. He was one of the men who, having spent the night in the Chapel, were taken in a lorry to the nearby village:

I don't remember him, but my mother said he was a good man. He didn't do anything wrong, but they took him ... and they took him. He never hurt anyone, my mother said. But that's what happened, and it happened to the others too. Some of them were released, but my uncle ... they killed him. Poor men, what a pity, for God's sake, what could they have possibly done? (Antonia 2015, my translation)

Visibly affected by this family memory, Antonia quickly changed the topic of conversation. From a discursive perspective, three points stand out from her response: Antonia's reiteration of her uncle's goodness; the use of 'they' to refer to the agents of the executions, presenting them as a faceless group, without naming any specific culprits but implying their irrationality; and the inclusion of the wider group of men who, like her uncle, were killed.

It appears that some of the men who spent the night in the Chapel were released in the morning. One of those who were released was Cupida's father. Cupida, whose mother was also a direct victim of the repressive actions taken in the village (see Chapter 6), narrates what she knows about her father's experience:

They put my father in the Chapel. My aunties brought coffee and food to him. When they were on their way, a man asked them where they were going. They said that they were bringing some coffee to his brother. The man told them to go back home because their brother had already been killed. Then, it turned out that they hadn't, but they took 18 men to Cala to shoot them, although my father was released. He hadn't done anything and they released him. But it was a massacre what they did. (Cupida 2014, my translation)

Another man, known as Joaquín 'Alegría', was released because the officers realised that they had the wrong person. Joaquín 'Pipita', who had the same (inverted) surnames, had been released, apparently, after paying a sum to the officers. The entire misunderstanding was then resolved and Alegría was set free that morning. It is thanks to Alegría's imprisonment in the Chapel that we know some details about what happened that night. Miguel (2015), for example, remembered that Alegría had told him that Pitarro had spent the night singing for the Republic (see above), while another man was so scared that he had defecated on himself.

According to Luis, a third man was freed in the morning. He recalls how one of the local doctors signed a paper stating that this man was ill and should be released:

The man had diarrhoea or something like that, and the doctor used it as a reason to send him home … saying that he was ill, he tried to save his life, so he was

Figure 4.3 Ermita de la Virgen de los Remedios, the Chapel in Arroyomolinos de León. Photograph by Ruth Sanz Sabido.

released. But then, when he was going back, someone saw him and said 'no, you go down that way', and they shot him dead anyway. (Luis 2014a, my translation)

This testimony resembles Aurelio's description of a man who was released from the Chapel but, on his way back, had the misfortune of coming across Trenado, the fascist mayor, who had him killed the same day (Aurelio 2002). To my surprise, towards the end of the research, one of my participants told me that my grandfather's brother, Manuel, had also spent the night in the Chapel. However, it appears that he was not imprisoned there for political reasons, and that he too was released in the morning.

EXECUTIONS IN ARROYOMOLINOS DE LEÓN

As is the case with Cala, the following list of victims who were executed within the village of Arroyomolinos is also incomplete. However, it offers a revision of Espinosa Maestre's tally in that some of the individuals whose names or nicknames figure as having been killed in one place appear again, with their full name, as having been executed elsewhere. For example, Ramón Mateo Núñez (killed in Arroyomolinos on 4 October 1936) is the son of Consuelo 'la Jaca', who is also included, with his nickname, in Espinosa Maestre's list of victims who were murdered in Cala.

Juan Manuel, one of my participants, lost his maternal grandfather during the wave of repression that took place in the village, on 23 September 1936.

Table 4.2   Residents of Arroyomolinos de León who were executed extrajudicially during the early days of Francoist repression in Arroyomolinos de León. Elaborated by Ruth Sanz Sabido.

Arroyomolinos de León		
Name	Date	Comments
Manuel Fernández Rubio	23 September 1936	Executed when Aurelio escaped
Ramón Mateo Núñez 'el de la Jaca'	4 October 1936	Consuelo la Jaca's son
Guillermo Moya	23 September 1936	Executed when Aurelio escaped
Florencio Ramos Mateo 'el Canario'		Antonio Ramos' son
Pedro Rufo Santos	26 October 1936	Tía Tambora's husband. Her real name was Aurora García Mateos, and they had two children, Juan and Petra
José Silva Almendro 'el Letrero'	Possibly in 1937	Executed and buried in 'La Romería')

His name was Manuel Fernández Rubio, and he was denounced by his own brother, 'el Latero' ('The Tinsmith'). According to his grandson, Manuel's crime was that 'he was well ahead of his time. He was always reading newspapers, so he knew about politics and current affairs' (Juan Manuel 2015, my translation). According to some judicial documents, in addition, Manuel may have been involved in some of the actions that were taken in the village to resist the progress of the fascist troops (e.g., he was one of the individuals whose names were mentioned in the original witness' testimonies in the case of the 'requisitioned' car that was used to travel to nearby villages, see above). Silvia, a friend of one of Manuel's daughters, said that

> Manuel left two or three daughters behind. Ana [one of his daughters] could tell you many things, about how she grew up without a father, it was unbelievable what people had to do to survive, especially when you didn't have a man in the house. … What that meant in those times, you cannot imagine. (Silvia 2015, my translation)

Aurelio (2002), who was interviewed by villager Rafael Cid in 2002, described how he, Manuel and another man, Guillermo Moya, were taken from the local prison to the cemetery to be executed. Aurelio escaped just before arriving at the place of execution (see section 'Living in hiding' below, for more details on his escape), but Manuel and Guillermo were shot dead.

In addition, the man that Espinosa refers to as 'El hijo del tío' Antonio Ramos (Antonio Ramos' son) was not one of Cala's 18, but was in fact executed in Arroyomolinos. His name was Florencio Ramos Mateo, also known locally with the nickname of 'el Canario' ('The Canary') because he used to sing for the Republic. According to his nephew, the reason why he was executed was, precisely, that he used to sing songs about freedom and workers' rights. He was, indeed, the son of Antonio Ramos who, according to his great-grandson, 'cried so much for his dead son that he was left blind'. There are various versions about what happened to Florencio. His great-grandson has confirmed that he was kept in the local prison and taken to the cemetery, and that Florencio's sister heard the shots from their house. In fact, the three villagers who have recalled Florencio's death for this study have confirmed that he had been shot in the cemetery. Nevertheless, one of the participants said that Florencio had survived the shooting and had managed to drag himself, with his broken legs, all the way down to his house. According to this version, someone who saw him lying by his doorstep finished him off. However, another villager rejected this story. According to what he had been told, it was true that he was still alive after the execution, but that he never made it out of the cemetery. This informant claimed to know this because his own grandfather, who was in prison, was sent to the cemetery with two other men to dig the graves, and that is the moment when they found Florencio still alive. One of the guards, who had accompanied the prisoners from the local prison to the cemetery, delivered the coup de grâce there and then.

It is also worth noting the circumstances of José Silva Almendro 'el Letrero'. Valeria (2014), whose father was asked to take part in José's execution (see above, regarding José's involvement in the 1932 *sucesos*), recalled that José was very young and had two small children:

> Bienve, a woman from the village ... her mother had two children, one boy and one girl, Bienve. Her husband was very young, and the children were very little, and they took him near Cala, I don't know where exactly, but it was near Cala, and they killed him. They shot him dead. ... Why did they take him? Because they said he was from the other side, but he hadn't done anything. My mum told me these things. (Valeria 2014, my translation)

Three participants narrated José's execution in rather similar terms, focusing on the fact that information about his whereabouts was passed on by a villager to the civil guards, who subsequently found him in the countryside (Miguel 2014a; Rafael 2015; Santiago 2014a). His case is even more significant because of the reaction that the knowledge of his execution elicited in their commander:

> When they got back to the headquarters, the guy said 'but why have you killed him, if we are not supposed to kill anyone anymore?'. I suppose they must have decided that people shouldn't be killed like that. The order must have come from above. (Rafael 2015, my translation)

Despite the slight variation in the description of its location, all the versions agree that the place of execution was La Romería, which is, indeed, situated by the road that connects Arroyomolinos with Cala. They also pointed out that José was buried under a tree in La Romería, a plot of land where some local festivities used to take place years ago, before they began holding them within the village. Miguel (2014a) explained that 'they placed a few stones on top of the grave, that's how they marked it, but that was all'. Some villagers recall how, many years later, his daughter had him exhumed and gave him proper burial in the cemetery in Arroyomolinos. According to Rafael and Mercedes, the exhumation took place 'fifteen or twenty years ago'. Although they were not able to specify the year, it appears that the re-interment pre-dates the process of scientific exhumations that the Association for the Recuperation of Historical Memory (ARMH) has conducted for the past sixteen years.

Executions in Santa Olalla del Cala

Juan Manuel, Manuel Fernández Rubio's grandson (see above), also lost his paternal grandfather in 1936. According to the local memories of the period,

Table 4.3 **Residents of Arroyomolinos de León who were executed extrajudicially during the early days of Francoist repression in Santa Olalla del Cala.** Elaborated by Ruth Sanz Sabido.

Santa Olalla del Cala		
Name	Date	Comments
Antonio Moya Dorado		Tío Moya's son
Antonio Parente		
Juan Sánchez Carrasco 'el Cuezo'	28 August 1936	
Pascual Hernández 'el Correo'	28 August 1936	

Figure 4.4 **Remains of the house where Pascual 'el Correo' used to live.** Photograph by Ruth Sanz Sabido.

Juan Sánchez Carrasco 'el Cuezo' was a baker and '*segundo alcalde*' (deputy mayor). His brother, Esteban, who was a member and treasurer of Unión Republicana, also had a judicial case against him. In the witness' testimonies, Corporal Benito stated that Esteban and Juan did 'much political propaganda in their bakery, and they would threaten anyone who did not vote for them in February 1936 with refusing to sell them bread on credit'.[2] Esteban was subsequently sentenced to six years in prison on 31 March 1938 for supporting the rebellion (C-869/37, my translation).

When Juan Sánchez Carrasco was transported to Santa Olalla to be executed, Pascual 'el Correo' was also taken with him. Called 'el Correo' ('the Post') because he was in charge of delivering the post in the village, Pascual 'used to go to Segura in secret to collect letters that perhaps he shouldn't be collecting, if you know what I mean' (Rafael 2015, my translation). Both Juan and Pascual were shot dead on the same day on the road between Cala and Santa Olalla, in a place known as La Parrilla.

LIVING IN HIDING

Some individuals managed to escape from the immediate effects of repression by fleeing the village, joining a column to fight in the war or hiding in the mountains or at home. The experience of Aurelio Domínguez Silva stands out, not least because the fact of his escape is one of the most frequently narrated local memories of this period. Indeed, Aurelio (local Secretary of the Libertarian Youths) managed to run away when he was being taken to the cemetery in Arroyomolinos to be executed, alongside two other men (Manuel Fernández and Guillermo Moya, see above). Rafael describes how

> Aurelio was in the middle, in a row, like this, between Serones' grandfather and Ramón Moya's father. He got loose and ran away and ... the other two, well, imagine their faces. People say he was allowed to escape, because it's strange that he managed to run away when he was the one in the middle. He wasn't at the front or the back, so how did the rope get loose in the middle? And he is related to the Campos family, you know, so people say it was staged. I don't know. But they went ahead and killed the other two. (Rafael 2015, my translation)

Aurelio spent the following three years in hiding, until he turned himself in after the war had ended. According to the prison files collected by Antequera Luengo and Luengo Jiménez in the prison of Huelva, Aurelio spent some time in the prison of Huelva and was then taken to the concentration camp in Huelva, together with other men, in May 1939 (Antequera Luengo and Luengo Jiménez 2008, 7–8). The case that was opened against him included testimonies from the new mayor, Supriano Vázquez, who was also a member of the local FET and JONS (Falange Española Tradicionalista y de las Juntas de Ofensiva Nacional Sindicalista, or Traditionalist Spanish Phalanx and the Committees of the National Syndicalist Offensive).[3] He stated that Aurelio had

> been affiliated to the CNT in this village, where he was Secretary of the Communist Youths. ... Its aim was to teach and propagate communist ideas, and he took a very active part in all the acts of vandalism that were committed by the red hordes during their domination of this village, such as house lootings,

Figure 4.5 Path where Aurelio managed to escape. The cemetery, where Manuel and Guillermo were executed, can be seen behind the trees. Photograph by Ruth Sanz Sabido.

> assaults on the Church and the Chapel, blowing-up of bridges, burning sacred ornaments, and in each and every action that they took, which he did with pleasure. (C-2375/39, my translation)

According to his nephew, Santiago, Aurelio acted in fact as Secretary of the Libertarian – not the Communist – Youths, although it appears that this group was not formally constituted, at least as far as an analysis of the files can tell. One of the objectives that were pursued in the legal proceedings against Aurelio was, precisely, to establish whether this organisation had any official status. The final text of the proceedings concludes that the following information about Aurelio is factual:

> The accused stood out in his village for his extremist ideas, being affiliated to the CNT and being part of a small group from which extreme ideas were propagated, although it has not been possible to clarify this matter during the investigation. When the Glorious Movement began, he stood on the side of the [left-wing] leaders, having participated in guard duties and house searches. For this reason, he went way from the village when the Forces arrived, going deep into the mountains. ... He was captured during a raid and, when he was going to be executed, he escaped again, fleeing and hiding in a farm owned by his

father, where he was hidden until the end of the war, when he voluntarily turned himself in to the Civil Guard in Arroyomolinos. (C-2375/39, my translation)

In 1940, Aurelio was sentenced to a term of twelve years and one day, although he was then released on parole with exile[4] in 1943. Aurelio himself remembered how

> When I returned from prison, I had to go to the Civil Guard headquarters every day. One day I didn't do it, and they issued a twenty-five-peseta fine. (Aurelio 2002, my translation)

According to his nephew, Santiago, Aurelio was banished to a village in Córdoba for a few years before he could return to Arroyomolinos, where he passed away in 2011.

Several other testimonies include references to villagers who hid in their houses or in the mountains to escape persecution. According to Juan Manuel, one of the residents in the village, Frasquito, used to keep watch on behalf of his father, who hid in their roof for a period of time and only came out at nights. Frasquito, as a teenager, was always on alert in case the guards were nearby. Juan Manuel also asserted that Frasquito used to help out others in the same situation. However, Frasquito himself supplied a more detailed and accurate account:

> I was always keeping an eye out, because my father and my uncle were hiding, and I was already a lad so it was my responsibility. At home, everything came through me. I went to the countryside with the goats, and my father was hiding inside a rock, with my uncle. There was a small hole at the top, and I used to drop food through there. I had to be careful because there were always Falangists hunting in the area, and they had dogs. If I thought it would be dangerous to come close to them, I would leave the food somewhere else, where they could come to get it whenever it was safe. The dogs sometimes ate the food, because they sometimes found that it wasn't where I had left it. (Frasquito 2015, my translation)

Frasquito, however, admitted that, while his family was a family of *rojos*, and at heart he was 'one of them', in public he had to pretend that he espoused Franco's regime, so he 'would sing "Cara al Sol" out there by the fountain, or by the Civil Guard headquarters'. He admitted that 'out there I was more of a fascist than they were', explaining that, had he been suspected, the guards would have watched him more closely and he would not have been able to help his family. Despite his many efforts to keep his father safe, his father's story had become more widely known in the locality because of his sister. Some villagers had told me the story of a man who hid, for months, inside some furniture in his house and only came out at night. People's interest – and the reason why this tale appeared in testimonies so frequently – is because of its status as a major local scandal. Valeria, a traditional and devout woman, explained what happened:

> He had run away, he left home and they couldn't find him. But it turns out that he was hiding inside a chest. After a while, his wife became pregnant and people started to criticise her. 'She has no shame, her husband is missing and she is pregnant.' Lots of people will tell you about this. You can imagine, in those times, without knowing whether her husband was dead or alive, and it turned out that he was hiding during the day for a long time, and when they closed the door at night, he came out. But the woman was heavily criticised, because … you can imagine. (Valeria 2014, my translation)

Frasquito's father and the man to whom Valeria is referring are one and the same person. Frasquito's father, Lorenzo, after hiding in the countryside for several months, moved into his house and hid in the cellar. He concealed himself there for a long time, only coming out of his hideout at nights. After a while, his wife – Frasquito's mother – became pregnant, but villagers thought that she had cheated on her missing husband. Due to the social pressure on his wife (see Chapter 6), Lorenzo decided to turn himself in just after the end of the war. On 10 May 1939, Lorenzo explained in his *Ficha Clasificatoria* (Classificatory Record) that he had fled the village when it was taken over by the troops on 20 August 1936, and had stayed in Cabeza la Vaca until 14 September, when it was 'liberated' by Franco's troops. He then hid in the countryside, and although he intended to turn himself in, he came across his brother-in-law, who informed him that he 'should not [do so] since the village was in a bad state'. He therefore stayed in the countryside until 24 January 1937, when he managed to reach his house and hide there. The role of his son in helping him to remain hidden is mentioned in the document, which states that 'he survived thanks to what his wife sent him through his son, who is eighteen'. The file also notes that Lorenzo had decided to turn himself in because Franco had claimed that 'nobody should fear his justice unless their hands are stained with blood' and, therefore, he thought that nothing would happen to him.

Lorenzo's 'classificatory record' was followed by a 'trial' that included evidence provided by a number of witnesses. The testimony of the teacher, José Rodríguez Humanes, stands out. When asked whether he knew Lorenzo, he said:

> This is an individual who had belonged to the socialist party. Before our Glorious Movement, he was considered to be a person of bad conduct and has a socio-political record. In October 1932, when some works were being

conducted on the road to Cañaveral de León, there was a clash between the workers and the Civil Guard, in which various guards were injured, leaving two of them in a serious condition, and Lorenzo Agudo Pizarro was one of the men who opposed the civil guards.

During the red period in this village, Lorenzo Agudo Pizarro was one of the most active elements in this locality, being one of the members of the revolutionary committee. He took part in the abuses of power that were committed by the Marxist hordes in this village.

He was one of the most active elements in this village, participating in guard duties with weapons. If he did not intervene directly in the requisition of cattle, house searches and burning of sacred images in the Church and Chapel, he did so indirectly by giving orders and organising said acts of vandalism.

The individual deserves a heavy sentence due to his criminal record, bad conduct and for being hostile to the new Spanish state. (C-2469/39, my translation)

The sentence considers, among other aspects, that the facts that are described in the various testimonies 'could constitute a crime of Military Rebellion,' according to article 237 and article 238 of the Código de Justicia Militar y Bandos de Guerra, which was supposed to be applicable to such cases. The siblings recalled how their father began his long odyssey from one prison to another: from Arroyomolinos, he was taken to Huelva, and then to Talavera de la Reina. By that time, Lorenza was six months old and that is when Lorenzo saw his daughter for the first time. He spent several years in prison and, when he was finally released, he was still unable to return to the village, as he was banished to Punta Umbría, a seaside village in the province of Huelva.

Lorenzo's brother, Francisco, was also accused, as one of the main members of the local CNT branch, of taking an active part in the 'criminal acts' that took place in the village during the 'red' period, including 'the burning of sacred images, the arrest of right-wing people, the seizure of cattle and the blowing-up of bridges' (C-2484/39, my translation). He was also accused of participating in the events of 1932, when he was 'one of the main instigators' and a 'propagator of extremist ideas'. He had, in fact, already served a seven-month sentence for his involvement in the *sucesos*, before he was pardoned under Lerroux's amnesty. According to his own testimony on 22 April 1939, when he turned himself in, he fled to Segura when Franco's troops entered the village, 'for fear of what they might do to him', and then hid in the countryside, 'eating fruits until these ran out, and bread that he obtained through a group of coalmen'. He lived in those conditions until February 1937, when he returned to Arroyomolinos and, with his brother, hid in his family's cellar until 1939. For his continued involvement in local socio-economic struggles, Francisco was again sentenced to thirty years imprisonment in May 1940, although he asked to be pardoned in October 1945. This pardon was conceded in April 1946.

NOTES

1. Led by his brother Antonio, this family not only owned some of the best and largest lands, but were also active in the flour-making business and other industries, thereby controlling the local economic and political scene.

2. The characteristic irregularity of income in rural Andalusia makes it acceptable for villagers to ask for credit in local shops. The features of the local context make this a feasible option for retailers: shop owners know their customers and their families. They also know where they live and tend to have a good idea of their financial circumstances. In a small village, where residents can only purchase their goods from a limited number of establishments (most of which are family owned), it becomes difficult to leave unpaid debts in one shop and to start buying elsewhere. Debtors would also have to face the shame of being known to have delinquent accounts in the village. As Barke (1997) notes, asking for credit is not shameful in itself – this is, in fact, almost expected at some points during the year – but it would certainly be dishonourable, as far as the local milieu is concerned, to become the focus of fellow villagers' gossip (see also Pitt-Rivers 1963, and Peristiany 1966).

3. Created in 1937, this was the only legal party during the dictatorship. It merged the Carlist Party with the Spanish Falange.

4. When political prisoners were released, they were often banished from their villages for an additional period of time (Gómez Bravo 2009). This practice served to continue marginalising the enemies of the regime after the end of their prison sentence.

Chapter 5

Class, Ideology and Local Community

The military coup of 1936 and the subsequent three-year conflict between fascists and anti-fascists needs to be understood within the political, economic and social context of the Second Republic. The democratic and reformist outlook of the new Republican system attempted, at least in principle, to deal with the socio-economic problems that pre-dated the Republic itself by facilitating the organisation of workers in all industries and occupational fields. It is important to note, however, that the favourable stance of the Republic towards workers' rights existed *largely* in principle: while the socialist government of the *Primer Bienio* (First Biennium 1931–1933) began a series of moderate reforms that would benefit the working classes, the conservative coalition that won the national elections of 1933 delayed or altogether overturned the socialist advances, leading to what has been described as the *Bienio Negro* (Black Biennium 1933–1936). Even though the programme of socio-economic improvements was resumed when the left-wing coalition Frente Popular (Popular Front) won the elections of February 1936, the newly elected government had only been in power for five months when the military uprising began on 18 July 1936. The coup was, in short, the military response to the legitimate election of Frente Popular, and to the progressive developments that trade unions and left-wing parties had initiated in 1931.

In the rural context, the left-wing government of the First Biennium sought to redistribute unworked lands, thereby improving agrarian production and increasing the peasantry's access to the basic necessities of life. The Agrarian Reform (*Reforma Agraria*) was one of the key initiatives promoted by the liberal Republican administration, not only because it was aimed at redressing long overdue inequalities in the management of agrarian issues, but also because it was at the heart of the social movements that developed between 1931 and 1936 among impoverished labourers. The historical division of the land into large estates (*latifundios*), particularly in the South and the West of Spain, led to the permanent socio-economic stratification of society, which is still manifest in the contemporary rural context. According to Malefakis, disputes over the distribution of the land from the end of the nineteenth century facilitated the entry of Spain into 'the world of capitalist relations of ownership', but failed to 'transform the units of ownership, which became saleable and mortgageable goods instead' (Malefakis 1971, in Sánchez Jiménez 1975, 18, my translation). In the southern provinces, large farm exploitations predominated over small farms, occupying 65% of the best land, leaving the marginal and less productive plots to small owners. Locally based administrators often managed the large plots on behalf of the landowners (who were rarely ever present), offering occasional work to day labourers at harvest times, while most people were landless farm workers who struggled to make a living in harsh and unstable economic conditions (Sánchez Jiménez 1975, 20).

This is the unequal socio-economic situation that the Agrarian Reform was devised to rectify. By formalising a number of measures that tried to achieve a more equitable distribution of economic resources, the first Republican government, in 1931, was attending to the rights of the disadvantaged while raising the levels of anxiety of the privileged classes. The Agrarian Reform included two clauses that were particularly controversial. The first one determined that any lands that had been systematically leased out by their owners could be expropriated from them (5a section 12). The second contentious clause enabled the requisition of certain '*ruedos*', that is, some of the fertile lands that surrounded the proximity of agrarian villages[1] (5a section 10). Cobo Romero (2013) notes that the latter directive must have alarmed the owners of small farms in the North of the country, where most localities consist of compact stretches of land. Day labourers welcomed these new measures while small landowners and the middle peasantry, who felt threatened by the initiatives, sought an escape mechanism and began to pay attention to the corporatist, anti-Reformist and anti-parliamentarian discourse of the conservatives, which was increasingly acquiring a fascist character (Cobo Romero 2013; see also Vincent 1996). Therefore, the efforts to tackle deeply rooted socio-economic challenges not only exacerbated the rifts between the conservative sectors and the working classes, but also led to divisions within these broadly defined groups (Cobo Romero 2012).

Meanwhile, trade unions and workers' collectives, which watched closely to ensure that the new reforms were implemented, organised strikes that would place increasing pressure on land and business owners. For this reason, the conservative government of the Black Biennium not only prioritised the suspension of the socialist reforms by approving a 'counter-reform', but also violently repressed any emerging protest actions.[2] The best-known revolts from a historical viewpoint are the ones that took place in Casas Viejas in 1933 (Mintz 1982) and the workers' revolution of 1934 (Casanova 2013). As discussed earlier, Arroyomolinos also had its own *sucesos* in 1932 (when the local council was administered by right-wing representatives), and so did many other villages across all regions in Spain[3] (Casanova 2010, 138).

Against this backdrop, contemporary depictions of the Republic as a progressive and revolutionary force in the history of Spain, need to be treated with some caution (Casanova 2013; del Rey 2011; Sanz Sabido 2015). Nevertheless, there is a central aspect of what has become something of a myth, that remains true: compared to other democracies in Europe at the time, the Second Republic was the first democratic form of government in the history of Spain and, as such, it brought a number of improvements to a politically backward and economically depressed country. Arguably, the left-wing governments did not have sufficient time to implement the changes and allow them to settle, but the actions that were taken, including the collectivisation of lands and factories, were sufficient to spark the military reaction that would later be described as Civil War.

A CLASS WAR

Rural workers in Andalusia have always manifested a strong sense of 'class consciousness'. This was particularly important in the context of the Second Republic and its agrarian reforms, but it had been apparent from the nineteenth century onwards, with the development of anarchist and revolutionary perspectives. The motto '*la tierra para el que la trabaja*' (the land to those who till it) is still uttered by the most class-conscious land workers today (see Bernecker (1982) for a discussion of anarchist collectives in the revolution, and Collier (1987) for a discussion of socialist-led revolutionary actions in the rural context). Miguel, for example, often refers to land and freedom as two related notions, not only in his conversations but also in his singing (which he pursues on a non-professional basis):

My only fatherland, as El Cabrero[4] says, is freedom. El Cabrero doesn't want to sing about any drippy topics. Me neither. I only sing about freedom and about the land, for poor people and social justice. That's why many men were killed, for singing about freedom and work. Kiko Molinerín, Tío Kiko, out there, sitting by the doorstep, used to say these words to me: 'People need freedom. People need work. People need a place to live' [he counts one by one with his fingers]. They need land and freedom. That's all that matters ... you don't need anything else. (Miguel 2015, my translation)

The issue of land ownership is integral to understanding the class struggles that characterised this period and, by extension, the philosophy of Miguel and others like him. Indeed, class consciousness emerged in the nineteenth century 'in response to the abolition of agrarian collectivism and the introduction of laissez-faire capitalism' (Gilmore 1977, 149). Society was divided into a landowning class and a landless proletarian class: in rural Andalusia, the unequal distribution of lands (see above) meant that about half the people were landless farm workers (*jornaleros*, or day labourers) who earned their day-wages (*el jornal*) by working in large estates owned by the landed gentry.

Before and after the war, there were three main farm estates in or around the village: Los Murtales, situated by the road to Cañaveral; La Vicaría, located between Arroyomolinos and Cala and owned by the Falangist Ramón de Carranza Gómez, Marquis of Sotohermoso; and El Castaño, situated outside the village, towards Badajoz. Many villagers found work and a place to live on these three farms. According to Rafael (2015), there were so many people working in El Castaño that the hairdresser had to spend 'one entire week in the farm in order to cut everyone's hair before coming back to the village'. Meanwhile, La Vicaría had also employed, for many years, a significant number of people, to the extent that entire families (coming from Arroyomolinos, Cala and Calera, among other nearby villages) lived permanently on its vast lands. These days, the farm has progressively reduced its number of employees, until it has practically ceased to operate.

In the large farms, the interests of the community were substituted by 'patronal obligations, communal institutions, and institutionalized charity', and by classes with distinct functions, needs and ambitions (Gilmore 1977, 154). As mentioned earlier, not only is it possible to observe differences between labourers and landowners, but also among the various 'types' of land workers. While *jornaleros* or day labourers work for wages, peasants cultivate their small (often inherited) plots of land. These groups consequently form distinctive categories within the working class, as they each have different interests, although the division between both groups is often blurred. In practice, *jornaleros* frequently own small plots of land that they use, as peasants do, to plant some vegetables, or to keep cattle, while still engaging in waged work. The lands are so small, however, that their subsistence economy can only be maintained through the combination of a variety of disparate resources. Therefore, peasants and day labourers do not necessarily constitute mutually exclusive categories, which means that their interests in land reform sometimes (but not always) coincide (Gilmore 1977, 159; see also Mintz 1953; Wolf 1966).

Oral testimonies shed light on the class divisions that existed among different families in the village, and how the power and position of the upper classes were linked to their ownership of lands and related businesses. In Arroyomolinos, these divisions materialised in a number of incidents, some of which took place in the larger farm estates mentioned above. For instance, during the *sucesos* of the village in 1932 (see Chapter 4), some armed clashes developed in El Castaño, where a goatherd broke his arm (Santiago 2013). Some civil guards were also injured during the clashes (Ahora 1932; Elena 2013; Juan 2014). Further details emerge in this regard when participants mention the *maquis*, that is, the group of people who fled to the mountains, where they continued the armed resistance against Franco (see, e.g., Marco 2006; Moreno Gómez 2001, 2006; Yusta Rodrigo 2003, 2008). According to Darnaude (2006), relatives and visitors of the Marquis of Sotohermoso at La Vicaría were well aware of the threat of the *maquis,* although this did not discourage them from horse riding in the farm.

According to Casanova (2008), this resistance became more organised as it began to follow the example of the French anti-fascist struggle. In the 1940s, there were approximately 7,000 *maquis* involved in armed activities across the country (Casanova 2008, 162–163). Although only three villagers made references to the *maquis* during the interviews, their descriptions provide further insight into their understanding of class divisions at the time. Rafael defines the group as follows:

> After the war, there were guerrillas in the mountains, they didn't adapt to the dictatorship that Franco set up. They stole from the rich, not from the poor. They were all caught in the end. These guys called them *maquis*. They were socialist, anarchist and communist. (Rafael 2015, my translation)

Carlos also describes what the *maquis* used to do in the countryside:

> There was this group of people ... the *maquis*. Like in the Pedro Jiménez film, they stole from the rich. The 'Gabrieles', for example, were very rich. They killed six or seven pigs every year so, when nobody was eating, they did eat. At night, the *maquis* got food for those who were in the mountains. They used passwords with flares to communicate with one another. They brought them things to eat, ham, and things like that, but they had to be careful because there were guards watching. (Carlos 2014, my translation)

According to Ramona (2015), the 'Gabrieles' owned a very large extension of land where they also kept cattle, although the property has more recently been reduced in size because it was divided through inheritance.

Actions conducted by the *maquis*, such as those described by Carlos, did not go unpunished, as the authorities would retaliate by attacking the villagers. Miguel explains that

If a pig disappeared, they came in people's houses to throw away the stewpots, with the food in it. They took away the light bulbs, and the doors had to remain open all the time. They forced you to leave them open, so they could see what everyone was doing. (Miguel 2014a, my translation)

Like Miguel, Luis (2014a) also recalls how 'the civil guards went into people's homes, and they kicked the stewpots so they wouldn't have anything to eat'. In practical terms, the war against the poor was waged, day after day, through targeted actions such as these.

THE IMPORTANCE OF IDEOLOGY

Historians and scholars in other disciplines have dedicated considerable resources to the analysis of the ideological battleground that was the Spanish Civil War. The significance of these political clashes transcended national boundaries, particularly when we think about the Civil War in relation to the European context and the broader international background. Despite the detailed examinations that have been conducted in this respect, the complexity of the various ideological stances are often simplified in contemporary Spain, as though the conflict consisted of two 'sides' only: the Republican Left and the Nationalist Right. This is often reinforced by the reference to close relatives, friends and neighbours who took different stances in the conflict. For instance, Carlos describes what his father had seen while he was at the battlefront:

My father was in the trench and he knew when the reds were coming ... the reds' planes, from Russia. There was a man who was in the trench with my father, he was the son of a pilot, and the man said 'that's my father, the son of a bitch.' He said that even when the boxes were empty, after using all the bombs, they even threw the boxes out of the plane. 'That's my father, the son of a bitch.' Literally, fathers and sons clashing, face to face. (Carlos 2014, my translation)

As part of a 'Civil' War, this is a raw expression of the two sides of the conflict, a localised and unpolished reference to the generalising notion of the 'two Spains' that has permeated the nation's collective memory. Nevertheless, the true complexity of these ideological divisions (from 'neutral' positions to clearly defined perspectives, including anarchist, communist, libertarian communist, socialist and fascist, to name the most significant) determined the course of the war and, ultimately, its long-lasting consequences. Santiago explains, succinctly, the ways in which these ideologies clashed:

The republican side was divided, because the anarchists didn't want the Republic, and the government was scared of the people, so they didn't give them weapons for the revolution. And the other countries ... the Germans helped the nationalists, but the capitalist countries were scared of communists and anarchists. Franco seemed a better choice for them. (Santiago 2013, my translation)

The lack of weapons emerges, once again, in Santiago's testimony (see Chapter 4, where Miguel (2014a) also discusses this problem), indicating that, for him, this was the fundamental difference that underpinned the ideas over which different factions were fighting. Considering both the national and international aspects of the war, he seems to conclude that the people were not given weapons to fight because it did not serve anybody's interests: everyone (the government, the capitalist countries) was 'scared' of what the people might achieve if they acquired the resources that they needed to fight. It was, therefore, not a balanced struggle, a perspective also suggested by Miguel in another interview. On this occasion, Miguel made a similar point, though he approached it from a different perspective. He reflected on the connections between people's ideologies, their socio-economic status and their behaviour towards other individuals. Miguel, clearly speaking from a

Figure 5.1 Santiago Campos: Magdalena's and Santiago's son, and Aurelio's nephew. Photograph by Ruth Sanz Sabido.

libertarian perspective (even though he does not adhere to a particular political stance), often echoes the principles of the CNT in his opinions about collectivisation, solidarity and freedom from any systemic forms of control. Not only does he abhor fascist repression, but also believes that the actions of communist leaders were equally reprehensible:

> What they want is to strike terror into the people. Everything was turned upside down, but the ringleaders got away. ... La Pasionaria, Carrillo, all those people ... they all went away, while they made a sergeant out of any shoemaker or carpenter. When fascist professional officers arrived, knowing what they were doing, what chance could the shoemaker have of surviving ... of defending anything? The people paid for the war ... the nobodies, the poor wretches. (Miguel 2014b, my translation)

Santiago and Miguel's arguments that people were not prepared for war (due to the lack of weapons and professional training) appear to be amalgamated, more or less explicitly, with moral judgements about the (lack of) involvement on the part of external governments and national politicians (for a discussion of the non-intervention pact and the support received by Republicans and fascists, see, e.g., Beevor 2006, 147–158; Bolloten 2015, 97–109; Moradiellos 1999).

The analysis of these testimonies also sheds light on a fundamental difference between the ways in which specific culprits are identified within the narratives. While participants, such as Miguel, do not hesitate to allude to individuals such as Dolores Ibárruri 'La Pasionaria' and Santiago Carrillo – both of whom are widely known at a national (rather than local) level – they refuse persistently to reveal the names of villagers who are known to have taken an active part in the violent acts that developed locally (see Chapter 4). The national level provides them with sufficient distance from the local sphere so as not to raise any concerns within the village itself.

WINNING BY HOOK OR BY CROOK

Historians have established, based on evidence gathered both at national and local levels, that the military coup of July 1936 was planned for months before it took place (Prada Rodríguez 2004). The conservative factions, which had opposed the constitution of the Republic in 1931, were now set against the legitimate government of the Frente Popular, the left-wing coalition that was democratically elected in February 1936. The attempts to topple the Republican system, particularly when the Left was in power, had already led to a number of failed coups, such as the one spearheaded by General Sanjurjo in

1932 (Abella 1982). Manuel Azaña, who was the first prime minister of the Second Republic[5] (from 1931 to 1933), was aware of these conspiracies and was concerned about the army's reaction to the military reforms that were being implemented. In the summer of 1931, shortly after the Republic was constituted, he wrote: 'The army, after the reforms, is quite raw and needs some peace and quiet to develop a new skin. Any incident could ruin everything' (Cardona 1982, 44, my translation).

It could therefore be argued that the coup of 1936 had, in fact, been in motion for years, although it was after the victory of the left-wing coalition – and the subsequent return to the socio-economic reforms that had been brought to a halt in 1933 – that preparations were put in place for the 'salvation of Spain' from the 'Marxist hordes'. When Santiago described how the events unfolded in Arroyomolinos between February and July 1936, he hinted at the forethought and scheming that had preceded the uprising:

> The Right was used to winning, and they lost this time. ... The Church couldn't keep deceiving people. They lost, so they said 'if we don't win the elections, we will win in a different way.' By force, they meant. And then the Civil War started, but there were revolutionary groups in the village that fought for the people, but we lost. Back then, class consciousness was much stronger than it is today. Today people are not bothered, but we were much more aware and active then. (Santiago 2013, my translation)

I asked Santiago to clarify what he meant when he stated that the Right would win 'in a different way' if they did not win the elections. He replied that

> at the time of the February elections, my father told us that he had heard them saying that they would win by hook or by crook. Later on ... years later, my granddad would sometimes remember this. He said: 'no wonder they said that they would win no matter what.' It was understood then. They didn't win the peaceful way, so they imposed it on us. And look, they really imposed it! (Santiago 2013, my translation)

Santiago's memory of what his father and grandfather had conveyed is in keeping with the thesis that both civil and military agents began to work on the organisation of the coup at a local level across the country (Prada Rodríguez 2004). Contacts among the civil population played an essential role in this large-scale movement, as they were able to provide vital information about individuals who might resist the coup locally while also contributing to the creation of a favourable stance towards the insurrection (Prada Rodríguez 2004, 130). In Arroyomolinos, there was also a local cabal of informants that included individuals from all social classes, from day labourers to business and landowners.

Despite all the preparatory efforts, the coup did not lead to the results that its leaders had expected. The rebels had planned to take control of the entire country, but their hopes were crushed due to two important facts: the active and passive refusal, on the part of many servicemen, to join and support the uprising, and the mobilisation of the working class, promoted by the left-wing parties and trade unions (Gil Honduvilla 2004, 99). Nonetheless, the coup served to unleash a conflict that would last three years, as fascist rebels and the loyal sections of the army engaged in battle, a fight that was also joined by the shoemakers, blacksmiths and carpenters that Miguel mentioned in his testimony (see above).

OPPORTUNISM, BETRAYALS AND TREACHERY

Although this period of repression is frequently described in terms of intense ideological struggles, a recurrent feature in this context was the emergence of opportunistic behaviour, betrayals and treacherous actions. Instances of repressive measures taken against villagers whose 'disappearance' was simply convenient for their rivals or enemies, abounded everywhere, particularly in the rural context, where residents of relatively small communities know a great deal about the intimate lives of other villagers. During an interview with a resident of A Fonsagrada (in the north-western province of Lugo), it emerged that a man had been executed because another individual wanted to take his ploughing machine (Raquel 2015). A woman from another village in Lugo explained that her uncle had been killed because he had a permanent post as a doctor and someone else wanted the job (Lorena 2015). Miguel heard that something similar happened in the nearby village of Fuentes de León: 'In Fuentes they caught a kid and stole his money, and they killed him right there, in the mountain. He was 14 or 15' (Miguel 2014a). Jealousy and personal interests, such as direct economic gains through the acceptance of bribes, or access to the victims' resources or positions, were at the heart of these executions.

According to Pedro, betrayal and treachery happened often and across all the political factions in Arroyomolinos:

> Someone from the anarchist trade union used to rat to the Naudes [the Darnaude family]. He told them what was going on in the union, the discussions they were having, which workers were saying what. They accused one another ... they told on one another, because they either changed sides, or they were scared and were trying to survive. In another village, I have been told, there was a guy who was shot dead because everyone noticed that he was always accusing everyone else of doing things. (Pedro 2015, my translation)

Luis also shared a similar story, perhaps about the same informant:

> I won't tell you who it was, but they used to say that a guy from the anarchist union was talking to the Naudes. The thing is, after a while, he bought something up there, a plot, or something. He bought it when nobody else could buy anything. Nobody could afford to buy stuff back then, but he could. Do you understand what I mean? He was getting money from the Naudes in exchange for information. Do you see what I'm saying? (Luis 2014a, my translation)

Presumably, both Pedro and Luis were talking about the same individual, although it would not be too farfetched to think that they may, in fact, be referring to different people. The participants' persistent refusal to name those who aligned themselves with fascism means that we may never find out.

Individuals who had escaped to the mountains lived with the constant threat of being seen by someone who would report them to the authorities. For instance, José Silva Almendro 'el Letrero', who was hiding in the countryside, was shot dead by the local guards in La Romería because somebody 'squealed'. We also find several instances when the victims' own relatives denounced them to the authorities. For example, Florencio Ramos Mateo 'el Canario', who was shot in the local cemetery, was grassed by his own cousins, according to the testimony given by his nephew. Manuel Fernández Rubio, who was also killed in the village, was denounced by his brother, known as 'el Latero' (see Chapter 4 for further details on the executions of José, Florencio and Manuel). Several participants mentioned the latter case, expressing, explicitly or implicitly, their repulsion at El Latero's action.

On a more positive note, Miguel often insisted that, despite the division between Left and Right, what mattered in reality were individual principles, which meant that there were 'good' and 'bad' people on both sides:

> Some poor people are bad, very bad. They denounced people and pulled the trigger for money. And then, the doctors ... there were two here. They said they would not kill anyone, because they had studied to save lives, not to kill them. Other people also said they didn't want to get involved in any way. They didn't want anyone to die. (Miguel 2015, my translation)

Luis also refers to the doctors in positive terms when he explains how one of them had signed a paper stating that one of the men who spent the night in the chapel (one of Cala's 18, see Chapter 4) was ill and should be released. Miguel's argument is that class and ideology do not necessarily determine a person's moral standing and how individuals would conduct themselves in certain situations.

Taking advantage, look, that's not about ideals. That has to do with the type of person. If you are in a battalion, don't go around killing children and women and raping them. That has to do with the type of person. The Left also had some who were bad, very bad. It happened on both sides. For example, here in the village, the biggest thieves have been those who call themselves socialist, and they were not socialist, because I have seen them singing 'Cara al Sol' in the casinos. They changed because of their interests. They killed one, the father of a woman who lives over there, in Segura, because he owed money. Socialism? (Luis 2014a, my translation)

In some rare cases, tip-offs also occurred the other way around, that is, officers informed certain people that they were in danger. Miguel narrates the occasion when a civil guard alerted a family of a threat to their existence, although the episode ended tragically, despite his efforts:

In Llerena, a civil guard told a woman that her husband was on the next list, and he should escape, so he did. He warned them because he was a friend of the family. So they started looking for him and he was never there. She wouldn't give away his whereabouts so, in the end, they took her brother instead. (Miguel 2014b, my translation)

In these times of revolt, the occasional attempts, on the part of certain individuals, to protect villagers, contrasted clearly with the viciousness observed in the behaviour of other local agents, as some residents took the opportunity to settle existing quarrels. During one of the interviews with Luis, he described the story of a man who, having already been in prison and released, was told by one of the guards to go back 'just to check in'. However, suspecting that they would not let him go again, he prepared his escape:

Postre's father ended up in Madrid. He fled the village. They thought he was stupid. They called him, with the intention of putting him in prison, or killing him, who knows, but he must have sniffed it out. He told them he would come but he needed to find some figs for his family, because they were hungry, and then he escaped. (Luis 2014b, my translation)

When asked why they wanted to imprison this victim, Luis replied that there was no political reason for it: 'Anyone could accuse you of anything.' The randomness implied in this statement emerges in nearly all conversations about this period in more or less explicit ways. In some cases, this observation appears within wider accounts that are critical of the political, economic and social setting, as is the case with the testimony offered by Luis, whose left-wing political stance and critical vision emerge consistently through his narrative.

For other participants, however, emphasising the randomness of the accusations and executions seems to serve a twofold function: first, the narrator can avoid a deeper engagement with the issues at stake and, secondly, he or she can steer clear of doing so in public, in front of fellow villagers. This type of response serves, therefore, as an avoidance mechanism that narrators incorporate into their testimonies in order to circumvent what they perceive to be a potentially awkward or dangerous situation. The desire to avoid 'problems' also underpins the instruction that parents and grandparents have passed on to their children (many of whom have already become parents themselves): '*no te señales*' or '*no hay que significarse*' – that is, that they should not 'stand out' or 'take sides', 'should things get ugly' ('*por si las cosas se ponen feas*'). So, for example, Mateo, who consistently avoided making any explicit political comments during our conversation, explained the executions as follows:

> Here people were killed for the sake of being killed. Nothing had been done. They weren't bad people. They hadn't done anything. People pointed at one another over the slightest little thing. (Mateo 2015, my translation)

Mateo's initial utterance – 'here people were killed for the sake of being killed' – is striking due to its grammatical construction. The use of the passive voice to express this idea contrasts with the more frequent 'they killed for the sake of killing', or other statements articulated in the active voice that would emphasise, rather than erase, the agency of the killers, even if their names are not revealed ('*they* killed'). For Mateo, alluding to the randomness of the acts provides him with a way to avoid having to examine the violence in further depth.

'*LOS AÑOS MALOS*': THE STRUGGLE TO SURVIVE

Another key theme that stands out from the testimonies is the daily struggle that the average citizen had to endure in order to meet their basic needs and those of their families. Here, participants do not seem to be making reference to any of the ideological issues that underpinned the war, even though their efforts to survive were meant to be at the heart of the very socio-economic struggles that led to the clashes. Many recollections, therefore, focus purely on the day-to-day experience of hunger and extreme necessity. In this respect, their narrations draw our attention to a crucial aspect of the history of the 1930s and the post-war years: that of the average citizen whose struggle was to survive from one day to the next (del Arco Blanco 2007). For them, the ideological and class battles were not formulated in abstract or theoretical terms, but materialised in real problems that they had to face on a daily basis.

For instance, Manuel, who was born in 1940, described what he remembers about his childhood:

> I was born in 1940, during the bad years. Everything was scarce. When I came to understand what was happening I was seven or eight years old. I didn't notice before, but things were hard. There was no bread because there was no wheat. There was no bread, no meat, nothing. We only had lice, because there was no health service, or social security, nothing. Lice, bed bugs … . There was also tuberculosis, because people didn't eat, and they died and that was it. (Manuel 2015, my translation)

Manuel's reference to the 'bad years' is not uncommon. Fran's (2015) first description of this period is that 'there wasn't anything to eat. We had nothing. We worked a lot but we were hungry.' *'Los años malos'* ('the bad years') or *'los años del hambre'* ('the hunger years') are typical descriptions of the 1940s, when economic insecurity, scarcity and empty stomachs were the greatest social problems, together with the subsequent health issues and dreadful sanitary conditions. When Costa y Martínez calculated, in 1912, how much money was necessary for the average Andalusian peasant family (*familia jornalera*) to meet the costs of food, rent and other living expenses, he concluded that there was an overall deficit between income and outcome, although the severity of the situation varied across different Spanish regions. This author noted that

> Peasants need, on each of the 365 days of the year, three pesetas, but only earn from one to one and a half pesetas; therefore, the state of things has to change: a change through which peasants should earn, every day, from six to eight *reales* in excess of what they earn now. (Costa y Martínez 1912, 63, my translation)

Similar descriptions of scarcity abound in the literature and in other oral testimonies, in which hunger is a recurrent theme. Santiago, for instance, recalls how he and his father, taken as one economic unit, did not earn enough money per day to buy bread for their household. Indeed, according to the Padrón de Familias Pobres (Municipal Register of Poor Families) collated in 1939, there were 283 families in the village that were classified as 'poor' (Padrón de Familias Pobres 1939).

According to Escudero Delgado (1995), poverty had been considered to be a serious social problem since the nineteenth century, when a number of regulations were approved in order to provide free health assistance (access to doctors and pharmaceutical products) to families in need. In practice, however, despite the positive intentions, the system was deficient in several ways, particularly due to the lack of resources (Escudero Delgado 1995, 61). Another problem was the use of particular criteria to determine which families could be regarded as poor. Some of the aspects that were taken into consideration included the type

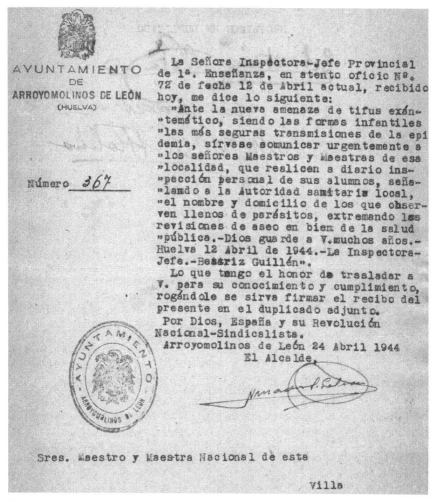

AVUNTAMIENTO
DE
ARROYOMOLINOS DE LEÓN
(HUELVA)

Número *367*

La Señora Inspectora-Jefe Provincial
de 1ª. Enseñanza, en atento oficio Nº.
72 de fecha 12 de Abril actual, recibido
hoy, me dice lo siguiente:
   «Ante la nueva amenaza de tifus exán-
»temático, siendo las formas infantiles
»las más seguras transmisiones de la epi
demia, sírvase comunicar urgentemente a
»los señores Maestros y Maestras de esa
»localidad, que realicen a diario ins-
»pección personal de sus alumnos, seña-
»lando a la Autoridad sanitaria local,
»el nombre y domicilio de los que obser-
ven llenos de parásitos, extremando las
revisiones de aseo en bien de la salud
»pública.-Dios guarde a V.muchos años.-
Huelva 12 Abril de 1944.-La Inspectora-
Jefe.-Beatriz Guillén».
   Lo que tengo el honor de trasladar a
V. para su conocimiento y cumplimiento,
rogándole se sirva firmar el recibo del
presente en el duplicado adjunto.
   Por Dios, España y su Revolución
Nacional-Sindicalista.
   Arroyomolinos de León 24 Abril 1944
              El Alcalde,

Sres. Maestro y Maestra Nacional de esta

                                    Villa

Figure 5.2 Document stating that, due to the threat of a typhus epidemic, teachers should check children for any symptoms of the disease on a daily basis. Ayuntamiento de Arroyomolinos de León.

of wages received (permanent or sessional), the total salary and the number of children. Escudero Delgado further notes that the number of men inscribed in the register was always higher than the number of women. The typical 'poor' man had 'an average of 3.5 members in his family, was born in the rural context, and was a sessional day labourer, while the average 'poor' woman was a 'widow, with or without children, born in the rural context, whose occupation was housework' (Escudero Delgado 1995, 62, my translation).

According to the testimonies, this assistance did not necessarily reach the villagers. When asked whether anyone died during this period, Manuel adds further details about the lack of resources that villagers had to endure:

People didn't have anything. What happened was very bad. Here in the village many people died during the war and also later. There was no men, but who could possibly go to work anyway, when there were no men to take food home. In the war many women were widowed because their men died in the war, or were killed here, or they were taken to prison. They took some of them to the cemetery wall and they killed them there. (Manuel 2015, my translation)

Manuel's statement regarding the lack of men to work the lands and provide a means of sustenance for their families is also observed by Sánchez Jiménez (1975), who points out that the lack of men and wheat were two simultaneous socio-economic problems that were closely interrelated:

Lack of wheat, economically speaking, becomes more noticeable, because nothing could be done about the human losses. The population then begins to grow again despite the deficit, the speculation, the lack of transparency and all the determining factors that took root during the war. (Sánchez Jiménez 1975, 124, my translation)

In reiterating the negativity of the situation, Manuel emphasised the practical elements of the struggle to survive. The lack of food and the fact that many people had died are amalgamated in his memory. It is notable, however, that in Manuel's mind, hunger and death do not appear as elements of a cause-effect relationship (people literally 'dying of starvation'), but both seem to appear as direct consequences of the war. In my approaching this respondent, I had purposely avoided any references to the armed conflict. As Bjerg and Rasmussen (2012) noted in their study of school memories, the use of different prompting techniques makes a difference to the narrative framework that participants use to present their memories. After asking Manuel when he was born, I followed with a general question about his childhood memories. In this case it was Manuel, rather than the interviewer, who mentioned the war, which suggests that his understanding of his childhood was marked by the conflict, even though it had officially ended by the time he was born.

Narratives about the need to survive on a daily basis also bring about memories of the rationing cards and the subsequent development of the black market, commonly known as *estraperlo* (Rodríguez Barreira 2013). Rationing cards did not provide sufficient amounts of essential products,[6] so people had to find alternative ways of obtaining them. These items disappeared from the shops and were hidden in cellars and back rooms until they could be sold at a higher price. While some individuals had to resort to *estraperlo* to survive, others profited from it (Ramírez Copeiro del Villar 1996, 85). This form of business effectively perpetuated the conditions of abject poverty in which the defeated lived, prolonging the situation throughout the 1940s and into the early 1950s (del Arco Blanco and Martínez Espinar 2009, 8).

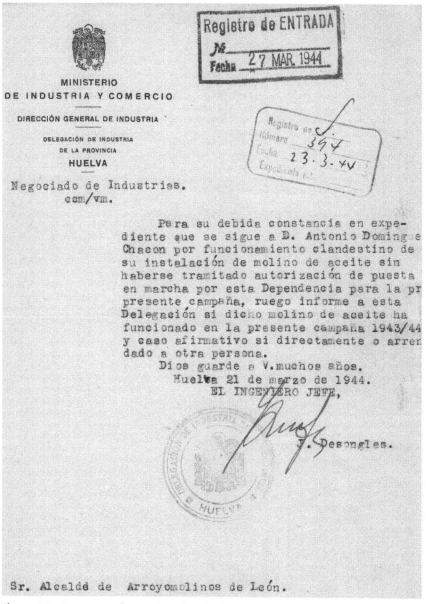

Figure 5.3 Document denouncing the clandestine use of a mill in Arroyomolinos.
Ayuntamiento de Arroyomolinos de León.

In the rural context, agricultural products were grown and sold locally or transported to nearby villages. For instance, in Arroyomolinos, water mills were used primarily to grind wheat for the production of bread, while some

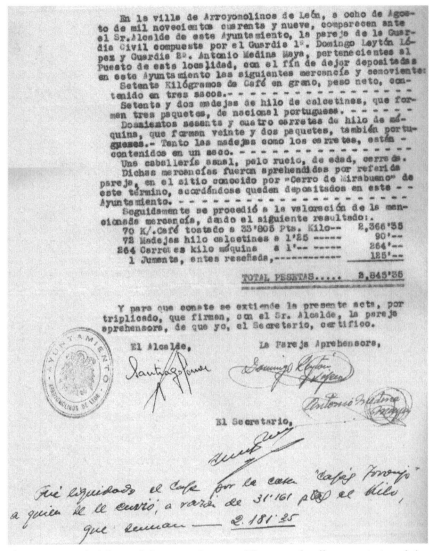

Figure 5.4 Local civil guards intercepted seventy kilograms of coffee, seventy-two skeins of yarn, 264 thread reels for sewing machines and one donkey. The goods, which were valued at 2,845.35 pesetas in 1949, were deposited in the local council. Ayuntamiento de Arroyomolinos de León.

of them were used to press olives. This tradition was documented locally in a special issue of *Cascarrabias*, a magazine that was published by and for villagers for a number of years. In 2006, residents of Arroyomolinos shared their knowledge of their heritage in articles that ranged from interviews to fictional stories inspired by actual events. In one of these stories, one of the villagers depicts the economic context of the time:

> It was 1941. Many people still did not believe that the war was over. In this village, lost in the Huelva mountains, everything seemed to happen later than in the rest of Spain. Hunger and lack of food made villagers sharpen their wits in order to fool the guard that controlled the rationing cards. (Criado 2006, 11, my translation)

Against this backdrop, the story describes how a small group of men used other people's mills to grind wheat illegally at night, employing different strategies so as not to be caught by the Civil Guard (Criado 2006, 11). This wheat would then be sold outside the village. According to Santiago, mills used to be so profitable that anyone who could afford it would invest in one. This was already the case before the war, but in the 1940s this tactic became 'very fashionable' and *estraperlo* was rampant (Campos 2006, 4). Santiago remembers that, when he was a teenager, his employer told him to take loads of wheat on his behalf to a mill in order to mislead the authorities.

In addition to the *estraperlo* that occurred around the mills, individuals also trafficked with other agricultural products, such as olives, olive oil, chick peas, sugar and pork meat. Other items included shoes, textiles and soap. Files located in the local archive provide details about residents who were caught transporting or storing products to be sold illegally. According to these documents, the penalties for being caught engaging in these activities included the closure of shops for three months, the ban on trading for a period of time, the confiscation of the products, house searches to find illegal stock (usually following the receipt of a tip-off), and the imposition of fines that villagers struggled to pay. For instance, a file opened against six individuals acknowledges their precarious economic conditions, but three of them were fined 1,000 pesetas while the other three were ordered to pay 250 pesetas (Fiscalía Provincial de Tasas 1941). These fines, which were excessive considering the economic circumstances of most villagers in the 1940s, were sometimes even higher depending on the case. In trying to eradicate these illegal practices, the state developed measures that served to push poor citizens further into destitution.

CHURCH, IDEOLOGY AND LOCAL COMMUNITY

References to the local Church and sacred images emerged at different points throughout the discussions recorded for this book. Indeed, the role of the Church was a crucial determining factor in the development of the Civil War and the ensuing dictatorship. When the Republic was established in 1931, its secular approach contrasted with Spain's long-standing religious tradition, not only on a social level, but also in terms of the ecclesiastic and aristocratic elites that controlled the power structures (Cuesta Bustillo 1984). Unlike the secular character of the Second Republic – of which conservative sectors thoroughly disapproved – Franco's regime re-established the centrality of religion in all aspects of Spanish way of life, imposing a strict ideological approach, known as National-Catholicism (*nacionalcatolicismo*),[7] through which both public and private life were governed by the Catholic Church. Catholic families were 'good' families, while the 'reds' – on the whole – were supposed to be atheists who destroyed the images of saints and therefore had no morality. Franco's espousal of these values was evidenced in all forms of state-sponsored religious indoctrination, from the design of the school curriculum to the production of political discourse. The Valle de los Caídos (Valley of the Fallen) in the valley of Cuelgamuros in Madrid, illustrates the intimate relationship that Franco's regime maintained with the Church. The monument, which includes a 150-metre-tall cross, was erected in commemoration of the 'heroic sacrifice', the 'crusade' and the 'victory' of those who fought for a 'better Spain' (BOE 1940).

Locally, veneration of the Church and acceptance of the regime were practically synonyms, whether parishioners were truly devout or only pretended to be in a situation where keeping up the appearance of 'respectability' became a survival tactic. So, for instance, the local archive in Arroyomolinos contains a letter, written by Joaquín Aramburu (Military Governor in Seville) for the attention of all councils, informing them of General Queipo de Llano's appeal, in 1938, to gather funds to build a new 'temple or chapel' for the Virgin of Macarena in Seville. Aramburu stated that the cash would be used

> to replace the [temple] that was destroyed by the Marxists on that glorious 18 July, when the General saved Seville and began the liberation of Andalusia and Extremadura.
>
> … Since we owe our freedom and our life to him [Queipo de Llano], the fact that this is his noble aspiration should be sufficient for us to be prepared to help him, through gratitude, through patriotism and to demonstrate our unwavering support.
>
> … The list of donors will be included in an Official Book of the Virgin of Esperanza, that will be published when the work is finished … and a copy will be given to the General.
>
> … This is an opportunity to express, once again, our affection and gratitude [to Queipo]. Therefore, it is very important that everyone, wealthy and humble people, employers and workers, cooperate with their donations, large or small, as the homage to our distinguished saviour will be more esteemed the greater the number of donors.

Needless to say that it is his wish that any contributions are absolutely spontaneous and voluntary, although this Executive Board is sure that it is from a sense of moral obligation that we must all take this laudable action. (Aramburu 1938)

Aramburu's letter is accompanied by a tally of parishioners and their donations: forty-six villagers from Arroyomolinos de León made individual contributions ranging from 0.50 to 25 pesetas, adding up to a sum total of 199.50 pesetas. The content of the letter and the list of local donors illustrate the attitude of the authorities in relation to religion, morality and money, regardless of each family's financial ability to meet these demands. The terms of Queipo de Llano's 'petition' become even more significant if we consider that these institutions, through their discursive interventions and material actions, were already established in this region in 1938, before the Civil War as such was over in the national context.

It is worth noting, however, that even before the war (and despite the secular intentions of the Second Republic) the Church remained heavily involved in daily life. It was influential not simply because of the religious services that occurred within individual places of worship, but also because it sponsored annual festivities that took place in the streets and squares of Spain. Local festivities, for example, were joined not only by religious people but also by atheists, agnostics and casual observers, who appreciated these activities as socio-cultural events rather than for their religious meaning: this attitude persists to this day. As Cintas Guillén (2006) points out, large Andalusian cities, such as Seville, had a strong tradition of religious fervour, but this trend was even more ingrained in the depths of Andalusia, where

> Social, political, economic and cultural struggles marked the lives of a people that lived through the typical contradictions of revolutionary decomposition: peasants without work, and socialist, communist, anarchist and syndicalist leaders who tried to keep the revolutionary fire burning, against the voices of the Right that called for unity. In the boundless landscape of an impoverished and illiterate Spain, some people raised their fists and others raised their arms, Roman style. Only religious festivities relieved, through the act of celebration, the intensity of the class struggle. People, whatever their beliefs, knew how to incorporate themselves into religious events where it seemed that political allegiance was not an obstacle to participation. (Cintas Guillén 2006, 69, my translation)

Similarly, Spanish films and various social and military events also served to divert the citizens' attention from the hardships they suffered after the armed conflict. Besides the escapism offered by religious devotion, the glorification of past imperial achievements – and more recent acts of 'heroism' displayed by the victors of the Civil War – were used to distract the populace (Ramírez Copeiro del Villar 1996, 35). Yet, despite these strategies, class antagonism remained in evidence. Cintas Guillén, for instance, cites a journalist who, describing a major religious festivity, exclaimed that 'every shout of "viva" to the Blanca Paloma [Virgin of Rocío] is a disguised shout of "death to the Republic"' (Cintas Guillén 2006, 69, my translation).

At street level, all villages tend to have a group of devout people who act as the custodians of local morality. According to Luis,

> *Beatas* are the worst dregs of humanity that you can find in the village. They are the worst. They think they can go to Church to clean their souls, but they are the height of hypocrisy. Hypocritical, self-righteous, two-faced … . If a poor woman got pregnant, it was a great sin, they were ready to criticise her and her family. 'Shame on her! What a scandal!' But when it is a rich woman, they don't waste any time to 'sort it out', or to find some way to justify it in front of everyone else. They fix it quickly, and nothing's happened. (Luis 2014b, my translation)

The double standards identified by Luis are also manifested in his recollection of something that Santiago's father had told him in the 1930s:

> The Naudes had some saints in their house. When Santiago's father went in, he crossed himself. When they saw him do that, they told him that the saints were there just so that the peasants would work. And then … they went around sleeping with women! (Luis 2014b, my translation)

Luis' testimony emphasises how the main landowners used religion as a way to exert pressure on the workers. The stark honesty of this revelation by a member of the Darnaude family (in effect, that 'the saints' were used as a tool of oppression) can only be explained by the fact that Santiago's father (a member of the Campos' family) was related to the Darnaudes through marriage (see Chapter 4 for a discussion of how Santiago's uncle may possibly have been allowed to escape execution for this very reason). Although I am unable to verify Luis' final remark regarding the Darnaude's behaviour, the point of his testimony is to highlight the double standards that were applied to different socio-economic classes.

When the participants expressed their opinions of the Church, information about its role in the 1930s is supplemented by insights into current attitudes. As noted in Chapter 4, Valeria's concern regarding the destruction of the saints was a key definer of her testimony, even though she also acknowledged the value of human life when the individuals 'hadn't done anything'. Carlos, a devout Christian from a right-wing family, never made any explicit references to religion, either positive or negative, but his narration indicates his perspective. Discussing the role of the 'reds' before the war, he addressed not only historical events, but the continuation of political controversy into the present

I think, they [the reds] should say, 'well, we did this wrong.' They burnt the saints! I say that we should talk about everything, not only about what the Nationals did ... although the reds didn't kill anyone here. But what wrong did the saints do? But Santiago sees it from his point of view. He says that the priests wanted women to have children, and more children. It was because they wanted to get the rich more hands to work. To produce slaves, he would say. That's what he would say. 'No, we shouldn't have any more children, because they will be hungry.' But this doesn't matter to the Church, he would say. To work and to go to war they are useful, men make wars, and if there are no men there are no wars. But he [Santiago] only talks about what happened on one side. Talk about what happened on both sides, I say. (Carlos 2014, my translation)

Valeria and Carlos' views contrast with those left-wing villagers like Valentina, who suffered the effects of Franco's repression within their own families:

They burned saints. They shouldn't have burnt them, but they were made of clay, they were not real, they were not people, but they killed people, real people, and the saints were made of clay. You can make new saints, but you can't replace men and women. Those families were left with nothing. (Valentina 2014, my translation)

Increasingly angry at the past experiences she recalled, Valentina wondered what would happen if something similar happened in the present. At that point, she could go no further and had to end the conversation.

EDUCATION AND IDEOLOGY

Culture was one of the main mechanisms through which the regime's ideology was instilled. Of all the elements of which culture is comprised, education is the one that is of most importance in the period under study. The Second Republic has frequently been praised for the advances that it achieved in intellectual life, and at the level of pedagogy. The foundation of the Residencia de Estudiantes was a prominent example of an educational institution, one where renowned scientists such as Santiago Ramón y Cajal and Severo Ochoa were educated. In a similar vein, the image of the 'Republican teacher' has often been depicted as a model of pedagogy that was founded in the values of freedom, democracy and equality. The Republican teacher is portrayed, for instance, in films such as *La Lengua de las Mariposas* (José Luis Cuerda 1999): a teacher that has the child's (and the country's) best interests at heart, only to be betrayed and punished when the persecution begins.[8]

Education had been, even before the beginning of the Second Republic, a major source of conflict and controversy in Spain. The endemic political instability and the clashes of competing interests aggravated the discussions over the curriculum, including the obligatory nature of religious tuition (Flecha García 2011, 19). Against this backdrop, an ambitious educational reform project was initiated in 1931. According to Flecha García, this project

> combined principles of Spanish liberalism, pedagogical theories of the Free Teaching Institution, and the program of public instruction promoted by the socialist party. This educational program was viewed as an indispensable instrument for creating social change, some in response to demands of specific groups. (Flecha García 2011, 22)

The existing Ministerio de Instrucción Pública was substituted by the Republican Ministerio de Educación Nacional, which was created 'to form men' rather than to 'instruct' them (Puelles Benítez 1999, 302). According to Puelles Benítez, the government became particularly concerned with the fact that one million children across the country did not attend school (Puelles Benítez 1999, 256; see also Rodríguez Barreira 2015).

The change to the Ministry of Education and its essential vision highlights the relationship that exists in every system between ideology and the need to control the education system. This is also reflected, of course, in the new changes imposed by Franco's regime. According to Langa Nuño (2001), Francoism learnt from the Republic that

> education is the most important element of sociability on which any state, government or ideology can count. For that reason, it is essential to control it, as it is the best way to educate docile citizens according to its own principles. (Langa Nuño 2001, 16, my translation)

For Franco's ideas to be communicated to new generations effectively, the regime had to ensure that the carriers of the National-Catholic message firmly espoused its principles. The first step towards this goal consisted of the physical annihilation of those liberal teachers that had previously educated children to value freedom and social justice.

Nevertheless, the typical image of the Republican teacher and the Republican view of education did not materialise everywhere. Once again, a close study of each local milieu is required in order to identify the variety of circumstances and local realities that existed. In Arroyomolinos, for example, there was never a teacher that espoused liberal perspectives on education and freedom, but one that remained faithful to the most conservative ideas. During our various conversations, I asked Blas to describe his teacher, and his answer was always similar: 'Don José, he was such a *facha* [fascist].'

Don José – José Rodríguez Humanes – held the post of National Teacher (*Maestro Nacional*) for the local boys, and was certainly an outspoken supporter of Franco's regime (see Chapter 4 for evidence of his fascist stance). A female teacher, who would share a similar ideological stance, taught the girls separately from the boys. Mercedes recalls what the pupils had to do as soon as they arrived in the morning:

> When we went to school, we had to stand in a line, boys and girls, and we sang 'Cara al Sol' or 'Viva España'. And then, in the classroom, the first thing we did was to pray. And that wasn't only here in the village, it was also in other villages, everywhere. (Mercedes 2014, my translation)

As shown by the testimonies discussed earlier in the chapter, the scarcity of resources and unequal living conditions between different socio-economic classes forced children to work from a young age in order to contribute to the family earnings. Files found in the local council include minutes taken in meetings during which concerns were raised regarding high rates of school absenteeism, the fact that the school building was in need of significant construction work, the lack of heating, and the low educational levels among the local population. Yet, action was barely ever taken to resolve these problems and, whenever the council attempted to address some of these issues, their efforts were soon deemed insufficient (Ayuntamiento de Arroyomolinos 1944, 1958, 1959).

Regarding the connections between education and class, Silvia (2015) recalls the differences that could be seen between those children who did have the opportunity to attend. When poorer families managed to send their children to school, their ability to concentrate was undermined by a poor diet and inadequate clothing, while their lack of access to additional academic resources put them at a further disadvantage. Frasquito mentioned that he went to school one day, but soiled himself, so he never returned. Instead, like most of his fellow villagers, he started working in the countryside in order to bring home an additional salary. Santiago never went to school either, but accompanied his grandfather to mind the livestock, a task that required the labourer to live in the countryside and thus away from home and from school. He later joined his father and worked on variety of agricultural activities, from harvesting to keeping beehives.

Despite the descriptions that challenge the idealised view of Republican achievements within the field of education, the situation was not always identical throughout rural areas. In Cala, for instance, the Republican mayor Teodosio Riscos played a key role in the construction of the school and other social initiatives, such as the installation of a telephone service and the attempt to build a public library (a project that did not materialise owing to the coup). These progressive initiatives were supported by Arturo Puntas Vela (teacher), Carlos Encinas González (doctor) and Julio Abril (nurse), all of whom suffered the effects of Franco's repression. Arturo Puntas Vela's brother was executed, while Julio Abril fled Cala with Teodosio Riscos and Carlos Encinas in order to escape the fascist troops (Larrinaga 2011). In Arroyomolinos, however, the noble ideal of the dedicated and selfless Republican teacher never existed, and the children of the poor were subjected to a regime of superstition, strict discipline and rigid class distinction.

NOTES

1. This clause specifically referred to lands that were located within two kilometres of the village centre, as long as the village had less that 25,000 inhabitants, and provided that the owner of the plot was also in possession of other lands, within the same administrative area, that had a cadastral value of over 1,000 pesetas (Cobo Romero 2013; Malefakis 1971).

2. For discussions of the failure of the Agrarian Reform, see, for example, Robledo Hernández (2014) and González de Molina (2014).

3. Cobo Romero (2013) calculates that, only in the rural context of four Andalusian provinces (Córdoba, Granada, Jaén and Seville), 1,271 strikes took place between 1931 and 1936. The highest incidence is concentrated between 1933 (389) and 1934 (337), although workers were also particularly active in 1931 and 1932 (with 220 and 246 strikes, respectively). The number of revolts decreased significantly in 1935 (3) when the resilient capacity of labourers to fight for their rights was progressively crushed by the conservative government (Cobo Romero 2013; see also Cobo Romero 1992; Garrido González 1990; López Martínez 1995; Moreno Gómez 1982; Pascual Cevallos 1983; Pérez Yruela 1979).

4. José Domínguez Muñoz 'El Cabrero' ('The Goatherd'), one of the most important flamenco singers in Spain, is best known for his commitment to the politics that underpin his music. Born and brought up in Aznalcóllar (a village in the southern province of Seville) in 1944, he grew up in a family of goatherds. Like many Spanish children during those years, he left school at a very young age to help his father look after the cattle. This is the socio-economic context in which his political ideas began to take shape. An outspoken collaborator of the anarchist movement and the CNT, El Cabrero's intense and highly critical lyrics, condemning Franco's systemic repression, often landed him in prison after his concerts in the final years of the dictatorship. As his wife writes in her blog '*El Cabrero, porque callar es morir*' ('El Cabrero, because to keep quiet is to die'), writing the lyrics is the most complex part of her husband's process of music production. The lyrics that he wants to sing, she notes, nobody else wants to recite, and the ones that everyone else is happy to perform, he rejects. 'He does not want his songs to talk about women, bulls, fairs, or saints. … Animals, the countryside and his way of thinking, his rebelliousness … those are the topics he likes to sing about' (Bermúdez 2012). My participant, Miguel, is well known in

Arroyomolinos for his singing. He often sings *fandangos* (a style of flamenco which is typical in the province of Huelva) in a local bar or in any improvised setting, with or without the accompaniment of a friend's guitar. He is appreciated to the extent that he has been invited to attend parties in other localities in Huelva and Seville in order to sing alongside more established flamenco vocalists. The *fandangos* that Miguel sings are deeply influenced by El Cabrero, not only because he often borrows his lyrics, but also because of the themes that he sings about.

5. Azaña became Prime Minister again in February 1936, before serving as President of the Republic between 1936 and 1939, while the Civil War unfolded. Azaña resigned when Franco won the war and died in 1940 during his exile in France.

6. According to Ramírez Copeiro del Villar, rationing cards allowed: between 100 and 250 grams of certain foods per person once a week; 250 millilitres of oil per week; 500 grams of potatoes, when there was enough stock, and bread nearly every day, in pieces of approximately 150 grams (Ramírez Copeiro del Villar 1996, 85).

7. Franco adopted this deeply entrenched religious approach when it became necessary to substitute the fascist discourse after the defeat of Germany and Italy in World War II. Franco's ideology could be defined as 'clerical fascism', which encompasses, according to Eatwell, 'links between the churches and fascism' in Italy and elsewhere (Eatwell 2003, 145; see also Trevor-Roper's (1981) typology of different forms of fascism).

8. See, for example, Dávila Balsera (2005), Flecha García (2011) and Gudín de la Lama et al. (2013) to read more on the developments of the education system in Spain.

Chapter 6

Rojas: Women and the Anti-fascist Struggle

The discussion has focused thus far on the male victims of Franco's repression, but this is not to suggest that women's experiences were unimportant: they played a crucial role during the war and its aftermath, and an account of their experiences will help us appreciate the full horror that was unleashed by the military rebellion. The reason why women have taken a secondary position in the present narrative is explained by the local application of repressive practices: unlike the situation that prevailed in many other localities, no women were killed in Arroyomolinos. They did, however, suffer other forms of violence and indignity.

It is also true that the experiences of women have received less attention within studies of the war as a whole, though several authors have discussed the lives of those more prominent individuals who demonstrated their commitment to social justice (Ackelsberg 2004; Mangini 1995). At a national level, the anti-fascist struggle included a significant number of women who served the cause of freedom, both on the frontline and in the rear guard (Yusta Rodrigo 1998, 2004). To some extent, women had already become more visible in public life during the Second Republic, when they took a number of important steps towards the goal of equality.[1] While the social order as a whole was dominated by reactionary factions, some women were emerging from the domestic environment and joining trade unions, taking posts of responsibility, and demanding their rights – assisted by the fact that the Republic eventually recognised women's right to vote (Oyarzábal 2013). Some of those who took an active part in politics during this period included Clara Campoamor (Partido Radical), Victoria Kent (Partido Radical Socialista), Margarita Nelken (Partido Socialista Obrero Español) and Federica Montseny of the CNT, or Confederación Nacional del Trabajo (Ackelsberg 2004; Preston 2002; Rodrigo 2013). These and other women had to fight the system from within, confronting the chauvinism of their male counterparts and the establishment as a whole. Victoria Kent, for example, was removed from her post as Head of the Penitentiary System in 1932 following the insistence of Prime Minister Manuel Azaña. In his diary, Azaña wrote that

> we have finally managed to remove Victoria Kent, Head of the Penitentiary System. Victoria is usually modest and pleasant, and the only one out of the three female members of Parliament [the others were Clara Campoamor and Margarita Nelken] who is likeable; I think she is also the only one who is … polite. But she has failed in her post. Too humanitarian, she has not had leadership qualities. The state of the prisons is alarming. There is no discipline. Prisoners escape whenever they want. For many days we have been trying to convince the Minister, Albornoz, to replace her. Albornoz ... blames everything that happens in the prisons on the employees, who are unhappy because they have not had any pay rises. (Rodrigo 2013, 100–101, my translation)

Azaña's condescending and chauvinist description of Kent (and of her sister parliamentarians) is an indication of his prejudice, further demonstrated when he assigned systemic failures to a woman who was never given the time or resources to accomplish the task. Criticisms of women who took an active part in political affairs went as far as to blame them for the defeat of the Left in 1933, when they were allowed to vote for the first time. Clara Campoamor, in her book *El voto femenino y yo* – originally published in 1936 – discussed the backlash that she experienced after fighting for universal suffrage for this very reason.

ANONYMOUS WOMEN

While works such as those by Rodrigo (2013) have focused on the life and experiences of well-known women, who are described as the 'great forgotten', I would argue that those who actually suffered from invisibility were the thousands of women whose life stories have, for the most part, remained unknown. These unsung heroines – or 'invisible' heroines, as Sánchez Sánchez (2009a) calls them – appear, where remembered at all, in the online annals or blogs of Spain's memory associations. Amongst other purposes, these online sites are used to commemorate the lives of Franco's victims: their articles and testimonies contribute to the circulation of subjugated knowledges. The ARMH – Asociación para la Recuperación de la Memoria Histórica — for instance, commemorates the life of men and women who contributed to the cause in one form or another, by re-posting relevant articles, or writing new material about events that have not gained the attention of the mainstream media. The news section of their website includes, among many other stories, articles on Vicenta López and her son, who were killed after giving shelter to five guerrillas in 1948 (Fidalgo 2015); on María Silva 'la Libertaria', who survived the massacre of Casas Viejas in 1933 but was eventually executed by the military rebels in August 1936 (her murder was only officially recognised 75 years after her death) (Carballar 2011); and the story of Juana Aguilar Pazos, who survived two executions in the summer of 1936, after all the men in her family were killed (Torrús 2014).

Some of these women have acquired a symbolic place in the collective memory of this period. One of the most renowned cases is that of the *trece rosas* (thirteen roses), a group of thirteen women (seven of whom were under 21, the age of majority at the time)[2] who were executed in Madrid on 5 August 1939 in Cementerio del Este, known today as Cementerio de la Almudena (Ferrero 2011; Fonseca 2011; López 2008). The women were accused, alongside a group of 43 men (who were executed in the same place earlier the same day), of aiding the 'military rebellion' (i.e. supporting the legitimate government of the Republic after the military coup). All the victims were members of the Juventudes Socialistas Unificadas (Unified Socialist Youth).

In recent years, a growing number of publications have focused on the experiences of women who had their heads shaved, who were forced to swallow castor oil, who were publicly humiliated and, in many cases, raped, imprisoned or executed (Barranquero Texeira 2012; González Duro 2012; González Fernández 2006; Nash 2006; Ramos Mesonero 2011; Vinyes 2010). Memory associations have also demanded that the women who were subjected to various forms of abuse should be recognised as victims of the repression. They argue that there is a need

> to conduct research into the practices that were carried out by rebel troops and citizens, which included shaving and forcing the ingestion of castor oil, and even raping women who, directly or indirectly, were part of the collectives that defended the Republic and the Revolution; to recognise all the victims of repression through any necessary rules, decrees or laws, and through the organisation of public acts, preferably in the same place where the events originally took place; and to repair the damages institutionally and economically. (Gordillo 2015, my translation)

In keeping with the tenets of a Critical Ethnography of Memory, and in line with its aim to uncover 'unknown' stories and struggles, this chapter focuses on the local memories about women in Arroyomolinos, paying particular attention to the experiences of women who were members of trade unions that operated within a rural environment, or who were related to men who were targeted for being on the Left. Their children's testimonies shed light on the reasons why they were targeted within the village, and the actions that were taken to punish them. Besides the various physical and psychological forms of abuse that they endured, they also suffered the consequences of losing the male figures in their families (husbands, sons, fathers, brothers or uncles). Not only did they have to deal with the emotional consequences of their men's forced disappearance, execution or imprisonment,[3] but the absence of men in the family also led to at least two additional consequences – which I discuss below in further depth – in a context where men were in charge of providing sustenance and protection: the first consequence was clearly economic, which became even more serious when there were young children in the family; in addition, women whose male relatives had been killed, imprisoned or forced to flee were exposed to becoming the target of further humiliation and abuse.

ROJAS IN ARROYOMOLINOS DE LEÓN

Santiago's mother, Magdalena, was one of the women who endured the repressive practices in Arroyomolinos. She is still remembered locally as someone who was both very literate and strongly political. Her son explained that she was a libertarian communist, and was always up to date with the latest political developments in Spain and abroad, which she read about in magazines such as *Tierra y Libertad*, which could be found at the local CNT centre. Her strong ideological stance and involvement in political debates are still recalled in the village, a memory that is reinforced by the fact that her son is also known for being equally outspoken regarding political matters. According to the oral testimonies, she is, in fact, the individual who is most often recalled when the issue of repression against women is discussed.

Magdalena was only one of the many thousands of women who suffered the effects of Francoist persecution across Spain. Abad argues that, within the broader framework of Francoist repression, there existed a *'represión sexuada'* (sexual repression) directed against women from the very moment of the military coup (Abad 2009, 65; see also Abad et al. 2012). In this context, Magdalena met the basic conditions as a target of local repression: first and foremost, she was a woman who displayed initiative, intellectual skills, an inquiring mind and ideas of her own, and she was not afraid to express them publicly. González Duro notes how Franco's judicial and extrajudicial 'systems' gradually created an image of the *roja* as ferocious, vulgar, dirty, hardly feminine and inclined to idleness, vice or violence (González Duro 2012, 110). They were also thought likely to invade public spaces by making themselves socially visible. Even when they acted in supporting roles in activities led by men, these women were described as agitators who encouraged and propagated anticlerical ideas. This was, in itself, highly problematic as a general rule in Franco's times but, for women, it was a double crime: in engaging in this sort of activities, they were breaking away from their traditional role of dependency and subordination to men. Men, even when they were *rojos*, were subjects in their own right. Women, however, were not, and had to be punished for not meeting the 'moral' behaviours that were expected of them (González Duro 2012; Nash 2006).

One of Santiago's first memories of his mother is a conversation that took place between her and several villagers at the local bakery.[4] He often recalls how, at some point before the elections of February 1936, the baker, Juan 'el Cuezo', a socialist who would eventually become mayor – and who was later executed in the summer of 1936 – had questioned her libertarian stance on the issue of voting. The fact that CNT members had refused to participate in previous elections had facilitated the recurrent victories of the Right within the village:

> My mum and I went to buy some bread, I always remember this day, because there was a huge debate down there at the baker's. The baker believed in socialism and he said to my mum, 'Don't you see, Magdalena, don't you realise that because of your refusal to vote the Right keeps winning?'. Of course, libertarians didn't want to get involved in politics, so he said 'if you don't vote, it's the same as giving the vote to the Right, don't you realise? You need to wake up.' It was a huge debate because they couldn't agree. (Santiago 2013, my translation)

Eventually, the local anarchists voted for the socialist baker, enabling a tilt in the polls that would give him the victory in the elections of February 1936, finally bringing socialism to the local council, albeit for five months only. By July 1936, Juan was shot dead for having taken sides in favour of the socialist cause (see Chapter 4).

Santiago also remembers how his mother was sentenced to death alongside other women in the village during the same period:

> She was sentenced to death because she had left-wing ideas. My mother had a grave ready for twelve days. In total, there were seven or eight women who had been sentenced to death and all their graves were ready. Some people said that women shouldn't be executed because they had children. In the end they decided not to kill them for that reason. (Santiago 2013, my translation)

Other participants also remember that Magdalena had been in prison, where the guards had shaved her head, and had been sentenced to death. Particularly when it concerns women, participants tend to connect the memory of their imprisonment with the fact that their heads had been shaved, which was a frequent tool designed to shame the victims publicly (González Duro 2012).

Valeria (2014), for example, recalls that 'some women were taken to prison and they were shaved, because they were … *rojas*. But I don't know who they are.' According to Santiago (2013), up to 100 women suffered this indignity at different points during the period.

However, being imprisoned and living through the threat of execution did not make up the sum total of Magdalena's experiences of repression. In 1937, Santiago's parents were both banished to La Corte, a small village near Aracena, where his father (a socialist) came from. Initially, Santiago accompanied them, although he would soon return to Arroyomolinos to work with his grandfather in the countryside at a young age, having barely attended school. In the meantime, Magdalena and her husband were forced to find alternative means of sustenance away from home. This practice was in essence yet another tool of systemic violence applied during the dictatorship (as discussed in Chapter 4, Magdalena's brother, Aurelio, was also banished to a village in Córdoba after he was released from prison). Carlos remembered that, years later, when Magdalena had returned to the village, she remained loyal to her ideas despite the risks:

> His [Santiago's] mother was a notorious red. She used to listen to Pirenaica, a radio station [which was forbidden in Spain]. I was 14 or 15 and I walked past her door, and her daughter said to her, 'mum, you don't know who is walking

Figure 6.1   The old prison. This building is now the local School for Adult Education (Escuela de Adultos). Photograph by Ruth Sanz Sabido.

in the street.' This was years after the war, but you had to be very careful. The woman listened to Pirenaica ... secretly of course. (Carlos 2014, my translation)

While some villagers are remembered as having fled to the mountains, none of the participants mentioned the fact that people had left Arroyomolinos to live in other villages or towns. Although everyone remembers Magdalena's politics and intellectual abilities, nobody, except for her own son, seems to recall that she was forced to leave the village for a period of time. This is not the case in other villages, where the fact that villagers took flight when the troops arrived is deeply rooted in their local memory. For example, people who originate from La Torre de Esteban Hambrán, in the province of Toledo, recall how in October 1936 there was a 'mass exodus of families' when Franco's military allies approached the village (Serrano 2015). The difference between these particular localities appears to be the scale of the flight: while in La Torre there was a general impulse to escape, it appears that in Arroyomolinos this option was taken on a more individual basis. In La Torre, the properties that were left empty were expropriated by the fascists.

The decision to flee was made throughout the territories occupied by the Nationalists, often because the victims wished to begin a new life free from the 'taint' of persecution. For instance, one woman that I interviewed in Madrid, as part of a broader though essentially parallel project, recounted how she and her family had to abandon everything in her village after her father was executed, so that they could make an attempt at starting again in a locality where people would not know their history. Therefore, the decision to flee sometimes had a twofold purpose: primarily, to save one's life, but also to avoid the stigmatisation to which the victims of Franco's repression were exposed.

SENTENCED TO DEATH

In Arroyomolinos, Magdalena was one of the most outspoken women at the time, but she was certainly not the only woman who was targeted in the village. Other women were also subjected to various forms of humiliation, although none of the participants mentioned that these women had been banished. Nonetheless, they all remember the fact that a group of women – including Magdalena – had been sentenced to death, indicating that these women were 'seven or eight' who were going to be executed. Nobody was sure of the complete list of the condemned, but some of them recall how their graves were dug in Alcántara's land, a local olive grove, in the days prior to the date set for the executions. Only one interviewee, Miguel, ventured to provide what appears to be the most complete list that I have been able to identify at this stage, eighty years after the events, although it is far from accurate and it has not been possible to verify the information:

> Seven or eight women were sentenced to death. One of my aunties, María, was one of them. They wanted to kill her because she had taken something from the Church, something that had been thrown away, out there, because you can't imagine the chaos around the saints ... I don't know. And Elvira, rest in peace, she lived over there, where I live now, because I live in a house of *rojos*, listen to what I am saying. When I was a kid, I used to go to her house. Cupida's mother, three. Santiago's mother, four. María 'Moya', who I appreciated a lot, five. There were seven or eight. They shaved them. They shaved them and everything. And I think that X's mother, too ... I think she was another one, I'm not sure. There were people who were against it. (Miguel 2014b, my translation)

The name of the last woman has been removed from my text, not only because Miguel was unsure of the truth, but also because he thought that her son might not have been aware of his mother's position. Valentina also mentioned the same woman's name, this time in front of the son's wife, who responded by saying that her husband had never mentioned it and that she, for her own part, knew nothing about it.

We can only gain some degree of certainty about the total number of victims and their names by crosschecking oral testimonies, as no relevant documents have been found, either in the local council or in other archives. There is, therefore, no official trace of the women that were sentenced or detailed information about the process that was followed to accuse the victims. As a result, the only tool available is to interrogate the level of certainty expressed by the participants, and to contrast different versions of the same events. The names that I have been able to crosscheck, based on all the testimonies, are: Magdalena Domínguez Silva, Ángeles Escobar García, Luisa García Valero, María Ramos Mateo, Elvira and María (Ramón Moya's wife).

If the list of the women who were sentenced to death is still incomplete, the attempt to provide a full list of those who had their heads shaved and who were subjected to other forms of humiliation, has proven to be even more difficult. This is caused, among other reasons, by the participants' difficulties in remembering the details of these events, which are sometimes conflated with other occasions. So, for example, during the course of the research, a general consensus was reached to the effect that there were eight women who were sentenced to death, though some participants were not clear if there were eight or only seven. In attempting to collate the list of all the women affected, I asked one more person, Ramona, whether she could remember any additional information. However, her testimony added more confusion, as it contradicted what all other participants had previously stated:

My mother, my poor mother, they shaved her head. The women that were shaved were the ones that were sentenced to death. My mother used to tell me that there were 18 women who had been sentenced to death, although none of them died in the end. (Ramona 2015, my translation)

Ramona was sure that her mother had told her that there were 18 women. However, when I mentioned this to Miguel, he refuted it:

There were eight women, definitely. Santiago can tell you. This woman must be confused with something else. She may be confusing Cala's 18 with the number of women. There were eight, for sure. Ask anyone. I don't know why she has told you this. (Miguel 2014a, my translation)

Santiago had pointed out that, in addition to those who were sentenced, about 100 women were shaven for being *rojas* (see above). The daughter of Ánge-les Escobar García confirmed that, with her mother, there were six or seven women who were sentenced to death and then liberated:

My mum was very innocent, she was a very nice woman, she was a saint. She read very well. Magdalena used to tell her 'Come to see me and we will read a little.' And she went, the innocent woman, not thinking, and they read things that perhaps they shouldn't be reading. Magdalena was very revolutionary and they read magazines that existed back then, about the war and things like that. (Cupida 2014, my translation)

Cupida also explains what happened in the summer of 1936, before her mother was arrested, in connection with the acts of vandalism that occurred in the Church after the news of the coup arrived in the village:

My parents were cooking *migas* [meal made with breadcrumbs] here, and she noticed that there were some big lights around there, and she asked my father what they were. My father told her that they were burning the saints, and that she shouldn't leave the house. But she went out to the doorstep anyway, and when they [the Nationalists] were passing by, they took her. They locked her in prison, which was where the school for adults is now. And they shaved them. They beat them and did horrible things to them. And we know who they are. What's the point of saying it now. My dear, you don't want to know about this. Don't get into it. (Cupida 2014, my translation)

Cupida cannot remember these events because she was a baby at the time, but her close relatives had told her what had happened as she was growing up:

I was nearly born in prison. I was a few months old and they brought me to her so she could breastfeed me, and she didn't want to do it. She didn't want to breastfeed me. My uncle spoke to them and they released her, but she never got over it. She completely lost it. She went mad. Years later she still thought they were going to kill her. Another woman had to feed me, because she wouldn't do it. (Cupida 2014, my translation)

Cupida became visibly upset when she narrated this painful family memory, clearly troubled by the psychological trauma that her mother had suffered.

The case of Luisa García Valero was also described by Rafael (2015), who explained that a man from the village, Ceferino, who was 'very right-wing', had married Luisa to save her from death. Rafael further pointed out that not only did they occupy diametrically opposed ideological positions, but that he was nearly thirty years her senior. Despite these facts, they married and, according to the Census of 1940, they had a two-year-old daughter by the end of 1939 (Padrón Municipal 1940).

LOCAL DECISIONS

According to Barranquero Texeira (2012, 91), across the nation as a whole, between 2% and 5% of the total number of executed victims were women, with the percentage varying depending on the province. She points out that, in the case of women, death sentences were definitive as no mitigating circumstances could be offered. In this respect, the case of Arroyomolinos is exceptional. Here, it was finally decided that no women would be killed, even though the graves were already prepared. Remembering one of the women, Elvira, Rafael alluded to this fact:

Elvira was sentenced to death, she was one of the most notorious of them. Santiago's mother, Cupida's mother, and there were more ... I can't remember the others but there were more. They shaved them and later ... they let them go. (Rafael 2015, my translation)

Some participants have discussed the reasons why they think that the women were acquitted. According to Miguel, the reason is simply that '"el tío Gregorio", from the tobacconist's, got involved in the matter so that they wouldn't kill them'. This individual was, in Miguel's (2015) words, 'a religious man, from a devout family. They still are, but he was a good man and didn't want anybody to be killed.' Although Miguel believes that Gregorio was the one who interceded, Santiago describes it as a 'discussion' that developed among certain individuals in the village, with people taking different sides:

The principals in the village argued because some of them thought that the women had to be killed, but others said they should think about their children.

They would have nobody to look after them, and that's why they didn't kill them. (Santiago 2014b, my translation)

Santiago's brother, Blas, described the women's experience as follows:

> They were sentenced to death. Their graves were ready, by Alcántara's place, but some people interceded so they wouldn't be killed. 'But are you also going to kill the women?', they said. When they took them out of prison, they were taken to Church, to attend a Mass service and to confess. Son of a bitch, huh? (Blas 2014, my translation)

While the nature of Franco's rule dictated the broader principles at a national level, specific actions were implemented and decisions were made locally, creating a generally consistent but somewhat varied map of repressive practices. Of course, thousands of women were killed elsewhere. In the province of Seville alone, for instance, at least 727 women were executed *after* the end of the war: most of them were not involved in political activities, but were targeted because they were the wives, daughters or sisters of *rojos*. Twelve of those women were pregnant: this is what García Márquez describes as one of the most concealed acts of repression (García Márquez 2010; see also García Márquez 2007). It is not necessary to travel too far to find instances of women who were executed. In Cala, the village that lies just to the south of Arroyomolinos, the possibility of saving them was not discussed. Valentina describes what happened to her friend's sister:

> A woman from Cala has a bar, and the clock they have … it looks like it doesn't work. Why? Because she had a sister and they killed her, and they stopped the clock at that moment. That woman was pregnant, and she was told they would let her live so she would have the baby, and then they would kill her. But she said no, if they are going to kill her, she would take her baby with her, she wouldn't leave it behind. A little baby, a newborn, without a mother. My God. Maybe they wouldn't have killed her later, but she said no. (Valentina 2014, my translation)

More widely known is the case of Manuel, a man from Segura de León (in the province of Badajoz) who lived by himself in a dwelling near Arroyomolinos. In this case, Manuel had been widowed when his wife was killed during the repression in Segura:

> Manuel, was an elderly man, he came from Segura. They had killed his wife there. He knew many people here in the village, because when people were on their way to Segura they stopped by his house and brought him food. Your parents used to go there too, maybe when you were a baby. Do you remember this? That man lived there on his own, in a house on the way to Segura. He had

been hiding, and they had killed his wife, and he stayed there. (Valeria 2014, my translation)

Manuel himself had managed to escape death when the firing squad failed to hit him. According to Mercedes (2014), who used to visit him in the 1980s, when the firing squad shot at the group in which Manuel was included, he dropped at the same time as the rest. The assailants assumed everyone was dead and he managed to escape, helping, at the same time, a pregnant woman who had only been injured in one arm.

OTHER FORMS OF REPRESSION

The approximate figures for female executions (see above) do not begin to scratch the surface of the repression endured by women under Franco's rule. As noted above, the absence of men in the family also led to social and economic exclusion: in a context where men were the primary breadwinners, women became responsible for the survival of their families (Barranquero Texeira 2012, 95; see also Prieto Borrego 2009; Quiñonero Hernández 2009; Sánchez Sánchez 2009b). Not only were women expected to meet the supposedly moral Catholic standards imposed by Franco (García del Cid 2012; Nash

Figure 6.2   Manuel, from Segura de León, survived his execution. Family Archive.

2006), but forms of economic repression placed them in particularly vulnerable positions, especially when they were under pressure to feed their children. Valeria mentioned these repercussions when she recalled the experience of one of the men who was executed. She could not remember who he was, but she describes the scene, focusing particularly on his wife and children:

> One day they came to pull him out of his house, just there, around that corner. And his wife and his three children were screaming by the doorstep, 'don't take him, don't take him', crying. Imagine, that woman, with three young daughters, to bring them up on her own, no salary, no pay, nothing. My mum witnessed this and she could never forget it. Imagine the situation, there was so much hunger and she had to bring them up on her own. Sitting there by her doorstep, crying. She and many others, it happened to many families, here and in other villages. In Segura it was worse. (Valeria 2014, my translation)

Women who were widowed were left in particularly vulnerable positions. For instance, Isabel, the sister of Luisa García Valero (one of the women who were sentenced to death) lost her husband in one of the executions in the summer of 1936. Later, the Nationalists shaved her head, although her nephew is not sure whether she was one of the women who, like her sister, had been sentenced to death. Isabel was punished for her left-wing ideas, and because she was alone: without her husband, she was a prime candidate for becoming victimised.

> My auntie ... what happened was that she didn't want to sleep with the sergeant, or the captain, whatever he was. 'I will kill you then.' And she said, 'You will have to kill me, I am not sleeping with you.' She didn't want to do it ... he couldn't do what he wanted, so he shaved her head. He left her bald, and he took her for a walk [*la paseó*] like that, bald, in the village. I don't know if she had been sentenced, but this is what happened to her. (Juan Manuel 2015, my translation)

Very rarely have participants alluded to cases of sexual abuse in Arroyomolinos, and even when they do so, references tend to be implicit and impersonal. In addition to Juan Manuel's mention of his auntie's ordeal, we have seen Cupida's description of the time her mother spent in prison: 'They beat them, and did horrible things to them. ... She didn't want to breastfeed me' (Cupida 2014, my translation). Cupida does not explain which 'horrible things' were done, most likely because she does not know, but the context enables us to infer that there may have been forms of torture and sexual assault. Miguel is more explicit, although he does not mention any specific names, either of victims or culprits:

They took charge in the village in a way that there was no way back. They killed the best in the village. Santiago can tell you. Women without husbands, how were they going to feed their children? Well, you can imagine … they didn't have many options, because some men came to take advantage of them, because the children needed to eat. Complete and utter brutality. I have heard lots of things from the elderly … it makes you sick. The workers' women have to be respected. (Miguel 2014b, my translation)

In Miguel's case, I suspect that he knew some details, but he was not comfortable sharing them, perhaps because he was concerned about how I – as a friend, as an ethnographer, but also, importantly, as a woman – might react to any sensitive revelations. Similarly, when I asked Santiago whether he remembered any cases of sexual abuse, he responded that he was not aware of any specific cases, although 'there may have been some' (Santiago 2014b). It is likely that these repressive practices may have been kept private by the victims in most cases.

From an economic perspective, the financial responsibilities that women had to face in these difficult times also had a knock-on effect on their young families. Most children in families of peasants and *jornaleros* (day labourers) had to work to help sustain the domestic economy, regardless of whether they had been orphaned or not (see Chapter 5). Juan (2015) describes how he had to work 'from a young age, because this is what we had to do, always working in the countryside, so I went with my father to work when I was a small kid' (my translation). In his description of the scarcity that prevailed in the village at the time, he points to the fact that the situation was even worse for children who had lost their fathers:

Women became widows and they had to bring up the kids. Some of them had to go to soup kitchens. They set up some soup kitchen somewhere around there, I don't know where, but I remember there were soup kitchens. This is the struggle there was. Just hardship and suffering. (Juan 2015, my translation)

These 'soup kitchens' were established by Auxilio Social, an organisation created during the war in order to assist the victims, the unemployed, the elderly, children and pregnant women (Rodríguez Barreira 2011).[5] Local councils also constituted Boards for the Protection of Minors (Junta Local de Protección de Menores), which consisted of the local mayor, the priest, a doctor, a judge, a male teacher, a female teacher, a mother, a father and a worker. In Arroyomolinos, the Board was formally created on 8 November 1940, and included the local representative of Auxilio Social, who became treasurer (Junta Local de Protección de Menores 1940).

Despite the creation of these 'humanitarian' organisations, a closer look at the situation of orphaned children demonstrates that there were different classes of orphans. Pàmies (1977, 17) notes that, although the 'orphan' condition was bad for all those who suffered it, the circumstances varied dramatically from family to family. The children of those who supported the coup, she argues, lived in a context of 'non-traumatic inconvenience': war orphans whose fathers fell on the National side were protected through the award of pensions,[6] scholarships and other privileges that were reserved for the relatives of those who died for the Fatherland.

Meanwhile, the orphans of the 'reds', whose fathers or mothers (or both) were executed or imprisoned for defending the Republic, had to endure particular difficulties. Not only did they fail to receive the assistance that was available to 'good' families, but they also had to disguise, for a long time, the reasons why their parents were killed, imprisoned or forced to flee. This is illustrated by the testimony of Laura Palomo about her father, Tomás,[7] an army officer who remained loyal to the Republic and fought against the rebels:

> In my family, one uncle died at the battlefront, but my auntie and their children received some benefits because my uncle was right-wing. Apparently, the children of right-wing people were better calved than the left-wing ones, because we did not have any benefits. I do not think this is right. It should be recognised that children are not guilty of anything. (Madueño 1976, 21; see also Pàmies 1977, 18, my translation)

Laura Palomo, from Navas de Santiago (in the province of Badajoz), remembers how her grandparents were *paseados* (taken for a walk) because they would not tell the fascists where Laura's father was. After a while, they were found dead in a road ditch. Laura, her two brothers and her mother were thrown out of their home. When they were in the streets, she recalled,

> we moved from one place to another, working in our uncle's house, sleeping wherever we could. ... I became ill with tuberculosis and I suppose my mum did too, because she died of that illness. ... I stayed there [in the sanatorium of Ávila] for two years until I got better. (Madueño 1976, 21, my translation)

The experience of Laura and her mother not only underscores the consequences of Tomás' death on his widow and children, but also provides a good illustration of the unsuitability of Franco's 'humanitarian' organisations to provide real aid to those who were in need, which is in keeping with the broader programme of repression.

COMISIÓN COMARCAL

DEL

BENEMÉRITO CUERPO DE MUTILADOS

DE

GUERRA POR LA PATRIA

ARACENA

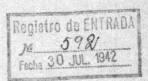

Registro de ENTRADA
Nº ___5921___
Fecha 30 JUL. 1942

El Iltm̃o.Sr. Presidente de la Comisión
Inspectora Provincial en su superior escrito nº
1,389,recibido con esta fecha me dice:
Tengo el gusto de comunicarle que esta Comisión Inspectora al objeto de facilitar a los Ca-
lleros Mutilados y Presuntos la extracción de r
raciones normales de viveres que mensualmente
suministran,ha acordado que las condiciones que
rijen desde el presente mes,la extracción de di
chas raciones sean las siguientes: Un Caballero
Mutilado o Presunto podrá extraer ademas de su
ración las correspondientes a dos mas,siempre q
que venga provisto de las oportunas autorizació
nes firmadas por ellos y selladas por la Comarcal,deviendo para ello el Caballero Mutilado
que autoriza a otro,para la extracción de su ra
ción,llevar personalmente dicha autorización
firmada a su Autoridad o Delegado de ella que
previa comprobación de su personalidad si esta
ofreciese duda la sellare.-
Debo significarle que los dias de suministr
durante el mes de la fecha, son 27,28 y 29,sie
do su composición 900 gramos de aceite,300 de
café y 300 de azucar.
Lo que tengo el honor de trasladar a V.S.
a fin de que haga llegar el presente a todos
los Caballeros Mutilados y Presuntos,residentes
en esa localidad.
Dios guarde a V.S. muchos años.
Aracena a 27 de Julio de 1,942.
El Presidente

Sr.Alcalde Presidente del Ayuntamiento de Arroyomolinos de León

Figure 6.3 Document stating that the Caballeros Mutilados (men who were maimed while fighting on the Nationalist side) have the right to claim the normal amount of food allocation through the rationing system, plus two additional portions. Ayuntamiento de Arroyomolinos de León.

MORAL EXPECTATIONS

Another organisation that was ostensibly created to support vulnerable individuals was the Patronato de Protección de la Mujer (Council for the Protection of Women). This was in charge, in theory, of protecting young women who were in need of help, or were at risk of exploitation. García del Cid (2012) explains what this protection really entailed in practice. The council focused on prostitutes, and generally arrested any women who did not meet the moral standards of the time. So, for example, young women who wore 'inappropriate' clothing or engaged in 'dishonourable' acts in public were considered to be immoral and were punished for it. Young women could be confined to this council – which was, in effect, a disguised penitentiary system – until they reached the age of twenty-five. In addition, the council dealt with victims of sexual abuse, particularly when fathers or brothers were the abusers. In these cases, the council did not rule for the detention and punishment of the aggressor, but of the victim. If the women became pregnant, not only were they disciplined and humiliated, but their babies were used in the child trafficking network that was developed from the beginning of the dictatorship: 'red' babies were taken away and given (or sold) to 'good' families that would bring them up in the National-Catholic values favoured by Franco's regime, thereby curing the 'Marxist' illness (Arroyo 2013; Escudero 2014).

Moral behaviour was, as discussed earlier, an expectation that fell much more heavily on women than it did on men, for women were considered to be the source of moral corruption, exemplified by the story of Adam and Eve. According to Franco's discourse of hereditary transmission, the political 'depravation' associated with the *rojas* was actually passed on through 'the poisonous germ of Marxism' that they carried, meaning that it was impossible to re-educate and integrate them in Franco's National-Catholic project (Narotzky and Smith 2002, 208–209). The very term '*roja*', used by right-wing individuals, has acquired a strong pejorative meaning. Valeria, who comes from a traditional right-wing family, describes some of the women who were sentenced to death as follows:

> The women were shaved and imprisoned, because they were *rojas*. Cupida's mother was one of them, she was also a *roja*, and Santiago's mother. She was very clever, it was amazing how much she read. But she was *rojísima* [as red as red can be], and her son is like her, he knows about everything and enjoys reading and writing. Cupida's mother was a *roja*, but Cupida isn't, and her father was a very good man, but her mother was *roja* and she also read a lot. (Valeria 2014, my translation)

Valeria's repetition of the term '*roja*' – and in particular the superlative '*rojísima*' – is useful insofar as it represents the extant views of certain sectors of the population, which still emerge in exchanges both at local and national level. In Arroyomolinos, Valentina explains how one of the *beatas* made fun of the *paseos* (walks) that some women were forced to take:

> She laughed at the women who were imprisoned. Women were given purgative so they would defecate, and they walked them in the streets while they were defecating. That woman said to Remedios, who was not a liar, as you know, 'last night it was so much fun', she had said. Remedios asked her why. Had there been a show or something? No, it turned out that the reason she was so amused was that the women were shitting themselves in the street. (Valentina 2014, my translation)

Valentina asked me whether I remembered this woman, who had already passed away. I responded that I knew who she was, but she then asked me not to write her name 'because she is no longer here'. She then described a clash she had experienced with that very same woman years later, after the end of the dictatorship:

> She said to me 'You were born out of the Church rubble.' And I replied, 'and you were born out of the rubble of those you killed.' And she never said anything else to me. But, you know, they used to say this as if this were a joking matter. When they take away one son, and then another, and then another, then you really see the joke, you know? (Valentina 2014, my translation)

Valentina ends her point on a sarcastic note. Of course, what seemed to be a laughing matter to some villagers, was a real tragedy for those who had to suffer it. The story of Lorenza's mother also elicits diverging responses (see Chapter 4 for background on her father's reclusion and imprisonment). Lorenza was conceived while her father was hiding in the family's cellar and everyone in Arroyomolinos thought that he had fled the village. When the local residents knew of her pregnancy, Lorenza's mother was criticised because everyone assumed she had cheated on her missing husband:

> I've been told my mum had a hard time. Everyone criticised her. How could she do that? Everyone talked about my mother making a cuckold of my father. They didn't know, of course ... they didn't know that it was actually my father's child – that I was his child – but she couldn't tell them. She soldiered on. (Lorenza 2015, my translation)

Lorenza's brother, Frasquito, remembers how his father started discussing the possibility of turning himself in so as to ease the social pressure on his wife, as it became unbearable. Lorenza was told that his father said the following words to his mother: 'My life is worth less than your honour' (Lorenza 2015, my translation). Even though she did not hear this sentence first-hand, she asserts that the knowledge of this statement had marked her deeply:

> My father eventually turned himself in. My mother didn't want him to do it, but he insisted that his life was worth less than her honour, because she was heavily criticised and scorned in the village. I was due in May, and he turned himself in to the Civil Guard in April, just so that people would know the truth and realise that she had not cheated on him. That was the whole purpose of it. (Lorenza 2015, my translation)

This was already 1939 and the war had just ended. In fact, according to Lorenzo's legal files, he turned himself in on 10 May 1939, a few days before Lorenza was born. Despite the seriousness of the matter, the memory of Lorenza's father hiding at home and her mother becoming pregnant is now remembered by some, not as the social scandal that it was in the 1930s, but as a funny anecdote. Nearly eighty years later, nothing much remains of the negative judgements and malicious gossip that had deeply marked the fate of this family. In hindsight, the social reading of the situation is different, but the drama that unfolded within the privacy of their home remains. Lorenza recalls their life without her father, and what happened when he finally returned home:

> I had it easier because I spent much time with my auntie, who didn't have any children. So, I ate more. Here, my mother and my siblings did what they could to survive. When my father came back, he had to rebuild ... build, really, his home, practically, from the beginning, as if he was a young man just starting out from scratch. Only that he wasn't really starting out. He had already built a life, and then he spent all those years in prison, and things were hard. (Lorenza 2015, my translation)

Ostensibly less dramatic, but equally reflective of the moral standards that were expected of women, is the case brought against Dolores Sánchez García, a villager who had moved and lived in Seville. Dolores' predicament illustrates not only the extent to which the legal system was designed to identify and punish any discordant elements, but also the fact that there were citizens who were prepared to report individuals in accordance with the regime's political and moral expectations. Dolores was arrested on 20 February 1939 after claiming, in a state of intoxication, that 'this regime should not exist' and 'communism is what should exist, instead of what we have now'. According to the person who reported the 'crime' (her landlord), Dolores then looked at Franco's picture and tried to pull it off the wall (C-6040/39). While her remarks were clearly offensive to Franco's regime, she was not 'simply' accused for uttering this string of 'provocations': Dolores was a prostitute and seemed to have been an alcoholic. The witnesses who testified in her case confirmed this:

> She is on the game but, when she is not drunk – something that rarely occurs – she has a good character and feelings, and she is not known to have taken part in any political activities, so it is supposed that she said what she said because of her complete state of inebriation. (C-6040/39)

In her defence, Dolores declared that she was very drunk and she could not remember anything, but she had not been a member of any political party. Another witness, however, clarifies that she attempted to pull down Queipo de Llano's – not Franco's – picture, and added that among her statements she had also said that 'this swine is the one that will execute me, because I am a *roja* and I still am'. The various witness accounts in Dolores' judicial case coincide in practically every detail, but there is one discrepancy that stands out. While the report issued by the Civil Guard states that it had not been possible to establish whether she had ever represented herself as an adherent of the Left, the investigation conducted by the Department of Surveillance (Comisaría de Investigación y Vigilancia) in Seville had found that

> this individual is an angry Marxist, of dreadful moral and public conduct. Every time she gets drunk – and she frequently does this – she starts to curse and swear at the *Generalísimo* [General Franco], General Queipo de Llano and other authorities of National Spain. (C-6040/39)

Considering the regime's essential moral rules, it is likely that the accusatory report issued by the Department of Surveillance is underpinned by prejudice, rather than verified facts, because of Dolores' 'dreadful moral and public conduct'.[8]

NOTES

1. Women's struggles for social rights had begun to develop in the nineteenth century, when women from the liberal bourgeoisie started to challenge the male-centred status quo. By the 1920s, freethinking women from all left-wing perspectives (such as Ángeles López de Ayala, Amalia Domingo Soler and María Baldó Massanet) had already fought for working-class women to have access to cultural and educational resources, encouraging them to join trade unions, which would in turn challenge capitalist exploitation and the obscurantism of the Church (Iturbe 2003, 20–23).

2. The thirteen women, all of whom were between 18 and 29 years old, were: Carmen Barrero Aguado, Martina Barroso García, Blanca Brissac Vázquez, Pilar Bueno Ibáñez, Julia Conesa Conesa, Adelina García Casillas, Elena Gil Olaya, Virtudes González García, Ana López Gallego, Joaquina López Laffite, Dionisia Manzanero Salas, Victoria Muñoz García and Luisa Rodríguez de la Fuente (Egido León

2009). A fourteenth woman, Antonia Torres Llera, was also to be executed on the same day, but an error in the spelling of her name delayed her death until 19 February 1940, when she was executed alongside 18 men (Fonseca 2011, 244–45).

3. See Abad (2008) and Abad (2013) for a discussion of prisoners' wives as silenced protagonists and their role in the pro-amnesty campaign.

4. In our conversations, Santiago often referred to this exchange, which he always remembered with a smile that suggested both nostalgia and amusement. Amusement because, as he explains, he was struck by the nature of the conversation as a young child, not so much for the political content – to which he had become accustomed at home – but because what initially seemed to be an ordinary conversation developed into an improvised public debate, which seemed to get louder at times. Santiago enjoyed the scene when he lived it as a child and still continued to cherish it in his eighties. Behind his smile, nonetheless, lay an additional meaning that revealed his adult opinion of his mother's libertarian politics. In one of our first meetings, when we were discussing the various ideological positions that were involved in the war, he declared that 'Libertarian Communists are so good, that they are good for nothing', expressing both admiration and well-meaning criticism at the same time. However, Santiago (2013) firmly believed that all factions on the Left 'want to achieve the same ends', but the difference is in 'how they propose to accomplish them.' In this respect, he did not reveal any hard feelings against any of the left-wing alternatives, as long as they pursued social justice.

5. The duties of this Board included keeping a register of everyone who was bringing up or looking after children, including wet nurses and guardians, and keeping records of the activities conducted by wet nurses, so as to regulate their work and keep track of the health of the children they fed. Auxiliary services for children included juvenile courts, reformatories and other institutions related to the 'protection' of women (Gobernador 1937).

6. The Board of Pensions and Aid for Orphans of the Glorious Movement (Junta Delegada del Servicio de Pensiones y Socorros de Huérfanos del Glorioso Movimiento) was created on 5 September 1938, according to a letter written by the Provincial Inspector of the Service (Huérfanos 1938).

7. Tomás Palomo wrote a letter to his wife and children, dated on the day of his execution on 20 December 1940, explaining that 'I only have two hours to live, but death does not frighten me. I am only concerned about the miserable circumstances in which I am leaving you with the children. I did not marry you to make you suffer. Although we only had a short time together, I know I tried to make you happy. But destiny changed our luck. Tell the children one day that they can walk with their heads up high, because their father did not die a criminal. He died because of his ideas' (in Madueño 1976, 21, my translation).

8. Either way, the sentence was ruled in her favour on 28 February 1940, one year after the charges were pressed against her. It concluded that: 'The proven facts [that she cursed the regime and its authorities] constitute the crime of provocation and glorification of the military rebellion. Taking into account the existing circumstances of her criminal responsibility, as she was in a state of transitory mental disorder due to her complete intoxication, she did not mean to commit this crime, as envisaged by article 173 of the Justice Military Code [Código de Justicia Militar]. The sentence henceforth rules that she be released on bail' (C-6040/39, my translation).

Chapter 7

Final Remarks

From Local Memories to Spain's Politics of Oblivion

FROM LOCAL TO NATIONAL MEMORIES

The themes that have emerged in this study are not exclusive to Arroyomolinos de León, nor do they encompass all the repressive practices that occurred across the country. For instance, the custom of 'walking' neighbours in local streets was a generalised tool of repression that served a dual purpose: to punish targeted individuals by humiliating them publicly, and to control the direct and indirect witnesses of these acts by generating fear in the minds of bystanders. Other tools of repression, such as murder and rape, were also widespread, although there were local variations in their implementation and in the ways in which decisions were made within each village. In Arroyomolinos, we find a clear example of this in the determination not to kill any women, which was entirely the result of local judgement. As we have seen, this does not mean that women were exempt from other forms of repression.

In addition to physical violence, social and economic forms of exclusion were also effective methods of punishment and control. During the post-war years, when food and other basic necessities were scarce, individuals who were forced to leave their homes were particularly affected. This was so in the case of Santiago's parents, who were banished from Arroyomolinos and had to find ways to survive in another village. In other cases, entire families left their homes in an attempt to escape the yoke of fascist rule, or to avoid the stigmatisation that came with being related to individuals who had been imprisoned or executed. Meanwhile, properties taken from Republican families (who sometimes were forced to live in the streets) were seized by the fascists and never returned to their rightful owners. These were only some of the repressive socio-economic measures that were taken against Franco's enemies.

I have argued that a Critical Ethnography of Memory, with orality as one of its core components, can help us to take account of the complex map of circumstances, actions and histories that develop within the framework of larger events. When people's local memories of events are placed at the centre of the enquiry, a wealth of stories can emerge from the apparent obscurity of the setting. By narrating their experiences, people help to keep their memories – and those of their peers – alive. As noted by del Río, these individuals 'are not intellectuals nor people trained in oratory, they come from very humble families, but one becomes absorbed in their testimonies. It is an unrepeatable generation that does not enjoy the public recognition it deserves' (del Río 2014c, 203). As this generation gradually disappears, it becomes increasingly important to preserve their message, and their knowledge of what happened, so that it remains of use to future generations.

LAYERS OF DENIAL

Stuart Christie's perceptive observation that the Spanish Civil War did not end on 1 April 1939, not even on 20 November 1975, when Franco died, summarises Spain's contemporary position in relation to its past. As Christie noted, there still remains much unfinished business:

> We owe an enormous debt to the hundreds of thousands of brave men and women who fought, suffered, died and lost loved ones in the cause for freedom, resisting the reactionary priest-ridden, gun and prison-backed Franco regime. They are the forgotten dead of generations to whom we owe a profound obligation of remembrance – and a duty of commemoration. (Christie 2011, 4)

Considering the way in which Spanish politics have been conducted since the death of the dictator in 1975, the essential task of preserving local memories has assumed the form of a struggle to recuperate them from complete oblivion. Consequently, eighty years after the military coup that led to the Spanish Civil War, Spain is still immersed in a cycle of recrimination, one that exists within various layers of denial, including those represented by private, local and national spheres. In his essays on Holocaust denial, Vidal-Naquet (1994) presents a critique of the 'assassins of memory', whose attempts to deny certain aspects of the past not only have direct consequences for the victims, but also produce a second period of aggression, when the causes and the reality of their suffering are doubted, de-contextualised and falsified. Against this 'mnemonicide' or assassination of memory (Morris 2007), and against any subsequent manifestations of 'social dementia' (see Chapter 2), the local memories unearthed by a Critical Ethnography of Memory provide important social-pedagogic tools to counteract any politically motivated distortions of the past.[1]

Anti-memory perspectives are usually supported by a number of premises, all of which constitute examples of how events can be misrepresented until there is little, or no real truth attached to them. First among these notions is the claim that the enduring scars in the Spanish psyche were caused by the equal involvement of all parties in the same kind of abuses. The intended outcome of this version is to erase the key fact that the war developed as a consequence of a military coup against the legitimate government of the Second Republic. The coup failed to 'liberate' the country, at least in the first instance, thanks to ordinary people who resisted the rebels.

Another point that is often ignored by the advocates of the anti-memory camp is that Franco was, in fact, the first one to monopolise the so-called 'memory business' when he won the war in 1939, a privilege that he maintained for the following 36 years. Not only did he dictate the public memory of his intervention in Spain's history – according to which he had saved the country from mayhem and social deterioration – but he also used his power to investigate people's pasts in order to find evidence of behaviours that would justify retrospective punishment. Ironically, from Franco's own perspective, it was acceptable (because politically convenient) to revisit the past.[2] It is not surprising that one of the key principles of the 1977 Amnesty Act was to ensure the non-retroactive nature of the crimes that could be punished under the new 'democratic' system.

Assigning all the failures associated with the 1930s to those who were present at the time, may also work against the cause of justice, since it shifts the focus away from those individuals who did not take the opportunity to redress these imbalances during the so-described 'model' transition to democracy. The problem is that this transition was built on the decision, made by Franco's socio-political heirs, that in order to maximise Spain's chances of establishing a democratic state, it was better to forget and move on. The victims of the war, and of the dictatorship, were not given any form of acknowledgement or reparation. Instead, they also became the victims of the transition.[3] Here, we observe another major irony: in their willingness to dismiss the past, these 'democrats' chose to ignore the first democratic period in the history of Spain: the Second Republic. Even the Spanish Home Office (Ministerio del Interior) stated in a tweet that the first democratic elections in Spain took place in 1977 (Público 2015).[4] Of course, the Second Republic was not without flaws. We should not forget, for instance, Azaña's repressive management of the protests in Casas Viejas in 1933, nor should we make the mistake, rather common in Spain, of assuming that the Republic and the Left are synonyms, since the left-wing government elected in 1931 was replaced, in 1933, by a conservative one that undid much of what the former had achieved. Nevertheless, despite these failings, the establishment of the Second Republic was, from the very beginning, a progressive project that tried to pull the country out of the endemic stagnation that affected every aspect of its development as a country.

In Spain, attempts to misrepresent the past and to advance the anti-memory discourse can be observed quite frequently. So, for example, on 8 October 2015, José Joaquín Peñarrubia, the Senate spokesperson for the Comisión de Hacienda y Administraciones Públicas (the Spanish equivalent of the Inland Revenue), was asked to explain why, once again,[5] there was no budget to support activities related to historical memory, namely exhumations of the victims of Franco's violence. Peñarrubia, visibly annoyed, stated that he found this question 'tiresome', and added that the people who continue asking for such support are 'a pain' (Torres Reyes 2015, my translation). According to him, the reason why there is no budget allocation for these activities is simply that 'there are no more graves to find, unless they insist on finding Federico García Lorca in all four cardinal points in Spain. Right now there is nowhere else to go' (Torres Reyes 2015, my translation). Yet, in the cemetery of Guadalajara alone, there are several unmarked graves with an estimated total of about 200 victims who are yet to be exhumed, identified and returned to their families. There is, in fact, much more work left to do (Escudero 2015).

Peñarrubia's words encapsulate the stance of the conservative Partido Popular, of which he is an active member, towards the memory of those who were defeated in the conflict, repressed for four decades, and silenced during and after the transition. The conservatives' standpoint is characterised by the unwavering refusal to enable effective channels for the open discussion of the past. The memory of the events that occurred over a period of forty years – events that affected the lives of millions of people – is sacrificed because circulation of this knowledge would inconvenience the current establishment.

Peñarrubia's intervention in the Senate was not an isolated event. Two years earlier, on 4 November 2013, Rafael Hernando, the spokesperson in the Congress for (once again) Partido Popular, claimed that 'some people only remembered their father when there were subsidies to find him' (Campelo 2013, my translation). The implication was that there is no real need to find anyone's relatives, and that the memory of the victims is merely an excuse to make a profit. Another similar view was expressed by writer Javier Cercas who, having made a name writing historical fiction about the war and the post-war period, claimed that memory is a 'great business', an industry, which has brought several types of profit to certain sectors of society, by which he meant not only financial gain, but also moral, political and artistic benefits (Espinosa Maestre 2015). Cercas' flippant remark is problematic not only because of its frivolity, but because it allows the anti-memory stance to gain strength.

Emilio Silva, founder of the Asociación para la Recuperación de la Memoria Histórica, or ARMH, noted that Peñarrubia's statement (see above) is not only untrue, 'but verges on an exercise in denial. It is almost like denying that there were concentration camps in Germany.' And he added,

> Right now we have a list of 1,539 people who disappeared and are being sought by their relatives. They meet the requirements of the protocol established by the United Nations. We know where they may be and, if we had the resources, we would be able to find them. (Torres Reyes 2015, my translation)

Denying the existence of the 1,539 victims that Silva mentions is part of the anti-memory stance, as is denying the estimated total of 114,000 'disappeared' across the country. According to Amnesty International, this figure places Spain in the second position in the rank of countries with the highest number of disappeared victims in a conflict: they are 'more than all the disappeared in South America's dirty wars of the 70s and 80s put together. Only Cambodia has more mass graves' (Westland 2013). As Kelly (1995, 9) points out in reference to the Troubles in Northern Ireland, perhaps only when we rid ourselves of the denials, can a stable peace develop.

Definitions of 'denial' range from refusals to comply with a request, to refusals to believe that a statement or allegation is true (Jackson 2006, 253). In medicine, denial serves as an important defence mechanism against some pressing reality, such as a threatening illness or some form of dependency. Denial can often impede or delay the necessary medical care, effectively making things worse for the patient and his or her immediate associates. The essential problem will not be confronted until the cycle of denial is interrupted. Jackson notes that 'living a life of denial can only be accepted as part of a personal religion (in its broadest sense): otherwise denial can only lead to deception'. On a social level, I would argue that denial can be best understood, in a broader context, in terms of ideology. Certainly, the pathological cycle of denial within which Spain is immersed is intrinsically political: not only is the root of the problem ideological, but so are the decisions that have been made since Franco's death. Of course, individuals also develop this form of defence mechanism at a more private level, in order to deal with the pain of their own experiences, or with the shame of having inflicted pain on others. Denial can be deeply embedded in the collective mindset, however, enabling societies to avoid having to deal with the deep human scars of a conflict that involved killing, torturing, betraying and repressing people who were often known to their executioners.

An extreme form of denial, Jackson (2006, 253) points out, 'is the rejection of a doctrine or belief in spite of historical evidence of its validity'. Failing to acknowledge the historical evidence of Franco's repression – and doing everything possible to eliminate that evidence – means that these events and the victims remain unrecognised. Different sides within the conflict deny facts about the other, but the state-sanctioned denial is an integral part of the official public or 'national' memory. All the 'democratic' governments that have followed the dictatorship have denied the need to revisit the past, the need to remember and, with that, they have also denied the rights of the victims, and the scale of their suffering. In a war that was essentially a class conflict, the opportunity to discuss and analyse what happened – openly and publicly – is also denied, rejecting the useful socio-political knowledge that may arise from such activity. The principle of denial, therefore, together with the consequences of individual acts, is intrinsically political.

This type of discourse spreads beyond the bounds of formal politics, and into other platforms for ideological messages, such as media representations. The education system, also, is rife with examples of historical oversimplification. In 2014, for instance, one of the language textbooks edited for the first year of primary school was withdrawn from the market, following criticisms about some of its content. Specifically, concerns were raised about the ways in which the deaths of two writers – Federico García Lorca and Antonio Machado – were described in the textbook. Of García Lorca, it stated that 'shortly after finishing his last play, *La casa de Bernarda Alba* [The House of Bernarda Alba], Federico *died*, near his village, during the Spanish war' (Anaya 2011a, my translation). Of course, García Lorca did not simply die, but was shot dead on 18 August 1936 in an execution characterised by fascist and homophobic undertones. Furthermore, the textbook explains that Antonio Machado became a member of the Real Academia Española (Spanish Language Academy) and, 'after a few years, he went to France with his family. He lived there until he passed away' (Anaya 2011b, my translation). Machado did not go to France with his family, but had to flee to Valencia and Barcelona with his mother in 1938, before being forced to cross the French border to escape the advance of the fascist troops in Catalonia. Machado died shortly afterwards, while in exile in Colliure, on 22 February 1939.

Luis Naranjo, former director of the Democratic Memory office run by the Junta de Andalucía (the Andalusian regional government), argued that there is a difference between adapting a complex concept for young children and twisting history through 'unbearable euphemisms' that 'betray historical truth and fail to meet the minimum standards of rigour' (García de Blas 2014, my translation). In effect, the example of this textbook is only one of the myriad instances in which historical references are simplified, to the extent that facts are completely distorted and the essence of the underlying truth is lost. Even certain books that have been marketed as attempts to address these gaps in pedagogic materials, have served only to perpetuate some of the old myths. So, for example, Arturo Pérez-Reverte's *La Guerra Civil contada a los jóvenes* (The Civil War told to youths) disseminates a number of misconceptions about the conflict, namely two deeply problematic notions: one, that there were two equally guilty sides in the war, hence erasing the fact of the fascist coup against a legitimate and democratic government (Becerra 2015); and two, that this was a fratricidal war, one that was waged between brothers for unexplained reasons, thereby depoliticising the conflict and concealing its ideological and socio-economic roots. Pérez-Reverte (2015) states that 'all wars are bad, but civil wars are the worst of them, because they bring friends, neighbours and brothers face to face with one another' (in Becerra 2015, my translation). The author's simplistic treatment of the events and the erasure of the rebels' responsibility – alongside the fact that the book is directed at young audiences – have outraged the victims and the memory associations.

Furthermore, Pérez-Reverte's book also emphasises that the war provided an opportunity for certain individuals to take revenge on others, and to take advantage of the situation to increase their personal assets. While it is true that there were multiple instances of opportunism and treachery (see Chapter 5 for some examples), underscoring this particular aspect of the conflict to the detriment of its core ideological and socio-economic causes, further reinforces the depoliticised reading of the war. Treacherous behaviour, after all, only took place within the framework of the conflict, and cannot be understood as a cause of the conflict. At most, it is one of the symptoms or consequences of the war (Becerra 2015). It is also true that the Republic was, in many ways, an unstable period (see, again, Chapter 5 for a discussion of some of the issues that characterised the period). However, the instability was, for the most part, caused by endemic socio-economic problems that were inherited by the Republic. The new state did not have sufficient time to redress these deeply rooted issues, but it did accomplish several social achievements, such as the establishment of universal suffrage in 1933, or the attempts to redistribute lands in favour of the labourers who worked on them. Yet, a frequent flaw in many assessments of the Republic is that these acts are seen, in retrospect, from the perspective of the war that ensued, as though this was the only and inevitable fate to which the Republic could possibly lead. While it is necessary to understand the context of the Second Republic in order to trace the political, economic and social developments in the 1930s, it is incorrect to suggest that the war was caused by the Republic.

MEMORY AND THE STATE

At the time of writing this conclusion, a landmark event has just taken place in the history of Spain: a mass grave has been exhumed, for the first time, following a court order (EFE 2016; Junquera 2016). The grave contained the bodies of twenty-one men and one woman, including the remains of Timoteo Mendieta, a trade unionist who was executed by a firing squad in 1939. His

Figure 7.1   Photographs of disappeared relatives, displayed in Plaza de la Gavidia (Seville)
the last Saturday of every month. Photograph by Ruth Sanz Sabido.

daughter, Ascensión Mendieta, travelled to Buenos Aires in 2013, when she was
eighty-eight years old, to provide her testimony before Argentinian Judge María
Servini. Given the refusal of the Spanish state to bring the culprits to justice, the
Argentinian case (commonly known as '*la querella argentina*') was opened on
14 April 2010, when the ARMH, together with victims and relatives, presented
a formal complaint in the hope that the Argentinian justice system would investigate Francoist crimes (Martínez 2010).

When I interviewed Ascensión in May 2015, Servini's petition to open
Timoteo's grave had been rejected by the Spanish court, and Ascensión was
still waiting for the next step in the judicial process. She told me that her sister
had passed away without being able to find their father's remains, and that all
she wanted now was to be buried with him (Mendieta 2015). Finally, in January 2016, Timoteo's remains, and those of twenty-one other victims, were
rescued from the plot into which they were thrown seventy-seven years ago.

Ascensión's private realm is marked by her family's story, her particular
experiences of Franco's repression, and her subsequent life trajectory and
emotions. However, her private sphere is deeply marked by the public context
of Franco's dictatorship and Spain's attitude to its authoritarian past. The distinction between both spheres therefore remains blurred. The act of reparation

that was celebrated on 30 January 2016 in the cemetery of Guadalajara, where Timoteo's grave was located, is also indicative of this indistinctness. Through this act, homage was not only paid to the twenty-two exhumed victims, but to all those who disappeared as the result of Francoist repression. Recognition is also paid to their relatives, who have not only suffered the loss of their loved ones and the myriad consequences of their absence, but have also endured the systemic oblivion imposed upon them by Spain's 'democratic' state. At this point, it is important to note that, while Timoteo's exhumation is the first one that has ever been conducted following a court order, it has not been the result of the Spanish government's work and cooperative attitude: an Argentinian judicial case, with an Argentinian judge and Argentinian lawyers, have been necessary to take action, based on the principle of universal justice: a concept that Spain's 1977 Amnesty Act refuses to recognise. The exhumations are conducted by the ARMH, a third-sector organisation that is primarily funded by a Norwegian trade union. The expensive DNA tests that follow the exhumations are conducted in an Argentinian lab on a voluntary basis. Not only is the entire process unsupported by the Spanish state, but as Escudero points out, the local council of Guadalajara (led by Partido Popular),

> after being forced to authorise the exhumation, has taken the opportunity to cash in: it applies the corresponding municipal taxes and charges 70 euro for every corpse that is exhumed and transferred from the cemetery to the place of interment chosen by the relatives. (Escudero 2015, my translation)

As usual, the act of reparation, which is part of the efforts to recognise the victims of past human rights violations (in line with international law), was organised by victims, relatives and associations. There was, once again, no official representation from the Spanish state to take responsibility, to acknowledge the fact that this is a state matter, to ask for forgiveness and to seek reconciliation with those individuals who lost their lives defending Spain's first democracy.

Even though most of the culprits are now dead, the victims' families have the right to know what happened to their disappeared relatives, to find out where their bodies are concealed, and to give them proper burial. Clara, a volunteer in the memory movement, alluded to more contemporary examples to describe people's need to locate their dead relatives:

> Today, if a person disappears, we hear about it in the news, the Police search for them ... that person's family wants to find out where they are, what has happened to them. For example, it is normal that Marta del Castillo's parents [a seventeen-year old girl who was kidnapped and murdered in Seville in 2009] want to know what happened to their daughter. They know she died, but they

want to know where she is. The authorities have searched for her everywhere, they have done all they could. And that's the way it should be. But then, I wonder, what's the difference between this person, or another, and those who disappeared years ago? Don't they deserve to be found too? Don't they deserve some dignity, to be recognized as human beings, rather than being treated as pieces of dirt, that can just be thrown anywhere? Don't their relatives matter? (Clara 2015, my translation)

Precisely because they do matter, international human rights law recognises that the concept of reparation should extend to the victims' families. The very notion of 'victim' also applies to the relatives of the individuals who were kidnapped, tortured or executed (Martínez 2010). For this reason, grandchildren, nieces and nephews are admitted as plaintiffs in the Argentinian case. They are also the current driving force of the memory movement that has grown to prominence since the beginning of the twenty-first century.

'IT WON'T HAPPEN AGAIN, WILL IT?'

Ramona, one of those children, now in her late eighties, described the experiences of some of her relatives after the fascist occupation of Arroyomolinos de León. After explaining that her mother had her head shaved and her uncle had been walked through the village after being forced to take castor oil, she covered her face with her hands and, deeply saddened by the memories, said:'*¿niña, esto no pasará otra vez, no?*' ('girl, it won't happen again, will it?'). Apart from the grief and desolation brought by the memory of those who suffered – to whom she often referred as '*pobrecitos*' (poor souls, or poor things) – there was real concern in Ramona's question. It was not a rhetorical question: Ramona looked straight into my eyes searching for a response to a very honest and very deeply felt anxiety. The directness of her question took me by surprise, but I tried to appease her by saying that something like that would not happen now.

   Perhaps a conflict of those dimensions would not develop in contemporary Spain, but the fact that there is an ongoing conflict is undeniable, when even the need to remember is questioned. However, as Lorenza explained when she talked about her father, it is important to remember the victims in order to give them their proper place, which was denied to them for decades:

For me, it is a reason to be proud, not a reason to hide. I am proud of my father, of my mother, of what they did, and what they went through, because there is no reason to hide. I am holding my head high. If they had stolen, or raped, or murdered anyone, I wouldn't be proud. Those would be reasons to be ashamed. But my parents didn't do any of those things. All they did was to work so they could provide for their family, and get on with life. That's all they did. Suffer, struggle, and have some ideas. As far as I am concerned, you can write all you like about what I am saying, because for me it is a reason to be proud. There is no reason why it should be hidden. (Lorenza 2015, my translation)

Lorenza's brother, Frasquito, agreed with her, although he also muttered, disheartened, that 'we are not going to fix anything'. His pessimism is the consequence of a lifetime of repression, but it is precisely for that reason that the cycle of silence, oppression and denial must be broken. Ramona's concern that a similar level of violence would return in the future, and the siblings' thoughts on the fate of their father, are local expressions of unresolved national issues. Their lingering fears are deeply rooted in the knowledge and experience of what it means to live in the shadows of a system that forced them and their families to disappear, if not physically, then in other ways that were designed to crush them economically, socially, culturally and morally – all because of their 'ideas'. Perhaps unknowingly, relatives often paraphrase Che Guevara's statement when they argue that Franco and his henchmen tried to kill people in order to kill their ideas. Yet, despite the destruction and the high toll of victims caused by Franco's ideological genocide, they did not succeed in obliterating the latter.

NOTES

1. Denial, however, is not performed only by agents who have an interest in concealing their responsibility in the repression of others. As argued by del Río, doubt and scepticism towards the victims' testimonies and towards the entire historical period 'constitute an indignity that makes us accomplices of the murderers' (del Río 2014d, 197, my translation).

2. A look into judicial cases that were opened during Franco's regime reveals countless testimonies that, in line with Franco's Law of Political Responsibilities (Ley de Responsabilidades Políticas), are based on memories of events that had occurred several years earlier (Narotzky and Smith 2002; Tamarit Sumalla 2011). These memories or narratives about the past were recognised as valid evidence during the course of trials, and were endorsed systemically to the extent that they were decisive in determining the fate of many men, women and their families. In these instances, the act of remembering was officially sanctioned insofar as it helped to reinforce the national cause and everything that it was built upon: the execration of everything that the Left – reformist or revolutionary – stood for, and the pathological retribution for the (moderate) changes that they had dared to pursue and implement during the Republic. The state's uses of memory in the judgement and punishment of the *rojos* therefore stands in clear contrast with the succession of post-Franco governments that

have always, from the beginning of the transition to democracy, publicly discouraged remembrance and obstructed any legal attempts to investigate and bring Franco's agents of repression to justice.

3. The leaders of the transition established an official framework that was based on oblivion but, in doing so, they shaped the ways in which the entire period would be remembered from that point. See, for example, Cuesta Bustillo (2007b) for a discussion of the development of memory *after* the dictatorship.

4. The tweet published by the Home Office (Ministerio del Interior) was described by the ARMH as an 'exercise in historical obscurantism', since the first democratic elections took place during the Second Republic (Público 2015). According to Emilio Silva, this type of historical distortion should never happen, much less so when the information is published by an official institution.

5. The government of Partido Popular stopped all budget allocations for this cause after it was elected in November 2011, contravening the 2007 Law of Historical Memory, according to which the state should help in the search and exhumation of mass graves.

References

Abad, Irene. 2008. "El papel de las 'mujeres de preso' en la campaña pro-amnistía". *Entelequia: Revista Interdisciplinar* 7:139–151.

Abad, Irene. 2009. "Las dimensiones de la 'represión sexuada' durante la dictadura franquista". *Revista de Historia Jerónimo Zurita* 84:65–86.

Abad, Irene, Iván Heredia Urzáiz and Sescún Marías Cadenas. 2012. "Castigos 'de género' y violencia política en la España de Posguerra. Hacia un concepto de 'Represión sexuada' sobre las mujeres republicanas", in *No es país para jóvenes*, edited by Alberto González González. Vitoria-Gasteiz: Instituto Valentín Foronda.

Abad, Irene. 2013. "Las mujeres de los presos: protagonistas silenciadas", in *Lugares de represión, paisajes de la memoria: aspectos materiales y simbólicos de la cárcel de Carabanchel*, edited by Carmen Ortiz García, 260–74. Madrid: Los Libros de la Catarata.

Abella, Rafael. 1982. "Los hechos del 10-A". *Historia 16* 76:48–55.

Ackelsberg, Martha A. 2004. *Free Women of Spain: Anarchism and the Struggle for the Emancipation of Women*. Oakland, CA: AK Press.

Adam, Barbara. 1990. *Time as Social Theory*. Oxford: Polity Press.

Aguilar, Paloma. 2000. *Memory and Amnesia: The Role of the Spanish Civil War in the Transition to Democracy*. Oxford: Berghahn Books.

Ahora. 1932. "Los graves sucesos de Arroyomolinos de León". *Ahora*, 8 October.

Alfaya, Javier. 2003. *Crónica de los años perdidos. La España del tardofranquismo*. Madrid: Temas de Hoy.

Amnistía Internacional. 2015. "Crímenes del franquismo: Cuatro mecanismos de Naciones Unidas piden a España 'investigar o extraditar'". *Amnistía Internacional*, 27 March. Available at: https://www.es.amnesty.org/noticias/noticias/articulo/crimenes-del-franquismo-cuatro-mecanismos-de-naciones-unidas-piden-a-espana-investigar-o-o-ext/.

Anaya. 2011a. "Unidad 7: El lagarto está llorando". Lengua Primero Educación Primaria. Madrid: Grupo Anaya.

Anaya. 2011b. "Unidad 11: Era un niño que soñaba". Lengua Primero Educación Primaria. Madrid: Grupo Anaya.

Antequera Luengo, Juan José and Juan José Luengo Jiménez. 2008. *Expedientes Carcelarios de Arroyomolinos de León y Cabezas Rubias*. Prisión Provincial de Huelva, 1936-1939. Sevilla: Facediciones.

Antonia. 2015. Interview, 20 August. Arroyomolinos de León.

Aparicio, Abel. 2015. "Cunetas". *Alboradas en los zurrones del pastor*. Available at: http://abelaparicio.blogspot.co.uk/2015/04/alboradas-en-los-zurrones-del-pastor. html.

Aramburu, Joaquín. 1938. "Expediente instruido para la constitución de esta Juna Local Delegada de la suscripción Queipo de Llano, para la Virgen de la Macarena". Sevilla: Junta Recaudadora de la Suscripción Queipo de Llano para la Virgen de la Macarena.

Aróstegui, Julio. 1998. *Historia, experiencia y coetaneidad. Ensayo de fundamentación de la Historia del Presente*. Madrid: Universidad Complutense.

Arroyo, Soledad. 2013. *Los bebés robados de sor María. Testimonios de un comercio cruel*. Barcelona: RBA Libros.

Ashford, L. J. 1960. *The History of the Borough of High Wycombe from its Origins to 1880*. London: Routledge and Kegan Paul.

Assmann, Jan. 1995. "Collective Memory and Cultural Identity". *New German Critique* 65:125–33.

Assmann, Jan. 2010. "Communicative and Cultural Memory", in *A Companion to Cultural Memory Studies*, edited by Astrid Erll and Ansgar Nünning, 109–18. Berlin: De Gruyter.

Atkinson, Paul. 1992. *The Ethnographic Imagination: Textual Constructions of Reality*. London: Routledge.

Aurelio. 2002. Interview conducted by Rafael Cid on 9 September 2002. Unpublished notes.

Ayuntamiento de Arroyomolinos. 1944. "Acta Sesión Extraordinaria". Arroyomolinos de León, 12 March.

Ayuntamiento de Arroyomolinos. 1958. "Actas de la Junta Municipal de Educación". Arroyomolinos de León, 28 October.

Ayuntamiento de Arroyomolinos. 1959. "Acta de la Sesión Extraordinaria de la Junta Municipal de Educación Primaria". Arroyomolinos de León, 10 September.

Barke, Michael. 1997. "The Survival of 'Archaic' Forms of Retailing in Rural Malaga Province, Southern Spain". *Journal of Cultural Geography* 16(2):77–98.

Barker, Richard. 2007. *El Largo Trauma de un Pueblo Andaluz. República, represión, guerra, posguerra*. Sevilla: Tréveris.

Barker, Richard. 2012. *Skeletons in the Closet, Skeletons in the Ground: Repression, Victimization and Humiliation in a Small Andalusian Town: The Human Consequences of the Spanish Civil War*. Brighton: Sussex Academic Press.

Barranquero Texeira, Encarnación. 2012. "Investigaciones sobre repression franquista en Andalucía desde una perspectiva de género", in *Andaluzas en la Historia. Reflexiones sobre política, trabajo y acción colectiva*, edited by María Dolores Ramos Palomo, 91–110. Sevilla: Fundación Pública Andaluza Centro de Estudios Andaluces.

Bauman, Richard. 1986. *Story, Performance, and Event: Contextual Studies of Oral Narrative*. Cambridge: Cambridge University Press.

Beatriz. 2015. Interview, 22 May. Madrid.

Becerra, David. 2015. "La absurda guerra de Pérez-Reverte". *El Confidencial*, 11 November. Available at: http://www.elconfidencial.com/cultura/2015-11-11/perez-reverte-guerra-civil-contada-a-los-jovenes_1091187/.

Beevor, Antony. 2006. *The Battle for Spain. The Spanish Civil War 1936–1939*. London: Phoenix.

Beevor, Antony and Artemis Cooper. 2004. *Paris After the Liberation: 1944–1949*. London: Penguin Books.

Bergson, Henri. 2007. *Matter and Memory*. Mineola: Dover Publications.

Berman, Marshall. 1982. *All That Is Solid Melts Into Air: The Experience of Modernity*. New York: Penguin.

Bermúdez, Elena. 2012. "Dale alas y volará, al pueblo de Andalucía". *El Cabrero, porque callar es morir*. Published 30 June 2012. Accessed on 18 August 2015. https://elcabrero40aniversario.wordpress.com/tag/antonio-sousa/.

Bernecker, Walther L. 1982. *Colectividades y Revolución Social. El anarquismo en la Guerra civil española, 1936-1939*. Barcelona: Crítica.

Bierzo Diario. 2015. "El premio recibido por la ARMH garantiza dos años al laboratorio. *Bierzo Diario*, 10 May. Available at: http://bierzocomarca.eu/index.php/sociedad/48/21217-2015-05-10-21-28-08.

Bjerg, Helle and Lisa R. Rasmussen. 2012. "Prompting techniques: researching subjectivities in educational history". *Oral History* 40(1):89–98.

Blackman, Shane. 2007. "Hidden ethnography: Crossing emotional borders in qualitative accounts of young people's lives". *Sociology* 41(4):699–716.

Blas. 2014. Interview, 21 August. Arroyomolinos de León.

Blas. 2015. Interview, 27 August. Arroyomolinos de León.

Bloor, M., and F. Wood. 2006. *Keywords in qualitative methods: A vocabulary of research concepts*. London: Sage.

BOE. 1940. "Decreto fundacional de 1 de abril de 1940". *Boletín Oficial del Estado*, 2 April. Available at: http://www.cuelgamuros.com/txt/historia/decreto.html.

Bolloten, Burnett. 2015. *The Spanish Civil War: Revolution and Counterrevolution*. London: The University of North Carolina Press.

Bowers, Claude G. 1954. *My Mission to Spain: Watching the Rehearsal for World War II*. New York: Simon and Schuster.

Boyer, M. Christine. 2011. "From *The City of Collective Memory: Its Historical Imagery and Architectural Entertainments*", in *The Collective Memory Reader*, edited by Olick, Jeffrey K., Vered Vinitzky-Seroussi, and Daniel Levy, 378–81. Oxford: Oxford University Press.

Brockmeier, Jens, and Donal Carbaugh. 2001. "Introduction", in *Narrative and Identity: Studies in Autobiography, Self and Culture*, edited by Jens Brockmeier and Donal Carbaugh, 1–22. Amsterdam: John Benjamins.

C-869/37. Case against Manuel García Sánchez.

C-2375/39. Case against Aurelio Domínguez Silva.

C-2382/39. Case against Adolfo Lozano Infante.

C-2468/39. Case against Vicente García Martín.

C-2469/39. Case against Lorenzo Agudo Pizarro.

C-2484/39. Case against Francisco Agudo Pizarro.

C-6040/39. Case against Dolores Sánchez García.

Caamaño, Javier. 2015. "Los españoles que huyeron de la Guerra y acabaron en otra pesadilla". *Público*, 12 September. Available at: http://www.publico.es/politica/espanoles-huyeron-guerra-y-acabaron.html.

Campelo, Patricia. 2013. "Denuncian a Hernando por decir que las víctimas de Franco sólo se acuerdan de sus familiares 'cuando hay subvenciones'". *Público*, 25 November. Available at: http://www.publico.es/politica/denuncian-hernando-decir-victimas-franco.html.

Campoamor, Clara. 2001. *El voto femenino y yo: mi pecado mortal*. Sevilla: Instituto Andaluz de la Mujer, Junta de Andalucía.

Campos, Santiago. 2003. "Poema escrito el 23 aniversario de la muerte de Federico García Lorca". *Cascarrabias* 16:14.

Campos, Santiago. 2006. "El pueblo y los molinos". *Cascarrabias* (April):4.

Carballar, Olivia. 2011. "La 'Libertaria' muere de forma official 75 años después". *Público*, 12 July. Available at: http://memoriahistorica.org.es/s1-news/c1-ultimasnoticias/la-qlibertariaq-muere-de-forma-oficial-75-anos-despues/.

Cardona, Gabriel. 1982. "La conspiración". *Historia 16* 76:44–47.

Carlos. 2014. Interview, 17 August. Arroyomolinos de León.

Casanova, Julián. 2008. "La historia social de los vencidos". *Cuadernos de Historia Contemporánea* 30:155–63.

Casanova, Julián. 2010. *De la calle al frente: El anarcosindicalismo en España*. Barcelona: Crítica.

Casanova, Julián. 2013. *A Short History of the Spanish Civil War*. London: IB Tauris.

Casey, Edward S. 2008. "Public Memory in Place and Time". In *Framing Public Memory*, edited by Kendall R. Phillips, 17–44. Tuscaloosa: University of Alabama Press.

Casey, Edward S. 2008. "Public Memory in Place and Time". In *Framing Public Memory*, edited by Kendall R. Phillips, 17–44. Tuscaloosa: University of Alabama Press.

CEAQUA. 2015. "España debe extraditar o juzgar a los responsables de violaciones graves de DD HH - Expertos de la ONU". *CEAQUA*, 27 March. Available at: http://www.ceaqua.org/espana-debe-extraditar-o-juzgar-a-los-responsables-de-violaciones-graves-de-dd-hh-expertos-de-la-onu/.

Chacko, Elizabeth. 2004. "Positionality and praxis: fieldwork experiences in rural India". *Singapore Journal of Tropical Geography* 25(1):51–63.

Chientaroli, Natalia. 2014. "Los 10 suspensos de la ONU a España en memoria histórica". *El Diario*, 28 August. Available at: http://www.eldiario.es/sociedad/ONU-Espana-Guerra-Civil-franquismo_0_297120710.html.

Christie, Stuart. 2011. "Introduction to 1st edition by Stuart Christie: The Spanish War that never died", in *The Aftermath: 75th Anniversary of Spanish Civil War (1936-2011)*, 4–5. Commemorative booklet of the Spanish Civil War by Trade Unionists in North West of England.

Cid, Rafael. n.d. Notes on judicial cases concerning residents of Arroyomolinos de León. Personal archive. Unpublished.

Cintas Guillén, Maribel. 2006. "Andalucía 1935: Retrato en el olvido", in *Pierre Verger: Andalucía 1935, Resurrección de la memoria*, edited by Fundación Centro de estudios Andaluces, 67–69. Sevilla: Consejería de la Presidencia de la Junta de Andalucía.

Clara. 2015. Interview, 12 May. Barcelona.

Cobo Romero, Francisco. 1992. *Labradores, campesinos y jornaleros. Protesta social y diferenciación interna del campesinado jiennense en los orígenes de la guerra civil (1931-1936)*. Córdoba: La Posada.

Cobo Romero, Francisco. 2012. "Nuevas categorías conceptuales y teóricas para el estudio de la represión franquista en Andalucía", in *La Represión Franquista en Andalucía. Balance historiográfico, perspectivas teóricas y análisis de resultados*, edited by Francisco Cobo Romero, 31–63. Sevilla: Centro de Estudios Andaluces.

Cobo Romero, Francisco. 2013. "La cuestión agraria y las luchas campesinas en la II República, 1931-1936". *Hispania Nova: Revista de Historia Contemporánea* 11(n.p.).

Connerton, Paul. 1989. *How Societies Remember*. Cambridge, MA: Cambridge University Press.

Collier, George A. 1987. *Socialists of Rural Andalusia. Unacknowledged Revolutionaries of the Second Republic*. Standford: Stanford University Press.

Costa y Martínez, Joaquín. 1912. *La tierra y la cuestión social*. London: Forgotten Books.

Criado, Lorena. 2006. "El ronronear del valle". *Cascarrabias* (April):11–12.

Cuesta Bustillo, Josefina. 1984. "Estudios sobre el catolicismo social español (1915–1930): un estado de la cuestión". *Studia Historica: Historia Contemporánea* 2:193–244.s

Cuesta Bustillo, Josefina. 2007a. "'Las capas de la memoria'. Contemporaneidad, sucesión y transmisión generaciones en España (1931–2006)". *Hispania Nova: Revista de Historia Contemporánea* 7.

Cuesta Bustillo, Josefina. 2007b. "Recuerdo, silencio y amnistía en la Transición y en la democracia españolas (1975-2006)". *Studia Historica: Historia Contemporánea* 25:125–65.

Cupida. 2014. Interview, 13 August. Arroyomolinos de León.

Darnaude, Ignacio. 2006. "Arroyomolinos y Guerra Civil.doc". Email correspondence with Juan Ortiz Villalba, 18 May. Available at: http://www.ignaciodarnaude.galeon.com/textos_diversos/index.html.

Dávila Balsera, Paulí. 2005. "The educational system and national identities: the case of Spain in the twentieth century". *History of Education* 34(1):23–40.

De Gaulle, Charles. 1944. "25 de agosto de 1944 - Discurso del general de Gaulle en el Ayuntamiento de Paris". *Fondation Charles de Gaulle*, http://www.charles-de-gaulle.es/25-de-agosto-de-1944-discurso-pronunciado-en-el-ayuntamiento-de-paris.html.

De Guzmán, Eduardo. 2014. *La muerte de la esperanza. Segunda parte: El Puerto de Alicante (Así terminó la guerra de España)*. Hastings: Christie Books.

Del Arco Blanco, Miguel Ángel. 2007. *Hambre de Siglos. Mundo rural y apoyos sociales del franquismo en Andalucía Oriental, 1936-1951*. Granada: Comares.

Del Arco Blanco, Miguel Ángel, and Nadia Martínez Espinar. 2009. "Conflictividad ambiental y poder local en el primer franquismo, el 'lobby de la madera' en Santa Fe (1936–1951)". *Historia Actual Online* 20 (Otoño):7–18.

Del Rey, Fernando. Ed. 2011. *Palabras como puños. La intransigencia política en la Segunda República española*. Madrid: Tecnos.

Del Río, Ángel. Ed. 2014a. *Memoria de las Cenizas. Andaluces en los campos Nazis*. Sevilla: Aconcagua Libros.

Del Río, Ángel. 2014b. "Sociología de la deportación andaluza", in *Memoria de las Cenizas. Andaluces en los campos Nazis*, edited by Ángel del Río, 75–85. Sevilla: Aconcagua Libros.

Del Río, Ángel. 2014c. "Haban los supervivientes: el valor de testimoniar", in *Memoria de las Cenizas. Andaluces en los campos Nazis*, edited by Ángel del Río, 203–04. Sevilla: Aconcagua Libros.

Del Río, Ángel. 2014d. "El deber de recordar", in *Memoria de las Cenizas. Andaluces en los campos Nazis*, edited by Ángel del Río, 195–202. Sevilla: Aconcagua Libros.

Drake, Philip. 2003. "'Mortgaged to music': new retro movies in 1990s Hollywood cinema", in *Memory and Popular Film*, edited by Paul Grainge, 183–201. Manchester: Manchester University Press.

Dronne, Raymond. 1984. *Carnets de route d'un croisé de la France libre*. Paris: France-Empire.

EFE. 2015a. "Margallo homenajea a los españoles muertos en Mauthausen y destaca el deber de la memoria". *El Mundo*, 10 May. Available at: http://www.elmundo.es/espana/2015/05/10/554f394d268e3e79268b457b.html.

EFE. 2015b. "Homenaje a los españoles que combatieron a Alemania en Rusia". *La Nueva España*, 8 March. Available at: http://www.lne.es/espana/2015/03/08/homenaje-espanoles-combatieron-alemania-rusia/1723925.html.

EFE. 2016. "Ascensión Mendieta consigue justicia: exhumarán el cadáver de su padre asesinado en 1939". *Público*, 15 January. Available at: http://www.publico.es/politica/ascension-mendieta-cumple-sueno-exhumaran.html.

Egido León, Ángeles. 2009. *El perdón de Franco. La represión de las mujeres en el Madrid de posguerra*. Madrid: Catarata.

El Cabrero. 2012. Fandangos Republicanos. Available at: http://grandesmontanas1204.blogspot.co.uk/2012/04/fandangos-republicanos-el-cabrero.html.

El Correo de Andalucía. 1932. "De los sucesos de Arroyomolinos de León". *El Correo de Andalucía*, 8 October, p. 3.

Elena. 2013. Interview, 27 August. Arroyomolinos de León.

Erll, Astrid. 2010. "Cultural Memory Studies: An Introduction". In *A Companion to Cultural Memory Studies*, edited by Astrid Erll and Ansgar Nünning, 1–15. Berlin: De Gruyter.

Escudero, Rafael. 2014. "Road to Impunity: The Absence of Transitional Justice Programs in Spain". *Human Rights Quarterly* 36(1):123–46.

Escudero, Rafael. 2015. "Necesitamos un gobierno de izquierdas". El Diario, 31 January. Available at: http://www.eldiario.es/contrapoder/memoria_historica-represion_franquista_6_479512064.html.

Escudero, Rafael, Patricia Campelo, Carmen Pérez González, and Emilio Silva. 2013. *Qué hacemos por la memoria histórica*. Madrid: Ediciones Akal.

Escudero Delgado, M. Lourdes. 1995. "La beneficencia municipal en Guadalajara: El padrón de familias pobres (1885-1936)". *Añil: Cuadernos de Castilla-La Mancha* 6:61–65.

Espinosa Maestre, Francisco. 2005 [1996]. *La Guerra Civil en Huelva.* Huelva: Diputación Provincial de Huelva. Fourth Edition.

Espinosa Maestre, Francisco. 2011 [2003]. *La columna de la muerte. El avance del ejército franquista de Sevilla a Badajoz.* Barcelona: Editorial Crítica. Fifth Edition.

Espinosa Maestre, Francisco. 2012a. *Guerra y represión en el sur de España.* Valencia: Universidad de Valencia.

Espinosa Maestre, Francisco. 2012b. *Contra la República. Los 'sucesos de Almonte' en 1932.* Sevilla: Aconcagua Libros.

Espinosa Maestre, Francisco. 2015. "Cercas y el gran negocio de la 'memoria histórica'". *Público*, 12 April. Available at: http://blogs.publico.es/otrasmiradas/4370/cercas-y-el-gran-negocio-de-la-memoria-historica/.

Ferrero, Jesús. 2011. *Las Trece Rosas.* Madrid: Siruela.

Fidalgo, Carlos. 2015. "Milagros pierde el miedo a contar que mataron a su madre". *Diario de León*, 9 November. Available at: http://www.diariodeleon.es/noticias/bierzo/milagros-pierde-miedo-contar-mataron-madre_1022127.html.

Finberg, H. P. R. 1973. "Local History", in *Local History. Objective and Pursuit*, written by H. P. R. Finberg and V. H. T. Skipp, 25–44. Newton Abbot: David & Charles.

Fine, Michelle. 1994. "Dis-stance and Other Stances: Negotiations of Power Inside Feminist Research", in *Power and Method: Political Activism and Educational Research*, edited by Andrew David Gitlin, 13–35. London: Routledge.

Fine, Michelle and Lois Weis. 1998. *The Unknown City: The Lives of Poor and Working-Class Young Adults.* Boston: Beacon Press.

Fine, Michelle, Lois Weis, Susan Weseen, and Loonmum Wong. 2000. "For whom? Qualitative research, representations and social responsibilities", in *Handbook of Qualitative Research*, edited by N. K. Denzin and Y. S. Lincoln, 107–31. London: Sage.

Fiscalía Provincial de Tasas. 1941. "Expediente 183". *Fiscalía Provincial de Tasas, Badajoz.* 18 April.

Flecha García, Consuelo. 2011. "Education in Spain: Close-up of Its History in the 20th Century". *Analytical Reports in International Education* 4(1):17–42.

Fonseca, Carlos. 2011. *Trece Rosas Rojas.* Madrid: Planeta.

Foucault, Michel. 2004. *'Society Must Be Defended': lectures at the Collège de France, 1975–76.* London: Penguin Books.

Foucault, Michel. 2011. "From 'Film in Popular Memory: An Interview with Michel Foucault'", in *The Collective Memory Reader*, edited by Olick, Jeffrey K., Vered Vinitzky-Seroussi, and Daniel Levy, 252–53. Oxford: Oxford University Press.

Fran. 2015. Interview, 28 August. Arroyomolinos de León.

Fraser, Ronald. 1979. *Blood of Spain.* London: Allen Lane.

Frasquito. 2015. Interview, 27 August. Arroyomolinos de León.

Freeman, Mark. 2001. "From substance to story: Narrative, identity and the reconstruction of the self", in *Narrative and Identity: Studies in Autobiography, Self and Culture*, edited by Jens Brockmeier and Donal Carbaugh, 283–98. Amsterdam: John Benjamins.

Galtung, Johan and Mari H. Ruge. 1965. "The structure of foreign news. The presentation of the Congo, Cuba and Cyprus crises in four Norwegian newspapers". *Journal of Peace Research* 2(1):64–90.

García Bañales, Miguel. 2015. "La Valderas Roja, 'Valderas, Moscú de España'" *Astorga Redacción*, 6 August. Available at: http://astorgaredaccion.com/not/9221/la-valderas-roja-valderas-moscu-de-espana-/.

García de Blas, Elsa. 2014. "Anaya retira un libro de primaria que endulzaba la muerte de Lorca y Machado". *El País*, 5 May. Available at: http://sociedad.elpais.com/sociedad/2014/05/05/actualidad/1399303325_297198.html.

García del Cid, Consuelo. 2012. *Las Desterradas Hijas de Eva*. Granada: Algón Editores.

García Márquez, José M. 2007. *La represión militar en la Puebla de Cazalla (1936-1943)*. Sevilla: Fundación Centro de Estudios Andaluces.

García Márquez, José M. 2010. "El triunfo del golpe militar: el terror en la zona ocupada", in *Violencia roja y azul. España, 1936–1950*, edited by Francisco Espinosa Maestre, 93–101. Barcelona: Crítica.

García Márquez, José M. 2013. *República, Sublevación y Represión en el Castillo de las Guardas (1931-1944)*. Sevilla: Atrapasueños.

Garde-Hansen, Joanne. 2011. *Media and Memory*. Edinburgh: Edinburgh University Press.

Garrido González, Luis. 1990. *Riqueza y tragedia social. Historia de la clase obrera en la provincia de Jaén (1820–1939)*. Jaén: Diputación Provincial.

Gavilán, Enrique. 2004. "De la imposibilidad y de la necesidad de la 'memoria histórica'". In *La memoria de los olvidados. Un debate sobre el silencio de la represión franquista*, edited by Emilio Silva, Asunción Esteban, Javier Castán and Pancho Salvador, 55–65. Valladolid: Ámbito.

Geertz, C. 1988. *Works as Lives: The Anthropologist as Author*. Cambridge: Polity.

Gil Honduvilla, Joaquín. 2004. "La sublevación de Julio de 1936: proceso militar al General Romerales". *Historia Actual Online* 4:99–113.

Gilmore, David. 1977. "The Class Consciousness of the Andalusian Rural Proletarians in Historical Perspective". *Ethnohistory* 24(2):149–61.

Gobernador. 1937. "Circular". Junta Provincial de Protección de Menores, Huelva. 28 July.

Gobo, Giampietro. 2008. *Doing Ethnography*. London: Sage.

Goebbels, Joseph P. 1998. *La verdad sobre España*. Bilbao: Iralka.

Gómez Bravo, Gutmaro. 2009. *El Exilio Interior: Cárcel y Represión en la España Franquista, 1939-1950*. Madrid: Taurus.

Gómez Bravo, Gutmaro, and Jorge Marco. 2011. *La obra del miedo*. Barcelona: Península.

González de Molina, Manuel. 2014. "La tierra y la cuestión agraria entre 1812 y 1931: latifundismo versus campesinización", in *La Cuestión Agraria en la Historia de Andalucía: Nuevas Perspectivas*, edited by Manuel González de Molina, 23–59. Sevilla: Centro de Estudios Andaluces.

González Duro, Enrique. 2012. *Las rapadas. El franquismo contra la mujer*. Madrid: Siglo XXI de España Editores.

González Fernández, Ángeles. 2006. "Víctimas y Heroínas: La Mujer en la Guerra Civil", in *Andalucía y la Guerra Civil. Estudios y Perspectivas*, edited by Leandro Álvarez Rey, 109–29. Sevilla: Universidad de Sevilla and Diputación de Sevilla.

Gordillo, Cecilio. 2015. "La memoria pendiente: reparar el dolor de las mujeres e inscribir a las víctimas en el Registro". *Andalucesdiario.es*, 6 December. Available at: http://www.andalucesdiario.es/politica/memoria-historica-y-elecciones-generales/.

Graham, Helen. 2012. *The War and Its Shadow. Spain's Civil War in Europe's Long Twentieth Century*. Eastbourne: Sussex Academic Press.

Grainge, Paul. 2003. "Introduction: memory and popular film", in *Memory and Popular Film*, edited by Paul Grainge, 1–20. Manchester: Manchester University Press.

Gudín de la Lama, Enrique, Gutiérrez Flores, Jesús, Obregón Goyarrola, Fernando, and Menéndez Criado, Enrique. 2013. "La depuración franquista del profesorado cántabro durante la Guerra Civil". *Historia Actual Online* 30:53–68.

Guillemin, M. and L. Gillam. 2004. "Ethics, reflexivity and 'ethically important moments' in research". *Qualitative Inquiry* 10(2):261–80.

Halbwachs, Maurice. 1992. *On Collective Memory*. Chicago: University of Chicago Press.

Hallowell, N., J. Lawton, and S. Gregory. 2005. *Reflections on Research: The Realities of Doing Research in the Social Sciences*. Maidenhead: McGraw-Hill.

Hamilton, Paula, and Linda Shopes. 2008. "Introduction: Building Partnerships between oral history and memory studies", in *Oral History and Public Memories*, edited by Paula Hamilton and Linda Shopes, vii–xvii. Philadelphia: Temple University Press.

Harcup, Tony and Deirdre O'Neill. 2001. "What is news? Galtung and Ruge revisited". *Journalism Studies* 2(2):261–80.

Harth, Dietrich. 2010. "The Invention of Cultural Memory", in *A Companion to Cultural Memory Studies*, edited by Astrid Erll and Ansgar Nünning, 85–96. Berlin: De Gruyter.

Harvey, D. 1996. *Justice, Nature and the Geography of Difference*. Cambridge, MA: Blackwell Publishers.

Heley, Jesse. 2011. "On the Potential of Being a Village Boy: An Argument for Local Rural Ethnography". *Sociologia Ruralis* 51(3):219–37.

Hernández, Miguel. 1937. "Vientos del pueblo me llevan", in *Viento del pueblo. Poesía en la Guerra*, edited by José Carlos Rovira and Carmen Alemany Bay (2010). Madrid: Ediciones de la Torre.

Hernández de Miguel, Carlos. 2015. *Los últimos españoles de Mauthausen*. Barcelona: Ediciones B.

Hernández Velasco, Irene. 2015. "Felipe VI, en París: 'Quienes intentaron acallar el espíritu de libertad mediante el terror fracasaron'". *El Mundo*, 3 June. Available from: http://www.elmundo.es/espana/2015/06/03/556e3e92e2704e4b338b4590. html.

Hodgkin, Katharine, and Susannah Radstone. Eds. 2014. *Contested Pasts: The Politics of Memory*. London: Routledge.

Hubbard, G., K. Brackett-Milburn and D. Kemmer. 2001. "Working with emotion: issues for the researcher in fieldwork and teamwork". *International Journal of Social Research Methodology* 4(2):119–37.

Huérfanos. 1938. Letter, Inspector Provincial del Servicio de pensiones y socorro, Huelva. Arroyomolinos de León, 5 September.

InfoBierzo. 2015. "El sindicato noruego Elogit destaca "el trabajo de la ARMH como una cuestión de dignidad y humanidad". *InfoBierzo*, 23 January. Available at: http://www.infobierzo.com/henning-solhaug-elogit-el-trabajo-de-la-armh-es-una-cuestion-de-dignidad-y-de-humanidad/148208/.

Iturbe, Lola. 2003. *La Mujer en la Lucha Social y en le Guerra Civil Española*. Barcelona: Gráficas Fernando.

Izquierdo Martín, Jesús and Pablo Sánchez León. 2008. "El (débil) desafío de la memoria". *Minerva: Revista del* Círculo de Bellas Artes 8:42–44.

Jackson, Graham. 2006. "Denial". *International Journal of Clinical Practice* 60(3):253.

Jacoby, Russell. 1975. *Social Amnesia: A Critique of Conformist Psychology From Adler to Laing*. Boston: Beacon.

Jones, Patricia S., and Martinson, Ida M. 1992. "The experience of bereavement in caregivers of family members with Alzheimer's disease". *Journal of Nursing Scholarship* 24(3):172–76.

Juan. 2014. Interview, 23 August. Arroyomolinos de León.

Juan. 2015. Interview, 7 April. Arroyomolinos de León.

Juan Manuel. 2015. Interview, 16 August. Arroyomolinos de León.

Juliá, Santos. 2004. *Historias de las Dos Españas*. Madrid: Taurus.

Junquera, Natalia. 2015. "Reprimenda de la ONU a España por no extraditar a cargos franquistas". *El País*, 27 March. Available at: http://politica.elpais.com/politica/2015/03/27/actualidad/1427485906_256091.html.

Junquera, Natalia. 2016. "Yo quiero que me entierren con él". *El País*, 21 January. Available at: http://politica.elpais.com/politica/2016/01/19/actualidad/1453194638_672822.html.

Junta Local de Protección de Menores. 1940. "Expediente". Ayuntamiento de Arroyomolinos de León, 26 October.

Jurado Almonte, José Manuel. 1995. "Arroyomolinos de León", in *Los pueblos de Huelva*, edited by Juan Agero, 161–76. Huelva: Huelva Información S.A.

Kammen, Michael. 1997. In the Past Lane: Historical Perspectives on American Culture.

Katz, Cindi. 1994. "Playing the field - questions of fieldwork in geography". *Professional Geographer* 46(1):67–72.

Kelly, Carol. 1995. "Denial". *Fortnight* 341(July–August):9.

Kingdon, C. 2005. "Reflexivity: Not just a qualitative methodological tool". *British Journal of Midwifery* 13(10):622–28.

Kleinmann, S. and M. A. Copp. 1993. *Emotions and Fieldwork; Qualitative Research Methods* (Vol. 28). London: Sage.

Knowles, C. 2006. "Handling your baggage in the field reflections on research relationships". *International Journal of Social Research Methodology* 9(5):393–404.

Koselleck, Reinhart. 2011. "From War Memorials: Identity Formations of the Survivors", in *The Collective Memory Reader*, edited by Olick, Jeffrey K., Vered Vinitzky-Seroussi, and Daniel Levy, 365–70. Oxford: Oxford University Press.

Landsberg, Alison. 2003. "Prosthetic memory: the ethics and politics of memory in an age of mass culture", in *Memory and Popular Film*, edited by Paul Grainge, 144–61. Manchester: Manchester University Press.

Langa Nuño, Concha. 2001. *Educación y Propaganda en la Sevilla de la Guerra Civil. Una aproximación a través de la prensa.* Sevilla: Ayuntamiento de Sevilla.

Langellier, Kristin M. and Eric E. Peterson. 2004. *Storytelling in Daily Life: Performing Narrative*. Philadelphia: Temple University.

Larrinaga, Carlos. 2011. "Don Teodosio Riscos Ortín". *Restauración y República en Cala (Huelva)*. Available at: http://teodosio-riscos.blogspot.com.es.

Ledesma, José Luis. 2012. "Enemigos seculares: La violencia anticlerical (1936-1939)", in *Izquierda obrera y religión en España (1900-1939)*, edited by Julio de la Cueva and Feliciano Montero, 219–44. Alcalá: Servicio de Publicaciones Universidad de Alcalá.

Lewis, Susan J. and Andrew J. Russell. 2011. "Being embedded: A way forward for ethnographic research". *Ethnography* 12(3):398–416.

Lincoln, Bruce. 1999. "Exhumaciones revolucionarias en España, Julio 1936". *Historia Social* 35:101–18.

Lledó, Emilio. 2015. Interview in *El Intermedio*, La Sexta, 4 June 2015.

López, Ángeles. 2008. *Martina: La Rosa Número Trece*. Barcelona: Seix Barral.

López Martínez, Mario. 1995. Orden público y luchas agrarias en Andalucía. Granada, 1931-1936. Madrid: Ediciones Libertarias.

Lorenza. 2015. Interview, 13 May. Lugo.

Lorenza. 2015. Interview, 27 August. Arroyomolinos de León.

Luis. 2014a. Interview, 8 April. Arroyomolinos de León.

Luis. 2014b. Interview, 20 August. Arroyomolinos de León.

Luis. 2015. Interview, 23 August. Arroyomolinos de León.

Macciuci, Raquel. 2006. "Singularidad, anomalía, diferencia, olvido: la derrota de los republicanos españoles en Francia. El testimonio de Diario a dos voces de José María y Manuel Lamana". *Olivar* 7(8):165–93.

Madison, D. Soyini. 2012. *Critical Ethnography. Method, Ethics and Performance*. London: Sage.

Madoz, Pascual. 1835. *Diccionario Geográfico-Estadístico-Histórico de España y sus posesiones de ultramar*. Huelva: Diputación Provincial de Huelva.

Madueño, Eugenio. 1976. "Los 'malos' no fueron solo los rojos". *Grama* 94 (November):21.

Malefakis, E. 1971. *Reforma agraria y revolución campesina en la España del siglo XX*. Barcelona: Ariel.

Malinowski, Bronislaw. 2014. *Argonauts of the Western Pacific*. Abingdon: Routledge.

Mancomunidad Intermunicipal de R.S.U. 'Sierra Minera'. N.D. *Mancomunidad 'Sierra Minera'*. Monesterio: Junta de Andalucía.

Mangini, Shirley. 1995. *Memories of Resistance*. London: Yale University Press.

Manuel. 2015. Interview, 26 August.

Marco, Jorge. 2006. "Guerrilla, bandolerismo social, acción colectiva. Algunas reflexiones metodológicas sobre la resistencia armada antifranquista". *Cuadernos de Historia Contemporánea* 28:281–301.

Martínez, Diego. 2010. "Aquí, allá y en todas partes". *Página 12*, 4 September. Available at: http://www.pagina12.com.ar/diario/elpais/1-152581-2010-09-04.html.

Mateo. 2015. Interview, 23 August. Arroyomolinos de León.

Matthews, Herbert L. 1939. "130,000 refugees enter France". *New York Times*, 7 February.

Mauthner, N. and A. Doucet. 2003. "Reflexive accounts and accounts of reflexivity in qualitative data analysis". *Sociology* 37(3):413–31.

Mendieta, Ascensión. 2015. Interview, 23 May. Madrid.

Mercedes. 2014. Interview, 7 April. Arroyomolinos de León.

Mesquida, Evelyn. 2014. *La Nueve. Los españoles que liberaron París*. Barcelona: Ediciones B.

Miguel. 2014a. Interview, 16 August. Arroyomolinos de León.

Miguel. 2014b. Interview, 28 December. Arroyomolinos de León.

Miguel. 2015. Interview, 13 August. Arroyomolinos de León.

Mintz, Sidney. 1953. "The Folk-Urban Continuum and the Rural Proletarian Community". *American Journal of Sociology* 59:136–43.

Mintz, Frank. 1982. *The Anarchists of Casas Viejas*. Chicago: University of Chicago Press.

Misztal, Barbara A. 2003. *Theories of Social Remembering*. Maidenhead: Open University Press.

Moradiellos, Enrique. 1999. "The Allies and the Spanish Civil War", in *Spain and the Great Powers in the Twentieth Century*, edited by Sebastian Balfour and Paul Preston, 96–126. London: Routledge.

Moreno Gómez, Francisco. 1982. *La República y la Guerra Civil en Córdoba (I)*. Córdoba: Ayuntamiento de Córdoba.

Moreno Gómez, Francisco. 2001. *La resistencia armada contra Franco: tragedia del maquis y la guerrilla : el centro-sur de España : de Madrid al Guadalquivir*. Barcelona: Crítica.

Moreno Gómez, Francisco. 2006. "Lagunas en la memoria y en la historia del maquis". *Revista de Historia Contemporánea* 6.

Moro, Sofía. 2006. *Ellos y Nosotros*. Barcelona: Blume.

Morris, Charles E. 2007. "My Old Kentucky Homo: Abraham Lincoln, Larry Kramer, and the Politics of Queer Memory", in *Queering Public Address: Sexualities in American Historical Discourse*, edited by Charles E. Morris, 93–120. Columbia: University of South Carolina Press.

Morrissey, Matthew V. 1999. "Love, loss and disappearing lives". In *Alzheimer's disease: beyond the medical model*, edited by Matthew V. Morrissey and Ann-Louise Coakley, 45–64. Salisbury: Mark Allen Publishing.

Narotzky, Susana and Gavin Smith. 2002. "'Being político' in Spain: An Ethnographic Account of Memories, Silences and Public Politics". *History & Memory* 14(1/2):189–228.

Nash, Mary. 2006. *Rojas: Las Mujeres Republicanas en la Guerra Civil*. Madrid: Taurus.

Neiger, Motti, Oren Meyers, and Eyal Zandberg. 2011. *On Media Memory: Collective Memory in a New Media Age*. Basingstoke: Palgrave Macmillan.

O'Reilly, Karen. 2009. *Key Concepts in Ethnography*. London: Sage.

Olick, Jeffrey K. 2010. "From Collective Memory to the Sociology of Mnemonic Practices and Products", in *A Companion to Cultural Memory Studies*, edited by Astrid Erll and Ansgar Nünning, 151–62. Berlin: De Gruyter.

Ordóñez Márquez, Juan. 1968. *La apostasía de las masas y la persecución religiosa en la provincia de Huelva: 1931-1936*. Salamanca: Universidad Pontificia de Salamanca.

Ortiz Heras, Manuel. 2006. "Memoria social de la guerra civil: la memoria de los vencidos, la memoria de la frustración". *Historia Actual Online* 10:179–98.

Oyarzábal, Isabel. 2013. *Mujer, Voto y Libertad*. Sevilla: Editorial Renacimiento.

Padrón de Familias Pobres. 1939. *Expediente instruído para la formación del Padrón de Familias Pobres con derecho a asistencia medico-farmacéutica*. Arroyomolinos de León.

Padrón Municipal. 1940. *Padrón Municipal de los vecinos, cabezas de familia, domiciliados, (presentes y ausentes), y transeuntes que se inscribieron en este término el día 31 de Diciembre de 1940 según el Censo de Población de dicho año*. Arroyomolinos de León.

Pàmies, Teresa. 1977. *Los niños de la guerra*. Barcelona: Bruguera.

Pascual Cevallos, Fernando. 1983. *Luchas agrarias en Sevilla durante la Segunda República*. Sevilla: Diputación Provincial.

Pedro. 2015. Interview, 25 August. Arroyomolinos de León.

Pérez Yruela, Manuel. 1979. *La conflictividad campesina en la provincia de Córdoba (1931–1936)*. Madrid: Ministerio de Agricultura.

Peristiany, John G. 1966. *Honor and Shame: The Values of Mediterranean Society*. Chicago: Chicago University Press.

Phillips, Kendall R. 2008. "Introduction", in *Framing Public Memory*, edited by Kendall R. Phillips, 1–14. Tuscaloosa: University of Alabama Press.

Pitt-Rivers, Julian, A. 1963. *Mediterranean Countrymen*. Paris: Mounton & Cie.

Pons Prades, Eduardo. 1975. "Republicanos españoles en la liberación de París", *Tiempo de Historia* 3:4–24. Available at: http://gredos.usal.es/jspui/bitstream/10366/22769/3/THI~N3~P4-24.pdf.

Pons Prades, Eduardo. 1985. "Republicanos en la liberación de París". *Historia 16*: 111.

Portelli, Alessandro. 1991. *The Death of Luigi Trastulli and Other Stories: Form and Meaning in Oral History*. Albany: State University of New York Press.

Portelli, Alessandro. 2006. "What makes oral history different?", in *The Oral History Reader*, edited by Robert Perks and Alistair Thomson, 32–42. London: Routledge.

Prada Rodríguez, Julio. 2004. "Memoria 'da longa noite de pedra'. La represión franquista en Ourense (1936–1939)". *Historia Actual Online* 4:127–39.

Preston, Paul. 2002. *Doves of War: Four Women of Spain*. London: HarperCollins.

Preston, Paul. 2012. *The Spanish Holocaust*. London: Harper Press.

Prieto, Joaquín. 2015. "Un buen gesto real hacia los republicanos". *El País*, 4 June. http://elpais.com/elpais/2015/06/03/opinion/1433350822_168091.html.

Prieto Borrego, Lucía. 2009. "El desafío a la escasez. Estrategias de supervivencia de las mujeres en la posguerra", in *Heroínas invisibles. Mujeres entre la represión y la Resistencia (1936–1950)*, edited by Pura Sánchez Sánchez, 30–35. Sevilla: Centro de Estudios Andaluces.

Público. 2015. "La ARMH se queja del tuit de Interior que dice que las primeras elecciones democráticas fueron en 1977". *Público*, 20 December. Available at: http://www.publico.es/politica/armh-queja-del-tuit-interior.html.

Puelles Benítez, Manuel. 1999. *Educación e ideología en la España Contemporánea*. Madrid: Tecnos.

Quiñonero Hernández, Llum. 2009. "Verlas y nombrarlas. El deber de recomponer la trama de los relatos no contados", in *Andalucía en la Historia. Mujeres entre la represión y la Resistencia (1936–1950)*. *Heroínas invisibles*, edited by Pura Sánchez Sánchez, 36–39. Sevilla: Centro de Estudios Andaluces.

Rafael. 2015. Interview, 25 August. Arroyomolinos de León.

Rafaneau-Boj, Marie-Claude. 1995. *Los campos de concentración de los refugiados españoles en Francia (1939–1945)*. Barcelona: Omega.

Ramírez Copeiro del Villar, Jesús. 1996. *Espías y Neutrales: Huelva en la II Guerra Mundial*. Huelva: Imprenta Jiménez.

Ramona. 2015. Interview, 28 August. Arroyomolinos de León.

Ramoneda, Josep. 1997. "Memoria, amnesia, perdón". *El País*, 7 November. http://elpais.com/diario/1997/11/07/opinion/878857204_850215.html.

Ramos Mesonero, Alicia. 2011. *Memoria de las Presas de Franco*. Madrid: Huerga y Fierro Editores.

Raquel. 2015. Interview, 12 May. A Fonsagrada (Lugo).

Reig Tapia, Alberto. 1986. *Ideología e Historia*. Madrid: Ediciones Akal.

Richards, Michael. 2004. "El régimen de Franco y la política de memoria de la guerra civil española". In *Guerra Civil. Mito y memoria*, edited by Julio Aróstegui and François Godicheau, 167–200. Madrid: Marcial Pons.

Ricoeur, Paul. 2004. *Memory, History, Forgetting*. Chicago: University of Chicago Press.

Riera, Milagros. 2016. "Exilio, Memoria y República". *Eco Republicano*, 16 January. Available at: http://www.ecorepublicano.es/2016/01/exilio-memoria-y-republica.html.

Robledo Hernández, Ricardo. 2014. "Sobre el fracaso de la reforma agraria andaluza en la Segunda República", in *La Cuestión Agraria en la Historia de Andalucía: Nuevas Perspectivas*, edited by Manuel González de Molina, 63–96. Sevilla: Centro de Estudios Andaluces.

Rodrigo, Antonina. 2013. *Mujeres Olvidadas: Las Grandes Silenciadas de la Segunda República*. Madrid: La Esfera de los Libros.

Rodríguez Barreira, Oscar J. 2011. "Auxilio Social y las actitudes cotidianas en los Años del Hambre, 1937–1943". *Historia del Presente* 17:127–47.

Rodríguez Barreira, Oscar J. 2013. "Cambalaches: hambre, moralidad popular y mercados negros de guerra y postguerra". *Historia Social* 77:149–74.

Rodríguez Barreira, Oscar J. 2015. *Pupitres vacíos. La escuela rural de post-guerra. Almería, 1939-1953*. Almería: IEA.

Rolls, L. and M. Relf. 2006. "Bracketing interviews: Addressing methodological challenges in qualitative interviewing in bereavement and palliative care". *Mortality* 11(3):286–305.

Ryan, L. and A. Golden. 2006. "'Tick the box please': A reflexive approach to doing quantitative research". *Sociology* 40(6):1191–200.

Sabat, Steven R. 2001. *The Experience of Alzheimer's Disease: Life Through a Tangled Veil*. Oxford: Blackwell.

Sabugal, Noemí G. 2015. "Reescribiendo la historia del 'Gasta'". *La Nueva Crónica*, 1 June. Available at: http://www.lanuevacronica.com/reescribiendo-la-historia-del-gasta.

Salas Larrazábal, Ramón. 1977. *Pérdidas de la Guerra*. Barcelona: Planeta.

Samuel, Raphael. 2012. *Theatres of Memory. Past and Present in Contemporary Culture*. London: Verso.

Sánchez Jiménez, José. 1975. *La vida rural en la España del siglo XX*. Barcelona: Editorial Planeta.

Sánchez Sánchez, Pura. 2009a. *Andalucía en la Historia. Mujeres entre la represión y la Resistencia (1936–1950). Heroínas invisibles*. Sevilla: Centro de Estudios Andaluces.

Sánchez Sánchez, Pura. 2009b. "Individuas y sujetas. Las andaluzas represaliadas por los tribunals militares", in *Andalucía en la Historia. Mujeres entre la represión y la Resistencia (1936–1950). Heroínas invisibles*, edited by Pura Sánchez Sánchez, 16–19. Sevilla: Centro de Estudios Andaluces.

Sanghera, Gurchathen S. and Suruchi Thapar-Björkert. 2008. "Methodological dilemmas: gatekeepers and positionality in Bradford". *Ethnic and Racial Studies* 31(3):543–62.

Santiago. 2013. Interview, 20 August. Arroyomolinos de León.

Santiago. 2014a. Interview, 7 April. Arroyomolinos de León.

Santiago. 2014b. Interview, 21 August. Arroyomolinos de León.

Sanz Sabido, Ruth. 2015. "'They call it democracy': Cultural memory and anti-austerity protests in Spain", in *Contemporary Protest and the Legacy of Dissent*, edited by Stuart Price and Ruth Sanz Sabido, 29–44. London: Rowman and Littlefield.

Sanz Sabido, Ruth. 2016. "Echoes of the Spanish Revolution: Social memories, social struggles", in *Memory in a Mediated World: Remembrance and Reconstruction*, edited by Andrea Hajek, Christine Lohmeier and Christian Pentzold, 142–57. Basingstoke: Palgrave Macmillan.

Sanz Sabido, Ruth, Stuart Price and Laia Quílez. Eds. 2016. "The Spanish Civil War 80 years on: discourse, memory and the media – introduction to the special issue". *Catalan Journal of Communication & Cultural Studies* 8(1): 3–9.

Saramago, José. 1998. *Cuadernos de Lanzarote*. Madrid: Grupo Santillana.

Savin-Baden, Maggi and Claire Howell-Major. 2013. *Qualitative Research: The Essential Guide to Theory and Practice*. London: Routledge.

Schacter, Daniel L. 1996. *Searching for Memory: The Brain, the Mind and the Past*. New York: Basic Books.

Schacter, Daniel L. 1999. *Wir sind Erinnerung. Gedächtnis und Persönlichkeit*. Reinbek: Rowohlt.

Serrano, Rose-Marie. 2015. Personal Correspondence, 19 May.

Silvia. 2015. Interview, 8 April. Arroyomolinos de León.

Simon, Roger I. 1993. "Forms of insurgency in the production of popular memories: the Columbus quincentenary and the pedagogy of counter-commemoration". *Cultural Studies* 7(1):73–88.

Soto Gamboa, Ángel. 2004. "Historia del presente: estado de la cuestión y conceptualización". *Historia Actual Online* 3:101–16.

Surra, Catherine A. and Carl A. Ridley. 1991. "Multiple perspectives on interaction: Participants, peers, and observers", in *Studying Interpersonal Interaction*, edited by Barbara M. Montgomery and Steve Duck, 35–55. New York: Guilford Press.

Tamarit Sumalla, Josep María. 2011. "Transition, historical memory and criminal justice in Spain". *Journal of International Criminal Justice* 9(3):729–52.

Thomas, Jim. 1993. *Doing Critical Ethnography*. London: Sage.

Thomas, Maria. 2014. *La Fe y la Furia. Violencia Anticlerical Popular e Iconoclastia en España, 1931–1939*. Granada: Comares.

Todorov, Tzvetan. 2000. *Los abusos de la memoria*. Barcelona: Paidós.

Torres Reyes, Alejandra. 2015. "Un senador del PP asegura que 'ya no hay más fosas que descubrir'". *El País*, 8 October. Available at: http://politica.elpais.com/politica/2015/10/08/actualidad/1444329004_489460.html.

Torrús, Alejandro. 2014. "La mujer republicana que sobrevivió a dos fusilamientos". *Público*, 28 September. Available at: http://www.publico.es/actualidad/mujer-republicana-sobrevivio-fusilamientos.html.

Valentina. 2014. Interview, 12 August. Arroyomolinos de León.

Valeria. 2014. Interview, 12 August. Arroyomolinos de León.

Van Dijck, José. 2007. *Mediated Memories in the Digital Age*. Stanford: Stanford University Press.

Vidal-Naquet, Pierre. 1994. *Los Asesinos de la Memoria*. Mexico: Siglo XXI.

Vilanova, Francesc. 2003. "En el exilio: de los campos franceses al umbral de la deportación", in *Una inmensa prisión : los campos de concentración y las prisiones durante la Guerra Civil y el franquismo*, edited by Jaume Sobrequés i Callicó, Carme Molinero Ruiz, and Margarida Sala, 81–116. Barcelona: Crítica.

Vincent, Mary. 1996. *Catholicism in the Second Spanish Republic. Religion and Politics in Salamanca, 1930-1936*. Oxford: Clarendon Press.

Vincent, Mary. 2007. "La Guerra Civil española como Guerra de Religión". *Alcores: Revista de Historia Contemporánea* 4:57–73.

Vinyes, Ricard. 2010. *Irredentas. Las presas políticas y sus hijos en las cárceles franquistas*. Madrid: Planeta.

Westland, Naomi. 2013. "Why Spain must investigate Franco-era crimes". *Amnesty International UK*, 18 June. Available at: https://www.amnesty.org.uk/blogs/press-release-me-let-me-go/why-spain-must-investigate-franco-era-crimes#comments-expand.

Wolf, Eric R. 1966. *Peasants*. Englewood Cliffs, NJ: Prentice-Hall.

Woodthorpe, Kate. 2009. "Reflecting on death: The emotionality of the research encounter". *Morality* 14(1):70–86.

Woodthorpe, Kate. 2011. "Researching death: methodological reflections on the management of critical distance". *International Journal of Social Research Methodology* 14(2):99–109.

Yoder, Edwin M. 1997. *The Historical Present: Uses and Abuses of the Past*. Jackson, MS: University Press of Mississippi.

Young, James E. 2011. "From At Memory's Edge: After-Images of the Holocaust in Contemporary Art and Architecture", in *The Collective Memory Reader*, edited by Olick, Jeffrey K., Vered Vinitzky-Seroussi, and Daniel Levy, 371–74. Oxford: Oxford University Press.

Yusta Rodrigo, Mercedes. 1998. "Un mito de la guerrilla antifranquista en Aragón: La Pastora". *Arenal: Revista de Historia de Mujeres* 5(2):361–77.

Yusta Rodrigo, Mercedes. 2003. *Guerrilla y Resistencia Campesina: La Resistencia armada contra el franquismo en Aragón (1939–1952)*. Zaragoza: Prensas Universitarias de Zaragoza.

Yusta Rodrigo, Mercedes. 2004. "Rebeldía individual, compromiso familiar, acción colectiva: las mujeres en la resistencia al franquismo durante los años cuarenta". *Historia del Presente* 4:63–92.

Yusta Rodrigo, Mercedes. 2008. "Una guerra que no dice su nombre: los usos de la violencia en el contexto de la guerrilla antifranquista (1939–1953)". *Historia Social* 61:109–26.

Index

About the Author

Dr Ruth Sanz Sabido is Senior Lecturer in Media and Communication at Canterbury Christ Church University, UK. She is the co-editor of *Sites of Protest* (2016), *Contemporary Protest and the Legacy of Dissent* (2015) and a number of journal special issues. She is also author of several book chapters and journal articles on memory and the Spanish Civil War, media discourse, conflict and social movements. Ruth is founder and Chair of the MeCCSA Social Movements Network, and co-editor of the book series 'Protest, Media and Culture' (Rowman and Littlefield International). Ruth also coordinates the project *Herencias del 36*, an online map of testimonies about Francoist repression in Spain (www.herencias1936.com).

Printed in Great Britain
by Amazon

58485552R00125